Flight of the Penguin

By Adam Brett

Flight of the Penguin

First published in Great Britain in 2014

Copyright © Adam Brett 2014

To Stuart Brown. For the great night shift in the sky.

1

I didn't want to dress up. I didn't want to dress up as a pirate, or a gladiator, or Robin bloody Hood. I certainly didn't want to dress up as a blue fluffy penguin. Worse was the niggling feeling that we'd got it wrong; that everybody else would be in regulation smart-casual, staring at me and laughing as I waddled to the bar. Granted, this was a host famed for his frivolity and ridiculous excess, but not all of his guests struck me as the sort to express an interest in budget novelty costume. I was told I'd blend in seamlessly among an army of film and TV characters, and probably some bloke on one of those pretend-to-ride-the-ostrich things. But surely, even amid drunken revellers, a six-foot flightless bird was going to attract too much attention when you were supposed to be working a case?

'It's perfect. It hides the wire,' said Colin.

'It's about four-hundred degrees in here,' I said.

'Well don't take the head off, whatever you do. Keep drinking water and lift your wings. There's a mesh under each one to help with ventilation.'

'I can barely hear.'

'You don't have to hear, the wire will record everything.'

'Do we *have* to paint my face?'

'Do you want him to recognise you?'

There was no point in complaining. My eyes ran down the length of the two-foot beak protruding from my forehead. I took deep, steady breaths, standing with my flippers at right-angles to my body while Colin clogged my pores with blue face paint.

I visualised the house; entry, record, exit. Simple. No unnecessary conversations; keep focused on the targets – but do not become isolated. If they twig, run. There was a hallway off the main reception room with a lockable door at one end. That would slow down anyone in pursuit long enough to escape through the western entrance, via the kitchen.

It was the kitchen, wasn't it?

I turned my head to look at the floor plan we had spread over my desk, but Colin gripped my jaw to face him again, dabbing my cheeks like a fussy mother cleaning chocolate from her brat.

There was no Plan B. It was barely a Plan A. It was illegal, and we'd be grabbing our ankles in court if he found out.

The prime target was Samuel McIntyre. He grew up on the mean streets of leafy Sevenoaks, Kent. It was a tough childhood. His parents could only afford to replace the family Volvo every other year, and his dad was a member of one of the roughest golf courses in the area. His mother never cared. She was too busy fundraising for Oxfam. Hard drugs and gang violence were the inevitable outcome. Yet, in spite of his humble beginnings, it turns out Sammy had an eye for business, and in making several savvy recruitments it took less than a decade to create one of the South's greatest empires.

Over the years we'd tried everything to shut him down. It became a routine farce, uploading his dummy accounts, following his wife, searching through his bins. We never did any better than a small article in the local press next to a picture of a dog on a skateboard. Nothing stuck. Everyone else had long since given up. Then out of the blue we get a tip-off. That night, while he hosted his annual sham charity gala, we were going to meet some of his new friends.

'Why are you dressed as a duck, Rose?' asked DI Martin, back from another meeting about the department's bog roll ration, or the correct way to lift a pot of paperclips.

'It's not a duck, it's a penguin, sir,' said Colin.

5

'Penguin? Since when were penguins blue?'

Martin's desk chair squealed as he fell into it. Pulling himself as close to the table as his girth would allow, he picked the last of the lettuce and tomato out of a BLT, slopping it onto a notepad. Cramming his ruddy jowls, he looked like a great mound of sausage meat slowly escaping from a cheap shirt.

'Why do you bother?' he gurgled through half-chewed bacon.

'New leads,' replied Colin.

Martin rolled his eyes, sucking hard on a strawberry milkshake.

He was unshaven again; easily two days' growth. He'd slept in the office plenty of times before, but it had become more frequent. Maybe Sandra had finally gotten fed up with it and changed the locks? She must have known. His favourite prostitute never did manage to shoplift a perfume of any quality. You could smell it a mile off.

'Hi guys,' said Sue, the civilian admin girl from CID, appearing in the doorway. 'Nice duck, Chris.'

'*It's not a duck*,' said Colin.

Whatever I was, it wasn't the weirdest thing she'd caught us doing. At least I was clothed.

The inspector's eyes peeled every last stitch from Sue's body as she crossed the office to the photocopier. A little pink slug licked the tip of his milkshake straw.

'Printing something off?' he asked.

'Yep,' said Sue, determined not to make eye contact. 'Plug's missing from our machine again.'

'Oh no. Who does that?' asked Martin.

'Can't think.'

Sue visibly shuddered, feeling the slime ooze across her shoulders and down her thighs as Martin watched on from behind. I doubt she'd finished printing everything before she left.

Easing back in his chair, Martin was nodding to himself when he caught me shaking my head.

'Don't be jealous,' he said. 'You might get promoted one day.' He looked me up and down, stuffing another mouthful. 'Then again...'

It used to amuse me, the notion that all those women were picky about their clients; that his wife or a handful of mistresses ever saw anything other than a fat, blank cheque looking back at them for the last twenty years. Every new female colleague suffered the same, but for all his inappropriate advances you're just not allowed to fire someone in the public sector, something that risks a protracted legal challenge, kicking the last breath out of an already wheezing budget. All they do is move problem people from one department to another, further away from the public. I assumed they dressed it up when they dumped him on us; 'You're part of a secret unit now!' The reality is that they're just waiting for you to retire or die quietly. Either suited me.

'Right,' said Colin, 'we have three microphones in total; one at the tip of each wing, and one in your beak. Try and keep them all as close to the subject as you can.'

'Yeah, give them all a big cuddle,' said Martin. 'Drug dealers are pussy cats really. They love it.'

'Now, the batteries are new,' continued Colin, 'but they won't last long. I've fitted a switch to turn the wire on and off in your left foot; press hard on it to activate, and again to deactivate. If you need to talk to me at any point, a normal radio mike is in your right foot. Ok, let's test it.'

I put my foot down. Nothing happened. I leant forward to put extra weight on the switch. Still nothing. So I stomped on the floor. Finally, I could hear a faint crackle. The right foot for the radio mike was just as stubborn. It looked like I was duelling with a particularly elusive insect and I knocked most of the files off a nearby shelf. Attempting to alternate between the wire and the mike alerted some more colleagues from next door, who helpfully took camera-phone pictures and laughed.

'Have you got a tambourine as well?' asked Martin, dabbing milkshake from each of his chins in turn with a napkin.

We ran through some test speeches; all the classics - *Baa-Baa Adjust Ethnicity According to Audience Sheep, Humpty Numpty Sat at His Desk*. I just had to learn to ignore the beak and make sure my tights stayed up.

So we were set. I was to be dropped off at the house of one of the country's most dangerous criminals, dressed as a six-foot penguin-slash-duck, and all I had to do to start recording the information I almost certainly wouldn't hear, was to instigate an impromptu Riverdance.

Welcome to Special Operations.

2

The house was ridiculous. On the outskirts of town it looked about half a mile in every dimension, walled in with eight feet of concrete. Rottweilers paced the runway that doubled as a drive, CCTV covered every entrance, and every now and again a suit and dark glasses would appear to scowl on the roof. So, all in all, exactly what you'd expect from someone 'in insurance'.

Naturally, the closest neighbours had always been suspicious, and it was the closest of all, a retired headmaster, that was credited with inspiring the original topiary on show. During the long-running battle for planning permission, McIntyre maintained the design was 'a rocket'. Anyone else with eyes knew differently, but of course it was allowed to stay, and successfully block prying eyes into one side of the house.

We had deliberately left it late, hoping the cumulative effect of alcohol, drugs and a few cosmetically enhanced secretaries would prove a suitable distraction. From the back gardens I would make my way to the side of the house and a lesser-used door. There I would wait for a group of revellers to congregate outside, when I would casually stroll over. We'd laugh and we'd joke in our ridiculous outfits, and then I'd follow them all back inside. Everyone would be far too drunk to question their new friend, but if they did, I had my cover story.

Colin would remain outside in the van, listening in to my every move and guiding me through the building with the floor plan. From the basement to the roof, he had every detail on the cameras, alarms and internet connections. We could target specific rooms, wasting no time in the search for evidence.

The initial signs were promising. Each and every one of the guests I'd seen arrive was indeed dressed like a coke-addled five-year-old. If anything I was underdressed. However, I noted that nobody was spared the unapologetic hands of at least one caveman on their way in, looking through coats and bags.

'There're more than we thought,' I said.

'*Oh god,*' said Colin in my ear. '*I haven't got enough wine gums for this. If you think it's too hot you can still turn back.*'

No chance.

The flow of peculiarities had slowed to a trickle, passing through the funnel of suited muscle into the main entrance. I edged along the hedge as close to the side door as I could, just out of range of the nearest camera. All I needed was a few people to decide they wanted a quick cigarette and I'd helpfully go up and offer a light...

It was nearly eleven and no one had left the building. Not one person stumbled out, trying to steady themselves for a piss in the river that ran past the back of the house. There must have been more than two-hundred guests, but the silhouettes jumping to thumping bass had all disappeared with the music. What the hell were they doing? What self-respecting major criminal turns it down at eleven? A twenty-five-foot dick in the garden said McIntyre didn't care about the neighbours.

'*He must be addressing the guests in another room,*' said Colin.

My beak was almost certainly on camera as I strained for a better view.

And then it appeared from around a bush.

I froze as the powerful dog, veins throbbing through its upper legs and shoulders, stood there staring at me. It was no more than thirty metres away, tilting its head inquisitively. Approaching from the other direction, just around the corner, was a meathead patrol, the distorted voices across a walkie-talkie becoming clearer with each step. The gate was too far away. I'd never make it back out onto the street before I became canine floss.

Music powered from the house once more, louder than ever, to cheers of the crowd. I was only ten metres from the side door, but I couldn't run in on my own.

I backed myself into the hedge as far as I could, frantically scanning the floor for anything I could throw to distract the dog. There was an entire packet of biscuits in the van, but I had nothing on me. The security was about to round the corner.

Then the door burst open, spewing drunken, rowdy colour across the lawn. That was my chance and I ran; except you can't run when you're dressed as a penguin, so I fell over. I looked up to see the four-legged teeth-mobile launch towards me like the Pac-Man from Hell.

'Whoopsy-daisy,' said one very unsteady Red Indian, approaching to dance around me. He was joined by his cowboy comedy partner, struggling to holster his toy guns.

The rest of the group stumbled over to me, laughing and slurping champagne, when the dog cut through them to bark in my face. I slammed my forehead into the ground, shielding my head with both flippers. Vicious incisors ripped mouthfuls fluff from my arms.

'What the 'ell's going on here?' asked the security, lunging in to grab the dog by its collar.

The drunken Indian placed a hand on the big man's chest, trying to convince his eyes to work as a team again. 'It's alright, it's alright, don't panic,' he said. *'Bit too much wine.'*

Grabbing a flipper each, the wild-west double-act pulled me off the ground to more cheers and a fountain of drink spillage. I recovered my balance, and in my best pretend-drunk way said, 'Yaaay!' throwing my flippers in the air.

'What are you lot doin' out here?'

'Duh,' said Marilyn Monroe, holding her cigarette to the man's face.

He eyed me suspiciously.

'Who are you?'

I spoke as if it was obvious: 'I'm Penguinman.'

The whole group cheered.

'Penguinmaaaan!' said some sort of dinosaur. 'Never heard of you.'

'Can I ask you all to return indoors, please?' said the guard.

'We're going, we're going,' said a leathery middle-aged woman, fast losing her Victorian wench dress to gravity. 'Give us a kiss, you big bugger.'

With a curled lip the enormous man declined the overwhelmingly awful offer. 'Shut-up!' he barked at the dog, yanking it by the collar to continue on his route. I watched until he disappeared from sight.

The haggard bint in the dress looked me up and down, taking a drag of her cigarette.

'Are you sure you aren't a duck?' she said, coughing radioactive breath.

'Pretty sure,' I said, trying to keep some distance.

'Hey,' said Gandalf, with his ear cupped to the open door. 'It's *Mamma Mia*.'

I had never been so delighted to hear that excruciating drivel in all my life, and I was more than happy to join in with another cheer and plenty of jumping up and down on the spot.

We were in.

3

Total and utter alcoholic devastation; everyone happily preoccupied with each other, completely oblivious to my arrival.

If the outside was ostentatious, the inside of the house was pure pantomime. I'd arrived in what I suppose was the lounge. Polished black and white marble checks reflected four enormous pillars, which in turn, framed ornate mahogany doors at either end of the room. The guests sat on black and white leather, obscured by sculpted curiosities – largely naked women doing weird things with fish. To my right a huge glass conservatory stretched into the gardens, full to brimming with drunk and stoned business types. To my left, a purpose-built bar served free drinks, and beyond that a DJ stood behind his decks, dwarfed by giant speakers. Across from me a hallway led into the rest of the house, though the presence of security confirmed everything beyond the toilets was off-limits, as was the staircase leading to the first floor and a balcony landing that encircled the room.

Looking more closely at the crowds a few faces became familiar.

The first was the local MP, Geoffrey Mellor, only half-heartedly disguised as Where's Wally? in a striped jumper, bobble-hat and glasses. Despite being warned about his host and the nature of his business by just about everyone he knew, Mellor conveniently acquired amnesia at roughly the same time every year. It was difficult to say who gained the most, but it was an arrangement that helped keep McIntyre's operation under the radar and maintained the slow erosion of Mellor's septum, not to mention the continual disappearance of his expenses claims. But he wasn't of interest. He had no real influence and was only in it for himself. If anything I was happy he'd taken to drugs. I'd had to sit through several community meetings with him when I was still on shift, watching lifeless eyes in the audience consider whether they could hang themselves with their shoelaces during the coffee break. At least the drugs sped the crap up a bit.

Our next puppet was a different proposition. The unlikely filling in a leggy blonde sandwich, Lee Carr was a former homeless junkie. Thanks to his long-established connections at the docks, the boss took him from living in a shipping crate to managing his import strategy. He was the details man, ensuring all the correct paperwork was in order for trouble-free distribution. This was usually via supermarket HGVs, so much so that contamination had become an issue. The Food Standards Agency had approached our drugs team several times, presumably concerned that people were eating bananas, only to look up and see a squirrel playing the banjo.

In his younger days Carr looked like a particularly ugly vulture chick in jogging bottoms. He'd have tattooed his eyeballs if he'd found someone willing to do it. But with his new found wealth and an increased familiarity with rich, over-priced foods he came to resemble a particularly ugly *fat* vulture chick in jogging bottoms. Dressed as Batman, the two ladies in his company seemed to find him improbably alluring, rubbing their hands across his padded foam muscles, surrendering a butt cheek each to his yellowing claws.

I started to make my way over to the bar, careful that I shouldn't bump into anyone who thought I looked familiar. I had almost arrived when the patient queue waiting for drinks was parted at the waist by the angry arrival of another old acquaintance.

Eric 'Bingo' Sewell had been in a wheelchair ever since a high-speed car accident some years ago. Before anyone feels too sorry for him they should know that this was the top man in a paedophile ring I was investigating. His background in IT security made him ideally placed to launch and run a site that specialised in child degradation. While serving far too short a time in prison he met some of Sammy's friends, who suggested he'd be useful to help secure their online presence. It was celebrating that new role that crushed any chance of becoming the next Maradonna, at least, on the footballing side of things. He'd sucked up enough powder to talc a whale's arse and drove his Cosworth into what was a fairly obvious bingo hall. It was nasty. Two pedestrians decorated the walls. His brother was cut in half by the impact, while a girl travelling in the back seat would die a few days later, following several failed attempts to salvage her mangled innards. Sewell was powerless to help, only just able to drag himself free from the wreckage. Still, he got over it.

Bingo had come to the party dressed as a pathetic cripple. He chomped at the heels of those closest to the bar, smacking his useless legs off their calves until he was close enough to demand a bottle of beer, snatching it from the barmaid's hands and turning to snarl at no one in particular. Our paths had crossed too often for me to risk getting up close. I waited until he thrust himself off into the crowds before I continued to the bar.

I needed a drink. I asked for water, but without hesitation the barmaid opened a beer and eased it in my direction with a smile framed in bright red lipstick. I wasn't going to complain. Three good gulps coated my throat in gold ice. I turned the bottle, looking at the label. I don't know what it said. Something in Czech I think. I threw the last of it back to be presented with another bottle and a bigger smile. The empty was nonchalantly flung onto a mountain of others in one of several open wheelie-bins. The whole event had to have cost thousands, and it seemed likely the Rest Home for the Terminally Flatulent would end up losing out.

Propped against the bar I continued to scan the rest of the room, trying to work out who everyone was, making sure I knew where not to be.

Where was the big man? And what about those new friends?

I downed my beer, wiping excess moisture away with a flipper. It was time to check in. As discreetly as possible I leant diagonally forward to put pressure on my right foot.

'Colin... Colin...'

No response. It couldn't have been broken already, surely?

I persisted, '*Colin...*'

'*I told you – Nest,*' said Colin.

'Oh, for – What does it matter?'

'*This isn't a secure line. I don't want my name out there.*'

'Colin! Colin, Colin, Colin, Colin, Colin! No one's listening.'

'*You are such a child, PC Rose.*'

'I made it through the side door. He's not here.'

Colin huffed in my ear and rustled some paperwork.

'*If these plans are right, he has a high-speed internet connection and several phones wired into a room on the first floor.*'

'The stairs are covered.'

'*So abort. There's no shame in it. We tried.*'

'We might not get another chance at this.'

'*Then you need to find a way upstairs.*'

4

Nearly two hours had disappeared into the smoky haze. Although I could hardly hear, I was reasonably happy that I must have been getting something useful from the assembled cronies, easing my flippers under the nose of anyone close by. Still no sign of McIntyre, however, and no one else I'd deemed to be a new face. They were up to something on that first floor, but the upturned mouth of the boulder embedded at the foot of the staircase guaranteed I wasn't getting past. He'd only left his post once for five minutes all night, and even then he was temporarily replaced with an even bigger animal.

We needed a distraction. It was time for the old honey lure.

I made my way back to the bar, discreetly looking over the small huddle waiting for another drink. I thought it best that I had another one, too, just to keep my cover solid. We needed blonde, we needed dizzy, and we needed drunk. We also needed alone, with the reassuring whiff of desperation, and as a cluster of people walked out onto what had become the dance floor, there she was.

Slumped on a stool at one end of the bar, Playboy bunny ears and twisting her wine glass with a stare into nothing was a platinum blonde, somewhere around the late twenties mark. Her lipstick was smudged across one side of her face, thin streaks of black fell from giant pupils, and she had allowed one of her pathetically thin dress straps to fall limp from her shoulder. It looked like we might have had a domestic somewhere along the line and boyfriend was nowhere to be seen. Perfect.

I edged my way along the bar towards her, finishing my beer - to be presented with another bottle, which I concede I needed as a crutch of sorts on the counter. She watched me on my final approach as I negotiated the stools between us.

In my best smooth voice I said, 'Hi,' belied by the wobble of my increasingly uncertain legs.

'Hello,' replied the girl from under her fringe.

I leant on my elbows. 'You seem sad. All on your own?'

'Have you seen my pants?'

'Your *pants*? I... I don't think so...'

Drunk or not, I wasn't entirely sure what she meant. *Can* I see your pants? Would I *like* to? I looked her up and down, frowning in some hope of explanation, but she just stared back like a lost child.

'I haven't seen them since dinner,' she said, her voice breaking. 'They have to be around here somewhere.'

'Have you got them chipped?'

'What?'

'Never mind.'

The wheel was spinning but the hamster had died. This was my girl and I moved in closer to the sobbing wreck.

'You see that big guy over there?' I said, gesturing to the bouncer in my way. 'He's been watching you all night.'

'Me?'

'Yeah.'

'Why?'

'He likes you.'

'Me?'

'Yeah.'

'Why?'

''Cause you're pretty.'

'Me?'

'Look, if we could just skip on a bit. Why don't you go over and talk to him?'

'Me?'

'Yes, you. Go over and say hello.'

'Do you think he'll know where my pants are?'

'I think he does know… I think he has them in his pocket.'

'In his pocket? That *bastard*.'

Before I could say anything else, the enraged girl flew off her stool and ran at full pelt across the room – completely bypassing the man I was talking about and launching with a flying head-butt into his colleague a short way up the corridor behind him. My face sank into my flipper as the spindly nutter removed her one remaining stiletto, hitting the stunned man repeatedly as he lay on the floor. The commotion brought over every security guard except the one I wanted moved.

I turned to the barmaid. 'Do you have any whisky?'

She obliged, pouring a decent measure into a tumbler for me as the rabid fury in the background was thrown out into the garden.

Drugs: don't do 'em, kids.

I couldn't leave with the scraps I may or may not have recorded in the crowd. I needed at least a glimpse at those new guys or I was on to achieve nothing but a hangover that night.

I threw the whisky back. Sod it. I was going to have to bluff my way past security. But how?

Before I could think of an answer I'd made eye contact with the obstacle at the foot of the stairs and my legs made off without me. I was committed, smiling like a fourteen-year-old boy at a disinterested sixteen-year-old girl, and I only had ten paces to make a decision on what to say. I'm afraid that decision wasn't my finest.

'Hi. I need a poo. Would you mind?' I said, gesturing up the stairs.

'The guest toilets are down that corridor, sir,' replied the bouncer, without a hint of empathy.

'Yes, but you haven't got any soap, and very little toilet paper, so if you wouldn't mind?'

'I'll have housekeeping sort that right away, sir. One moment.'

The bald thug took his radio from his belt, discreetly requesting my sanitary upgrades. I had to try harder.

'I'm very sorry, I don't mean to be pushy, but I have this... *condition* where I can't go if there are people around me. It's a nervous thing, so I'd really appreciate it...'

'I'm sorry. We're under strict instructions tonight.'

'I know Sammy, I'm sure he'll be fine with it.'

'Sorry, sir.'

Useless. I may as well have been talking to mental pants woman. But that was my only way forward, so forcefully, and at far too loud a volume, I slapped my trump card onto the table: 'Look – I am going to *shit* myself.'

My exclamation coincided exactly with the death of the music. Everyone turned to stare in complete silence, stony faces broken only with an occasional smirk or the pug-like grimace only true disgust can provoke. I would have been bright red if I wasn't bright blue.

'It's IBS, alright?' I protested to the sea of shaking heads. 'It's a genuine condition, I can't help it. Don't all stand there staring at me. I don't laugh at your afflictions, do I?'

Unfortunately at that point, my gaze turned to another man in a wheelchair, while all my years of Respect and Diversity training ran out of the building and committed suicide under a lorry.

'I don't look at wheels here and say, "Oh, your legs don't work? But mine do. I think I'll do a dance. Look at me, Mr Cripple, wouldn't you love to be able to do this?" So go on, then, have a good laugh. Laugh at the man who has to throw away yet another pair of pants, while you lot slip yours off later for a gentle cleanse at forty degrees, ready to hug your over-paid arses for another day.'

I can't say where I was going with that, but it brought about a curiously calm reflection in the crowd. Even the bouncer had his head bowed, possibly recalling all the people he'd battered senseless in recent months for speaking to him in sentences.

I brushed past the big man and up the stairs, shaking with adrenalin and waiting for someone to call my bluff. No one did. A few steps onto the first floor landing and the music and raised voices resumed as though nothing had happened. It worked. Who needs dignity, anyway?

But I had to compose myself. I'd pretty much alerted the entire house as to where I was and I needed to be quick before suspicion set in.

'I'm going to shit myself,' repeated Colin in my ear. *'I'm going to use that the next time there's a long queue in the supermarket. But 'wheels'? That's going to get us letters.'*

5

'About twenty metres further, third on the left. It's just a standard door, no security.'

The party was a distant hum as I paced the far end of the corridor, careful to listen in to each door as I passed, only too wary that someone could fly out at any point.

It was beginning to look like Sammy had given us the slip, perhaps sneaking out with his new chums just before I got in. That said, all his cars were still parked up. I asked Colin to get a few of our colleagues on the radio to see if he'd turned up at any of his usual haunts, but there had been no sightings.

'Maybe he's gone to the shop?' said Colin.

'Why?'

'Well, he's got a lot of people over. He might need some milk.'

'Yeah, that's a point. And it's buy-one-get-one-free on the party rings at the moment.'

'You're just being silly now.'

'I still can't believe MI5 turned you down. I'm at the door. Are you sure it isn't alarmed?'

'There are no electrics I can see. According to this it isn't even lockable.'

That wasn't very reassuring. I was led to believe that there was a computer in that room containing anything from drug transactions to his wife's boob-job notes. Why would you leave the door unlocked and introduce hundreds of strangers into your house unless you were certain it was safe?

I reached out a flipper to grip the brass handle, looking left and right along the corridor. I had to have one more listen-in against the door to make sure there was nobody on the other side, but if there was they weren't doing much. I closed my eyes, held my breath, and in one swift motion yanked the handle down and pushed the door wide open.

I stood there for a few moments before peeking round.

It was a small library of sorts. Tall book cases bursting with coloured spines surrounded a single desk, on which sat a computer and companion printer. There was one small window looking out over the rear gardens. The room was dingy, only barely lit by two vulgar elephant-foot lamps, both far too big for their shelves. Surrounding those were various ornaments from around the world, but nothing that even tried to look expensive. It was all the kind of crap you brought back from holiday and gave to people you hate. No wires or junction box above the door frame, and no detectors in the corners of the room or under the desk. Even the computer was still on. It was all far too easy, and at any other time I'd have given in to the cold wave of anxiety washing through my body and left. It had to be a trap.

But I didn't think about that. I didn't think about it because this was Samuel McIntyre. I didn't think about it because it had taken years to get to this point, and no one had anything on him, ever. But above all, I didn't think about it because I was really quite pissed.

There was nothing obvious on the computer's desktop. I clicked a few of the icons but every file demanded a password.

'Any ideas?' I asked Colin, pulling my flippers back from my hands and searching through the drawers in the desk.

'I'd have used Splat.'

'What?'

'My gerbil when I was six. People always use pets as passwords.'

23

Looking around the room for inspiration I couldn't think of a better idea. I was pretty sure Sammy only had dogs, trouble was, he 'only' had about fifty of them and I didn't know what any of them were called. They were all Rottweilers, so it was unlikely to be anything cute.

Nothing worked. From 'Gnasher' to 'Toothy Bastard' and everything in between, they were all incorrect passwords. I was making too much noise, hammering the keys in frustration. I calmed myself down again and returned to the desk drawers, pulling everything out onto the floor. There were several dog-eared brochures for Costa Rica, which was obviously going to be the next holiday destination. Very nice. Receipts for nothing interesting. Blank CDs...

Then, alone at the bottom of the drawer, a solitary scrap of paper looked up at me.

I said: 'Hang on... Bollocks.'

'What is it?'

A friendly beep. 'Bollocks.' Of course; why would it be anything more eloquent?

'You can't call your dog Bollocks,' said Colin. *'I've half a mind to report him to the RSPCA.'*

The hard drive whirred into life, flicking icons onto the monitor. I clicked on the first, egging the machine on, conscious I had been upstairs for too long already. I loaded one of the CDs into the computer, ready to copy the first file that turned up on screen.

I checked the hallway while the first burn was underway. The party was very much in full swing. *Billie Jean* was bursting from those huge speakers. Great choice. I immediately attempted a short moonwalk, as is the law, but my fluffy feet provided too much friction on the carpet.

Then there was a noise from outside the window; a low hum and the crunch of gravel. A vehicle was approaching via the secluded rear driveway. I walked over to the window to see a dark MPV pull up to the house. Two of the security guys opened doors on either side, and from the tinted windows emerged several immaculate Asian, or perhaps Middle-Eastern, men. One of them carried a robust metal briefcase.

I stepped onto my mike. 'Nest, we have late arrivals.'
'Where?'
'Back entrance. Black Chrysler, six-up.'
'Who is it?'
'No one I know. Foreigners.'
'Can you see the registration?'
'No.'
'I can't see anything from here. Get what you can from the computer, I'm going to walk round.'

I watched as security helped unload several heavy-duty cases from the back of the car. Bingo had wheeled himself into position to supervise. Given the grimaces and the short, unsteady steps into the house it was obvious these things were heavy. It wasn't drugs. Guns, maybe?

That would have indicated a serious departure from McIntyre's long-standing policy of 'no machinery'. However deep he got, he knew that if he started carrying guns the game would change up a gear. That didn't mean that nobody got hurt, far from it. There were knives, there were beatings, kidnap. But never guns. They attract too much attention. A computer and forward planning are far greater weapons these days, and anyway, this is the UK, not the Bronx; who else is armed on this over-regulated, CCTV-plagued island that you'd need a gun to even things up?

The last case to emerge from the back of the car was a good six-feet-long and three wide. The goons sweated and strained at either end as they tried to negotiate the short staircase to the back door. They were nearly level with each other when suddenly the weight was too much and the man at the front lost his grip. The case thumped hard off the jagged edge of the concrete step. At once everyone jumped back, shielding their faces like vampires in the light. One man ducked behind the car and another jumped into a flowerbed. Sewell furiously yanked at his wheels to back away. Following their lead I stepped back from the window with a squint, holding up a protective flipper.

For a few seconds there was nothing, only anticipation.

The case remained still but untrusted. Everyone maintained a nervous glare for a few moments longer, as though it might come to life at any moment. To tangible relief, nothing happened.

Bingo launched himself at the man at fault, screaming up at him. Everyone else eased from their shelter and carried on, careful to sneak past the case at the very edge of the stairs before scurrying the last few steps into the house and safety. For the second attempt two extra men were brought in to delicately and nervously hoist the suspicious cargo up and inside.

What the hell was that?

Still watching out of the window I turned to walk back to the desk, only to bump into something solid that stopped me dead in my tracks. Looking forward again my view was completely obscured by a wide, suited chest.

'Someone wants a word with you,' came the gruff voice, a good six-and-a-half feet off the ground.

A solid right arm to my midriff knocked all sense out of me. As I jerked forward, the wire connected to my beak came loose and dangled in my face.

'I'm in position,' said Colin. 'I think I can see the car. Have they all gone inside..? Penguin One..? Is the coast clear..?'

I was pinned against the wall by my throat, only just standing on tip-toes. I kept flicking my leg down trying to activate the mike, but I couldn't connect with the floor.

'What have we here?' said my assailant, grabbing the thin, black cord and ripping it from my costume. 'Where's the recorder, then?'

He looked me over before launching another huge fist into my gut.

'It's not there,' I wheezed.

He hit me again on my other side, crunching plastic into my ribs.

'Yeah. That's it.'

I hit the floor, bent double. I sensed a second man round me and I was unceremoniously hauled up and out of the room.

6

I could only see my feet scuffing the carpet as I was dragged to the far end of the corridor and into another room. It was sterile in plain magnolia; nothing like the rest of the museum I had encountered to that point.

The two men pulled me up to a glass desk and dumped me on the floor. Through the blur of my vision I could just make out a pair of feet cradled in expensive shoes.

Then the voice: 'Will you excuse us for a moment, please, gentlemen?'

The tone was assured, laced with just a hint of cockney. The two brutes obliged and left, closing the door behind them.

I creaked to my knees and raised my head for the inevitable. As the last of my beak passed upwards from view, a black masquerade mask on a stick moved to one side to reveal a smiling, craggy face, eyes sunk deep in a forehead that must've been hit with every blunt instrument known to man over the years. The hair was thinner now, but found its dark, gelled strands supported by the year-long tan underneath. His gold hoop earring sat loose in its torn piercing, another war wound from the countless bar fights and gang beatings that defined his youth. The bridge of his nose no longer had any idea which way it was supposed to fall. It was all sat on a broad frame; thin, somewhat muscled, wiry greying clock springs ejecting from a crisp white shirt.

'Boo,' he said lifelessly, perched on the end of his chair.

'Sammy,' I acknowledged, too embarrassed to look at him.

'I hate it when people grovel,' he said, referring to my position on the floor. 'Why don't you take a seat?'

28

With slightly more than a grimace owing to the pain in my ribs, I climbed upwards and allowed myself to fall back onto a cold leather sofa. My beak sagged into view, which I was quick to swipe away with an angry flipper. McIntyre sat back in his chair, legs crossed, looking me up and down.

'I must say, I appreciate the effort, officer, but I don't seem to remember inviting you. I take it that's your partner parked out there in the van?'

I said nothing. But what could I say? I had already taken one beating and at that point I couldn't see a way out of the room. I don't mind admitting that I set trousers for brown, hoping that the ridiculous outfit might absorb some of the punishment that would follow. The radio was broken, the recorder was smashed, and for all I knew Colin had gone back to the van for another chapter of *The Da Vinci Code* and a cheese sandwich, just waiting for me to waddle back out.

While there was relative calm I studied the room carefully for anything I could use, but for a man with a career based on violence there was a disappointing lack of weaponry on show. Despite the myriad peculiarities elsewhere, there was nothing heavy or ornate to wield or throw. No pens on the desk, or one of those oversized staplers. Only flimsy books and paperwork, arranged neatly about the walls on shelves.

What about the window? It was certainly large enough to jump through, but the drop must have been twenty-five feet or more from that position. Maybe I'd be lucky and land on more carefully sculpted topiary, but if I'd got my bearings right there was only stone patio down there.

No. It was no use. It was just me, and him. And the thirty-odd steroid-fuelled gorillas just a whistle away.

'D'you like the place, then?' asked McIntyre.

'Yeah, it's… nice,' I said.

'Thanks. Takes a while to put your own stamp on it, you know? But I'm happy with it now.'

29

'Did you get someone in, or..?'

'No, no. My design. Well, I say mine, obviously the missus has got to have her say, and clutter the place with bloody lamps, and photos and bronze bollocks, or whatever.'

'Tell me about it,' I agreed. 'Times I've come home to some crap gurning at me from the mantelpiece.'

'Yeah. She came back with a life-sized painted sheepdog the other day because "we didn't have anything by the conservatory door." Well fuck knows who sculpted this thing, but it's got this expression on its face like it's trying to fart a pineapple. And guess how much?'

'Go on.'

'Two grand.'

'*No.*'

'*Yeah.* I said I could have shot and stuffed one of the ugly mutts we've got out there for free if you wanted one that bad.'

We both laughed, so much so that my ribs felt ready to splinter out of my chest. It must have been a full ten seconds, each of us performing impressions of our ridiculous ornaments, before it dawned on me: what the *hell* was I doing?

But then: 'So, did you find anything interesting?' asked McIntyre, his face returned to its regulation scowl.

'How d'you mean?'

'I dunno. Whatever it was you were looking for.'

We were back where we started. Whether you liked it or not, McIntyre was a master at charming all those around him. He'd lure you in, figure you out, and make sure you knew nothing that he didn't already.

'No,' I replied.

'Ah, well you were in the wrong place, see? That computer you were looking at, my nephew uses that mostly for his homework. There's nothing much on there unless you've got a particular interest in GCSE geography. *This* is the computer with the *really* interesting stuff on it.'

He tapped a laptop case on the desk.

Anxiety took a hold again. He could sit there in perfect arrogance and what could I do? Arrest him? Suppose I could get him out of the house, how was I going to explain to a judge what I was doing there in the first place, snooping around without a warrant and on camera almost every step of the way? Any evidence is immediately inadmissible, not that I had any anyway. Even if I had finished burning that disc, I was unlikely to challenge a defence counsel with details on how an oxbow lake is created and the rough migration figures for Outer Mongolia.

I had to hope Colin managed to get the index on that car; perhaps a few photos of the new guys who, after all the effort to get up onto the first floor, would have been sat relaxing in plain sight below me, sipping cocktails. In the meantime, my one and only consideration was how to get out of that house alive.

Then the tone changed again.

'What's your problem with me, Rose?' asked McIntyre, almost like a man trying to figure out why his date wasn't interested.

'What do you think?'

'Drugs? Is that it?'

'Well, I can think of one or two other things. D'you want a list?'

'Did you happen to notice what this little event was for tonight? Everyone here is supporting a charity – my charity. For children. Perhaps that passed you by while you were breaking into my house?'

'It's drugs money, Sammy.'

'So? Don't you get it? It's for kids.'

'Yeah, you're a real hero. You've killed more kids than you'll ever know about.'

'Choice, officer. I'm a businessman supplying a product. I only offer the option; I don't hold the needle to their arm. It's the same as if you and I go to the pub; we can have a few and enjoy ourselves, or we can take it too far and ruin our lives.'

'Except that if I want to stop drinking, the landlord at my local won't chase me down and smash my kneecaps.'

'Ha. He might have done if you'd lived round my old manor.'

My old *manor*. The *product*. I didn't know what was more pathetic, the transparent excuses for his business, or the delusion that he really did used to live in the ghetto.

McIntyre continued, 'All the lads working for me tonight; I took 'em off the streets, gave 'em a new start.'

'You gave them cocaine and a baseball bat.'

'You're jealous, Rose, I understand. You earn nothing, sorting out fights in a school playground. People want what I have to offer. Ask your sister.'

My eyes flicked up at the touch of that nerve.

'Have you said hello to Bingo?' he asked. 'Such a shame. They used to really love her. Both of them. He might still have some of the pictures if you want to buy 'em?'

Words were useless, I could never win. I wanted him to call it; take me on, hit me, whatever it was he was going to do. I'd go down fighting, penguin or no penguin. But true to form he wasn't going to get his own hands dirty if he didn't have to, especially when it came to police officers. He shouted out for the two stooges who instantly stomped into the room. They were informed that I was leaving, their cue to grab a flipper each. It was almost disappointing.

'A bit of friendly advice;' said McIntyre, approaching me in my meat harness, 'give up. You lot have been onto me for years now, and to be honest, I'm starting to get a bit embarrassed for you.' He grabbed at my beak and yanked my head back, eyeballing me intensely as he'd no doubt done to countless victims before they disappeared. 'Now, if you're good boy from now on, I promise I won't sue your pathetic little police force, but if I catch you anywhere near my property again... Do you understand? Good lad.'

With a playful slap to the cheek he gestured to the door and I was dragged out.

7

It was early afternoon when I finally came around.

Shadows from the pictures on the windowsill stretched across the room, half-masking my face from the sunlight. I hadn't managed to close the curtains that night, and as my eyes resumed some sense of focus, I clearly hadn't managed to get any further than the living room either, crashing through the door at God-knows-what time and crawling onto the sofa.

I leant forward to sit, reaching my arms out in front of me to see two blue matted rags, darkened with what looked like blood, among other liquids. I was still wearing that costume.

I swivelled on the spot to sit properly, kicking an empty bottle of whisky to the floor and inducing several deep, wasp-like stings to the left side of my torso. At least two of those ribs were broken. I winced from the pain as I touched my face on the same side.

And then the memories of the night's humiliation started to filter back through.

It seems that 'show him out' was understood code in goon land for 'beat the living toss out of him'. To make matters worse that crippled bastard, Sewell, had seen what was going on and wanted to join in. Trouble is, when you're in your late forties, wheelchair-bound and suffering from chronic osteoporosis, your boxing days are largely behind you. As compensation he had two men hold me while he travelled as fast as he could down a slight incline in the lawn, arm outstretched to connect with my face. Sadly for Bingo, his run-up took so long I had time to think. As he was almost in striking distance I transferred all my weight onto my supporting thugs and kicked out with both legs, sending him flying backward off his chair in a shower of urine from his burst catheter bag. As the security stood there, stunned, and newly moistened, I jumped, waddled, half-ran, fell over and waddled some more until I was out of the gate and slammed against the back door of the van to be hauled in by Colin.

That was the last thing I could remember.

Perhaps the embarrassment would subside if I could write the day off to sleep. I might well have tried if it wasn't for the sudden clank of metal on metal coming from my kitchen.

I listened... It happened again. That wasn't something falling off the side, there was someone in there, and that someone appeared to be putting things into bags.

I reached down for the whisky bottle and, as quietly as my ribs would allow, rose to my feet. Edging along the wall I tried to dodge the used plates, crisp packets and an escaped Bryan Adams CD. I wondered where that was.

I was about to peek around into the kitchen when my beak flopped into view. Without another thought I tore it off and threw it across the room, leaving what was left of the wire dangling to one side of my face.

I could just make out an open heavy-duty bag on the floor, feasting on my pots and pans as they were flung from a cupboard. Next to that were a couple of other bags, full of old ornaments and inexpensive picture frames. What a shit burglar.

My head spun round to the sound of an engine approaching tight to the front of the house. The getaway car? I bobbed and weaved, trying for a better view of the car and its driver beyond the light reflecting off the window. No one got out, but the engine kept running.

I had to act, not only in defence of my home, but also to save the public at large from one of the worst car boot sales ever. I backed myself tight up against the wall and lifted the bottle above my head, but as sunlight pierced my eyes: 'AAH!' *Bong!*

I crunched through the plates and assorted debris, twisting and falling backwards. Looking up, disorientated from a Tefal to the temple, I readied a defensive forearm for another strike, but instead, the light was blocked out by a familiar shadow.

'You scared the hell out of me!' she said.

She went back into the kitchen to pick up her useless bounty and returned to drop it by the front door. I eased myself back up onto the sofa, pulling the head of my costume back over my own and out of the way. That was another lump to add to my collection. I was just happy I'd opted for cheaper pans, and not the heavy-base stuff she always insisted we had to buy at some point.

The attacker was my sometime girlfriend, Jennifer, a physiotherapist I'd been seeing on-and-off for around three years or so. We'd met after my last serious injury, sustained when I was trying to free several children from a gang of Romanian people traffickers. I think she liked the hero story, and even three years ago, the old body was in serviceable shape. Sadly, the growing realisation that my job was much more paperwork than legwork, and the wage more acceptable than outrageous seemed to have gradually put her off. We grew apart to the point where we could only really stomach one another when we were drunk, though admittedly, that was an increasingly regular occurrence.

Having lived together for a grand total of five months, we decided it was best to have our own places again and see other people. Thing was, no matter how hard we tried, we always seemed to be the last two in the pub. As the jukebox faded out its last miserable song we'd walk off to get a kebab – chicken for her, donner for me - we'd argue about nothing in particular, get a taxi, argue about something else, and go back to my place or hers. And argue. Then, for old time's sake, with not a drop remaining in the house, and wiping the last of the chilli sauce from our mouths, we'd set about each other.

Jen's only other long-term boyfriend was massively into porn, watching almost nothing else whenever he got the opportunity. They were together nearly seven years from the age of sixteen, and as such, Jen had developed a slightly skewed view on a woman's role in the bedroom. She would contort herself into bizarre shapes that are designed only to give a camera a look at what you've had for lunch. She often shrieked so loud that when it was over the neighbours had a cigarette. I couldn't get her to shut up. If I tried to put my hand over her mouth she bit me and slapped my arse with the back of a brush. I'd look around the room sometimes, wondering who it was she was performing for. These ridiculous liaisons continued for months, up until the point where she met Travis.

That's his real name. Travis.

Like most traffic officers, Trev, as I liked to call him - because it wasn't his name and he hated it - stood around six-foot-seven and had about as much charisma as a bowl of cornflakes. He never really said much to me, but what he did say was delivered in the sort of sterile drone only the truly personality-devoid can muster, an absolute requirement of those officers charged with upholding the law on the correct space between digits on a number plate.

Trev didn't like to drink – I'm not sure he was even old enough – and I was pretty certain he couldn't tell you what a kebab was. He was of the generation that had grown up with these labels we have on every type of food, designed to give you some idea of at which point you'll be dragging your butt cheeks along the floor. Not that this particular metrosexual need worry about that. The slightest sign of sag, and it'd be off down the gym with an arm full of protein shake, before showering and moisturising away those tired eyes.

'Late night, was it?' said Jen, walking back in to stand over me with her hands on her hips. 'What the hell do you look like?'

She was wearing her unnecessarily expensive gym wear, though admittedly it looked great on her. The tight Lycra trousers hugged her lean thighs and pulled her bum into perfect symmetrical order. The vest top ran smoothly around the tennis balls she was smuggling under a secure sports bra – 32C – and it raised just enough on her abdomen for her belly button to peek out. There was the faintest hint of wobble, testament to our nights out drinking. Her long, dark hair was tied back in a tight ponytail. In any other outfit this was her 'business' hair. It meant she was on a mission; purposeful, not to be interrupted; you had to be careful what you said. If her hair was down, and I preferred it that way, then you were ok. She would be in a good mood, feeling fun and giving off the kind of friendly, excitable aura that was the reason I was attracted to her in the first place.

'When did you get here?' I asked, rubbing the bridge of my nose at the onset of another headache.

'About an hour ago. Don't worry, I'm not staying. I'm just here for the rest of my stuff. Is that *wee* all over your groin?'

Jen pointed out a fairly expansive wet patch at my midriff I hadn't noticed.

'No, that's whisky,' I said, rubbing a finger across the blue fluff to take a taste, before I gagged on the sharp, unexpected flavour. 'Oh no, you're right.'

I hope that was my piss.

'You're disgusting. I'm taking the hoover. You obviously don't use it anyway.'

'Fine,' I said, finding some stale water in a pint glass next to the sofa to try and wash my tongue.

'I've got the TV from the bedroom.'

'Yeah.'

'The alarm clock.'

38

'Yep.'

'And I'm sorry, I'm taking the fondue set, too. I'm not leaving it here to rust in this hole.'

'Jen, even if I knew what to do with a fondue set, I still wouldn't care. It's all yours.'

She always had to try and illicit a reaction from me. I never understood why she became so irrationally incensed when I never took her choice of vinyl flooring "seriously", or why I wouldn't come down off the fence to decide on either light purple or dark purple cushions. Not that it would matter anyway; she'd still choose what she wanted.

'Out with your Russian tart, were you?' she asked.

'She's not Russian, she's Polish.'

'Same thing.'

'No it isn't, and no I wasn't.'

'She'll only try and marry you so she can stay in the country. You know that, don't you?'

'She's been in the country for years.'

'Illegally, no doubt.'

Then a heavy knock at the door. Jennifer opened it to Travis' towering figure, every inch of him tight under his close-fitting uniform and heavy stab vest. His dark hair was sculpted with the putty a men's lifestyle magazine told him to use and, no doubt, there would have been cause on more than one occasion to rearrange the plums in some designer's pathetic pants whilst driving over.

'Are we ready?' he asked. 'I need to be back at work soon.'

''Ello Trev,' I said.

There was something of a jolt at the furry blue blob on the floor.

'Chris?'

'The same. Why don't you come in? I think I've got some strawberry milkshake if your mum says you're allowed it.'

'Ignore him, he's drunk.'

'Jen. Not in front of the kids.'

'Oh, grow up you idiot. Come on, we're going.'

Jen picked the bags up from the doormat.

'We're going? Hang on; are you two moving in together?'

She wouldn't look at me.

'What I do now is none of your business.'

'After two months?' I said.

She continued to ignore me, walking down the driveway.

'But you just got here. At least let me get you something to eat. He must be due his mid-afternoon feed by now.'

Trev neatly tessellated the bags in the boot of a marked traffic car. Jen turned and threw her key at me before jumping in the passenger side and slamming the door shut.

'Are you sure?' I asked, hanging out of the doorway. 'If she's started you on solids I've got some nice pineapple chunks..?'

And off they drove without looking back.

I couldn't believe she'd want to live with another man so quickly. It was more than two years before we'd even considered it, and clearly, it wasn't a roaring success. I didn't know who was getting the worst deal, but it couldn't last, surely?

Easing back into the sofa, I used my weight to mould a comfortable position, trying to avoid jarring my headache any further. I could have happily dozed off again when the landline screamed in my ear. Fumbling for the insistent receiver, I was now in more pain than ever.

'Hello?' I winced.

'About time,' said Colin on the other end. *'I've been trying your phone all day. Where have you been?'*

'Nowhere.'

'Are you okay?'

'Nothing a few Asprin won't sort out.'

'Have you been to the hospital?'

'No... I don't think so.'

'Well get yourself cleaned up and over to the station. The chief superintendent wants a word with us.'

'Now?'

'About three hours ago.'

8

I kept my head down in the corridor, well aware that there were elderly tramps with a particular aversion to soap that looked better than I did at that point.

I couldn't get all the blue face paint off, despite scrubbing my cheeks raw with a scouring pad. Luckily the bruising had disguised most of it, but the taste of pure alcohol still burned through a mouthful of mint imperials. I could peel the paint off the walls with my breath. Speak only when necessary, I thought, and maybe no one will notice.

Once word of what happened spread around I was in for relentless grief. Anyone carrying what they thought was a secret through the front door of the station soon found themselves greeted with a knowing smile. Coppers are notoriously incestuous, forever trapped in a bubble that contains personal and professional lives, often blurring the two beyond recognition. The simple reason for that is that nobody else gets it; the hours, the hysteria, the red tape, the genuine hatred for your every move. When you're on shift you're never allowed to switch off. If you've just done a fourteen hour day and you still have five statements to take, then you're taking those five statements. And when those are done, and the call comes over the radio that there's a domestic in progress and no one else is closer, you're going to that shit hole of a council house yet again to take some more statements. Sixteen hours in and it might become necessary to arrest the violent husband, but you can't leave the wife at home to look after the kids because she's drunk and lashing out at the neighbours, all watching on with shaking heads. You call in Social Services, but they don't have anyone available, so you have to hang onto the children yourself and obtain a Police Protection Order - once you've completed the domestic risk assessment form, which the wife doesn't want to go through again because she's already done three that week. Even if you manage to get out of that house before it's light again, you still need to book your prisoner into custody, only to go through his pockets to find that he's additionally in possession of cannabis. You'll need to sort the paperwork out for that as well. After eighteen hours, with the tattooed scumbag finally secured in a cell, pissing up the wall and spitting at the civilian jailer whenever she comes close, you'll get a call from the wife demanding that he be released, refusing to support any charges. A lawyer you had to appoint for the prick for free warns you that action may result over the excessive manhandling of his client. Several irate phone calls over the course of the week precede an official letter of complaint, then the senior management become involved. To halt the growth of local media attention you are eventually issued with a verbal warning. You are told not to go anywhere near the house again or any of its occupants - until the following week, when the wife calls again the in the middle of another drunken episode and the cycle begins once more.

And that's just the first day of the week.

Needless to say I jumped at the chance to escape the uniform, taking secondments wherever possible to CID, Special Search and Rescue and even the airborne unit, until the opportunity arose to join a new team, created specifically to target high-value individuals and their interests. In just under five years we had made some genuine progress with a number of telling arrests. We disrupted supply chains, seized weapons, stopped grandparents getting ripped off in pyramid schemes, all undercover in a unit that was just allowed to get on with it. Sure, it meant there was no fanfare when we tasted success, but for once it felt like we were almost winning, and somewhere, maybe, in a quiet corner where they didn't sell the *Daily Mail*, someone might have been happy about that.

I turned into the Crew Room to see Colin standing with a tea. Any smile I may have forced was short-lived, however, as I continued around the corner to find a familiar huddle, all grinning at what was obviously a retelling of the night's fiasco.

It was the usual line-up of three, locked in a continual battle for alpha status, each one taking turns for the title with an ever more inventive prank, or a decent conquest that didn't warrant a trip to the clinic the following morning.

John Webb was generally the ringleader. He was a keen rugby player; tall and prematurely balding, with a thick thump of a body somewhere between muscle and fat. He was absolutely incapable of speaking at an acceptable volume, like the twat on public transport who insists on screaming into his Bluetooth earpiece even when both hands are free. Everything had to be big and urgent with him, which made him ideal in crowd situations but little more than annoying at any other time.

His diminutive sidekick, Tony Riley, was the worst kind of officer. Short and angry, he'd joined the police straight out of school, forgoing the life experience and 'normal' employment elsewhere that invariably produces an infinitely superior public servant. Without that time in the real world you find yourself talking to a procedure, not a person. He was all about the kudos the uniform affords, wielding his ill-deserved power to make up those lost inches in height. The victim had become the bully.

Ross Briggs, on the other hand, had always been confident in himself. He was one of Trev's mates and also looked like a Ken doll. He was a hit with the ladies on shift, and if he got tired of those he found an excuse to wander over to the Control Room and sample the civilian menu. He was officially single, but much to his annoyance, suffered from The Ex Got Pregnant Syndrome, which drained his party fund with the legally enforced need for Pampers each week.

John was the first to notice me.

'Here it is,' he said.

'Hey, Chris,' said Tony, '*duck.*' He threw something which I caught at my chest.

The laughter raised with my arm, reaching a crescendo as sat in the flat palm of my hand, a small, yellow rubber duck they'd tried to colour blue with a biro smiled up at me.

'We got you this trophy to commend another fine performance in Special Ops,' said Ross. 'We'll sleep easier tonight, knowing there's one less crap fancy dress costume out there.'

And the laughs went up again.

Sheepish in the corner, Colin mouthed the word 'sorry' at me.

'Busy then, gentlemen?' I asked.

'Oh, we've been running around all day. I'm spitting feathers,' said Tony, to more inexplicable laughter.

'It was a penguin actually, boys. Check your colouring books for the difference.'

'Seriously, Chris,' said Tony, 'what were you doing?'

'I can't tell you, it's classified. You grunts don't need to know anyway.'

'Ooh, grunts are we now?' said Ross.

'Does that make you a quack?' said John.

And off they went again.

At that Colin downed his drink and led me out into the corridor amid duck impressions of various authenticity. As we left the room I saw Trev engaged in conversation with a few of his traffic colleagues. He pretended not to notice me, but I could see him looking over and watching me leave.

Colin closed the door, holding it shut behind his back.

'Sorry. They wouldn't shut up about it,' he said.

We began to walk for the lift.

'It was going to come out eventually,' I said. 'Might as well get it over with.'

'I should have been in there with you last night.'

'Why? So we could both take a kicking?'

'If I'd known I would have called for back-up.'

'Forget it. Let's just make sure we put this experience to some use. McIntyre's working on something bigger. Much bigger.'

'I would have come and got you but the boss wanted a statement done. Did Jen drop you off?'

'No. She left this afternoon.'

'Again?'

'I think it's permanent this time. She's with someone else.'

The lift arrived and I was about to step in when Katya saw me at the other end of the corridor. I held the door and asked Colin for a moment, but she intimated that she was coming up with us anyway.

Katya, or Kate, as she had become known, came to Britain when Poles were still a relative novelty, as opposed to the haven for hard-working U-bend enthusiasts we are today. Her family made huge sacrifices to land her on these shores, but having left university she encountered just about every type of discrimination we have a law for. Her otherwise promising career as a solicitor ended with her boss straddling the corner of her desk for yet another unwanted advance, and she stapled his scrotum to the woodwork. Undeterred, she left her pride at the door and joined our force in the Control Room, strengthening her English beyond that of most of her native colleagues until she was ready to sign up as an officer. She excelled, and was the perfect candidate when Special Ops was looking for someone new to join the team around eighteen months ago. It also won't have escaped DI Martin's attention during the interview process that she was stunning. Shoulder-length, natural blonde hair framed the sort of face that stuck the pages of lads' mags together. Two pale blue gemstones drew you in to the point where you had to arrest yourself before you were powerless to bite on those full lips. She was feisty; slight, but no waif, and in the right top she certainly made a couple of interesting points.

I admit I liked her and admired her, though despite Jen's assumptions we'd never got close. I had the feeling it might not have been beyond the realms of possibility, but she was annoyingly good at separating business from pleasure. I always assumed she had a massive boyfriend waiting for her at the end of each day - successful, money, car, hung like a yeti. Knowing my luck it'd be another of Trev's mates.

As she approached I backed into the lift, quickly checking my reflection in the steel button panel, squashing a few hairs down with a saliva-wet palm and adjusting my shirt. I jumped straight again as she walked in and the door closed behind her.

'Hi,' she said, moving straight into my personal space and completely ignoring Colin, who had a look of 'typical' etched on his face.

'Hi,' I said.

'You look like zshit.'

'Yeah.'

'And you stink of booze.'

'Yeah.'

'And your zshirt's on inside-out.'

I looked down. She was right. Whatever impression I had wanted to make, I was making the opposite.

'It's a fashion thing. All the kids are doing it.'

'Come on,' she insisted, 'let's sort you out before the chief sticks his other foot in your arsz.'

Colin watched with raised eyebrows as Katya undid my buttons. I thought about stopping her, but it was the briefest thought I'd had in a while. She flicked my shirt open and pulled it off my shoulders, causing a loose button to fall at my feet, which Colin knelt down to retrieve. She almost had it the right way round again when the lift dinged to an unexpected stop.

The opening doors immediately halted a conversation between a sergeant and two suited VIPs he was showing around. I covered my nipples with my fingers as we stood there in silence, except for Colin who was still kneeling, trying to ignore his proximity to my groin.

'Sergeant,' I nodded, keeping my hands in place, stepping up and down on the balls of my feet. 'It is warm, isn't it?' I smiled to the VIPs.

Why weren't the doors closing?

Katya feigned an interest my shirt, pulling at the sleeves until one of them ripped off in her hand. Colin pretended to forage for more buttons on the floor. I began absent-mindedly tweaking my nipples, maintaining a ridiculous grin at the bemused VIPs.

Finally, the doors closed again.

'Zsorry,' said Katya, handing me back my shirt, then the sleeve.

'Never mind. Hopefully the chief will just shoot me and you two can worry about the fall-out on this one.'

'What d'you want on your headstone?' asked Colin, handing me back the button.

'I don't care. As long as there's nothing about ducks.'

9

Colin and I stopped outside Detective Chief Superintendent Straughan's door, pausing for a moment to half-heartedly psych each other up. Katya disappeared up the corridor, offering us a final 'Good luck' as she went.

I tapped pathetically, hoping he wouldn't hear, but 'Come in!' came the instant, no-nonsense, Scottish reply.

The chief didn't bother look up from a file he was reading. We dragged our feet up to his desk like we were in detention. I didn't know if I should smile, cry or bend over.

'Ah, good afternoon, gentlemen,' said Straughan, looking at his watch. 'Sorry to have dragged you out of bed so early today. Sit down. You look great, Christopher.'

An ex-military man now somewhere in his late fifties, the chief was still powerfully broad, leaning forward on elbows that supported huge arms and shoulders you could have bent steel around. His proud ginger-brown-grey moustache sat on a heavy bust, sculpted with a defiant frown. He probably had to chisel rather than shave. Yet, from under the two furious caterpillars gripping his forehead there was still a telling hint of humanity in the hazel sparkle.

On the desk was a photo of his two even bigger sons in Afghanistan, now both marines themselves, proudly standing in full rig with an arm on each other's shoulder. Next to that, the boys' mother, Alice, sadly passed away around three years prior.

Straughan was a true veteran, having seen serious action in several of the world's most dangerous countries. He retired as a Regimental Sergeant Major and progressed rapidly up the ranks with us. When he talked, you listened, but he was always courteous enough to take everyone's viewpoint into consideration and never tripped over pride if proved wrong. But while he had always been someone I could trust, and someone who I think trusted me, I couldn't deny there had been some frost appearing on the surface of our relationship. I didn't know if it was just the pressure of the cuts and losing staff, or if I'd done something, but there wasn't the time for us at Special Ops in the same way there used to be.

Flicking through the last of the pages in the file, Straughan pulled the glasses from his nose.

'So, whose idea was the duck?'

I hate ducks. I wanted to go down to the park and shoot them off the pond. I wanted to know if there was a sanctuary somewhere I could drive a bulldozer through. I could have happily bought a ticket to Disney Land, there and then, just so I could have smashed Donald Duck's stupid, smug face in, while Mickey and Goofy watched.

Colin half raised his hand to speak.

'Yes?'

'Nothing, sir. I was just going to say that it wasn't a duck... it was a penguin... but it doesn't matter.'

'No. It doesn't matter,' said Straughan, holding an incredulous glare.

'It was a team decision, sir,' I said. 'We weighed up our options and I was the man sent in.'

'Special Ops is a reconnaissance unit. You're supposed to be invisible. I put it to you that dressing up as a bloody-great furry animal in the middle of the target's own house runs contrary to those principles. What were you thinking?'

Colin stepped in again: 'We had information that McIntyre was meeting with some new people, but we didn't know who. The intel was late, so we had to come up with something quick, hence the... costume.'

Straughan looked at me. 'And DI Martin sanctioned this little stunt?'

'Yeah. Well, I think so.'

'You *think* so?'

'He had a lot of food in his mouth at the time; it's not always easy to tell.'

'Why not place the house under surveillance and organise a tail? What was to be gained by infiltration?'

'There was going to be more than two hundred people in there, all in fancy dress,' said Colin. 'It was impossible to tell who was who unless we got up close.'

'And yet, in the statement you prepared for me this morning, you say that these new people weren't even at the party when you arrived, and they weren't dressed up, they were wearing suits.'

'That's true, sir,' said Colin. 'They arrived at the very end of the evening.'

'And for good reason,' I said. 'Sammy was taking a delivery he didn't want anyone to see; huge boxes full of equipment, at least one of which contained -'

I hesitated for a moment, suddenly realising the magnitude of what I was about to say.

'What?' asked Straughan.

'A bomb. Or something dangerous, at least.'

'A *bomb*? Your colleague here thinks it was disco equipment.'

Colin shrugged. 'I saw some metal cases, but it looked like DJ stuff.'

'Carried by a troop of immaculate foreigners at half-one in the morning?'

'They were packing up.'

'So what about that reaction?'

'Why d'you think it was a bomb?' asked Straughan. 'Did you see it?'

'No.'

'Were they discussing any such weapons?'

51

'I don't know... maybe there was something I missed. We managed to salvage some of the recording. There might be something on there.'

'Oh, there is, I have the transcript here.'

The chief pushed his glasses back on and began reading the file again. Colin slumped forward with his head bowed.

'You spoke to Melissa Dean, a wealthy woman in insurance who offered some great tips on the best handbag to accommodate a Chihuahua... there's some absolutely fascinating advice from a banker named Gerald and his friend on the etiquette when spit-roasting your secretary... oh, and then there's a rather confused young lady who seems to have mislaid her underwear. I could go on, but I think those are the highlights for me. It's hard-hitting stuff, but no mention of any explosives I'm afraid.'

'Is that all we got?' I asked Colin.

He didn't look up.

'Sir, I'm telling you there was something in those cases. I saw how scared those men were just carrying them in.'

Straughan sat back and upright, gripping the edge of the table. He looked at Colin, who was struggling with the failure, or perhaps trying to work out what a spit-roast was.

'That'll be all, PC Whyte.'

'Oh. Okay,' said Colin, standing slowly to double check that it was just him leaving.

A quick trout mouth and a faint shrug signalled that I had no idea why I was staying either.

'Right, well I'll meet you downstairs,' said Colin, opening the door to the office. 'Unless you want to go to the pub and grab some food? Or we could do the sandwich shop? But I'll need to get some money, because - '

'Colin,' said Straughan.

'Yes sir?'

'Piss off.'

'Right you are, sir.'

Colin left, closing the door.

The boss expelled a trademark huff, shaking his head at the footsteps making off up the corridor. He seemed to wait until he could hear the lift doors open before he said anything else.

'Do you trust him?' he asked.

'Colin? Yeah. Only one I do.'

'What about the rest of your lot?'

'I don't really know the others - though I have been trying. Well, with some of them. Well, one of them.'

'I'll bet.'

Straughan got up and walked to the back of his office, boiling his kettle for two cups of tea. He was clearly distracted, but every time he was about to let go another drawn-out sigh steamed the words from his throat. He tapped on the cups with a spoon and looked at nothing out of the window until the silence became uncomfortable.

'Why aren't you doing my job?' he asked, squeezing the teabags hard against the ceramic.

'How d'you mean, sir?'

'You could have been promoted almost every year since you started with the force. I would have vouched for you all the way. Why are you still a PC?'

It wasn't the first time I'd been asked that question. Lots of officers go their entire careers achieving no greater rank than police constable. There are only ever so many supervisor roles that come up, and the ones that do are often on patches miles away from your usual turf. Senior officers are also little more than policy machines, obliged to consider mountains of bureaucratic tripe before we can actually go and investigate the dropped 999 call from the woman being threatened with a gun. Health and Safety legislation has increasingly ensured over the years that we arrive just in time to wipe the woman's brains off the wall and ask her budgie if it saw anything. At least none of our officers get shot and go off sick.

I was in the wrong company to say it out loud, but in the main, a supervisor's role is one long French kiss with the government's rusty hoop; a futile exercise in the avoidance of being sued from all angles, and delegating blame to the lowest common denominator when we invariably are. I didn't much care for kissing butt and quite frankly, I couldn't be bothered with the responsibility. My pay increments kept coming regardless.

'D'you think it's got anything to do with your drinking?' asked Straughan.

The question caught me off guard.

'Drinking..?'

'A few people have noticed it.'

'Noticed what?'

'The smell, for one thing. Not exactly fragrant today, are you?'

'I've been undercover...'

He clearly didn't buy into that as an excuse. He sat down, easing a hot tea under my nose. I took a quick mouthful, trying to swill away some more of the alcohol while hiding behind the cup, but I only succeeded in burning the roof of my mouth.

'Look,' said Straughan, 'the official announcement won't be made until next week but you may as well know now... Special Operations is being closed down.'

The words didn't register at all at first, but that solid, unblinking glare reinforced what I thought I'd heard.

'*Why?*' I asked.

'The independent review has concluded your services are best employed elsewhere.'

'And don't we get a say in this?'

'There've been several meetings. Forum's been on the intranet for six months. DI Martin should have briefed you on the procedure.'

DI Martin was a walrus in chinos. He redefined useless. *Six months.*

'What about our cases?' I asked, trying to ignore the image of Martin with an axe buried in his face. 'All the progress we've made? It's not just McIntyre, we've got loads on the board. What happens to all that work?'

'Any existing commitments will be taken over by CID.'

I cocked my head. We both knew what that really meant. I was almost afraid to ask, even though the acid burning in my stomach nearly made me spit the filthy word out onto the table – where was I going to end up?

'You'll be amalgamated back on shift.'

Shift. I knew it. I fell forwards, clenching my fists and tightening my body until my aching ribs crunched and forced me upright again. It was a punch out of nowhere. We were never considered at risk, even amid the sweeping cuts that were being made across the force. We were a successful team and hit every pointless target the government had tried to trip us up with, only designed so some gimp in Westminster can justify his pointless job and draw a pie chart, claiming his Crayolas on expenses. Why us, and why now? It didn't make sense.

'No, *not* shift,' I said. 'There has to be an alternative. Anything but shift.'

'The Chief Constable is anxious to get people out onto the streets, visible. That's what it's all about these days. For what it's worth, that includes me, and all the other senior officers.'

It was worth nothing. I had worked for years to climb out of that festering hole and now I was being thrown straight back in. I felt sick.

'What about McIntyre?' I asked. 'What if I'm right and he is planning to blow something up?'

'We've got no evidence for that.'

'Oh, come on. Credit me with some experience if nothing else.'

'Do you really think he'd be wheeling bombs through the door with two hundred people at home?'

'It's the perfect cover; plenty of cars in and out all night, all his cronies on site to talk plans.'

'I can't believe that.'

'I know what I saw.'

'Then you know what you need to do. Submit an intel report and they'll – '

'Ignore it, yeah… I need to go.'

I stood up - and nearly fell straight back down again as my body tugged to one side. My anger wasn't going to let me stop, and I dragged myself to the door.

'Chris, get to the hospital, now. And don't come back until the doctor clears you.'

'I'm okay,' I said, trying to reach down for the handle.

The boss came over to assist, watching my steps carefully so I didn't trip as I turned into the corridor. Then a hand came to rest on my shoulder. Straughan looked around and spoke quietly to my ear.

'Look, they're closing the department, but you don't have to like that. Get last night down on a statement and hand it to me A.S.A.P. In the meantime keep your ear to the ground. If you stumble on anything new, come to me first, not that blob, Martin.'

I nodded and we exchanged half-smiles. I turned to walk back to the lift when the grip on my shoulder tightened.

'But Chris, stay off the booze. I can't defend you forever.'

Straughan closed the door, leaving me staring at the wood.

I couldn't understand where this drinking thing had come from, especially in a building full to brimming with young coppers who did nothing but piss it up in their every spare moment. And who was he defending me from?

There was no question that now more than ever I had to come up with something. I'd never really thought of what I had as a career, but whatever it was, it had just smashed all over the floor in front of me.

10

I couldn't get my head out of my hands.

'Another one, mate?' asked Keith, the landlord.

'Yeah, why not, it's Christmas,' I said, with all the enthusiasm of an arthritic sloth on his day off.

I dropped a handful of coins on the beer mat and returned my face to my palms. I shouldn't have come out at all. Three cracked ribs and another four hairline. Nothing anyone was going to operate on, but the swelling was going to take a week to calm down and I'd still be bruised for a month or more. The doctor said I needed to rest and gave me some tablets. He also said that I shouldn't be at work for at least a fortnight, but when I was discharged I called Straughan and told him I'd be in the next morning.

I also wasn't allowed any alcohol, but I had a point to prove. Sure, I liked a drink as much as the next man, but I could handle it. I never drank on duty, or at least very rarely undercover. And if so many people were that worried then why hadn't anyone said anything before? Did someone have it in for me, starting a rumour that had somehow hardened into a malicious truth? Anyway, I'd had a burger and a few packets of crisps so I reasoned I should be fine.

Keith slopped the pint in front of me and I threw a few gulps down my neck.

'You got any more of that monkey whisky in?' I asked.

'Monkey Shoulder? Yeah, came this morning.'

'I've got my credit card.'

'Where's your mate gone?'

'Colin? I dunno, probably at chess club or playing bingo with his nan.'

58

'Nice lad. Bore the tits off you after a while, but nice lad. I would have thought he'd stay out a bit longer. Is he alright?'

'They're putting us back on shift.'

'Oh. Double, is it?'

'I think so.'

Colin was a nice lad, which made me resent Straughan's attitude that little bit more. We were a tight unit and our results spoke for themselves. Okay, McIntyre still eluded us, but handing him over to a CID team buried under their own problems was only going to set us back. It made me wonder who was really making the decisions. Had Sammy planted someone among the top brass? Our seniors had all been with us longer than you'd get for murder. Straughan was probably the freshest face, but even he had sixteen years' service under his belt. Was he looking at increasing his pension? I couldn't see how that would fit. He wasn't the type.

Keith reappeared with two tumblers of whisky.

'This one's on me, mate.'

With a 'Cheers' we both knocked it back. Beautiful stuff. Not sure what the monkey connection was, but I'm sure the distillery would tell you if you paid twenty quid for their tour and promised to buy some tenuous tat from their gift shop.

'I was going to ask you, actually,' said Keith, leaning on the bar next to me, 'how many times can you punch someone before it becomes assault?'

'Just the once will do it normally.'

'Even if they've Flymo-d your tortoise?'

'Is this your neighbour again?'

'Oh, don't get me started. Who gets up at six in the morning to start mowing the lawn? He thinks he's helpful doing the beer garden, and then bits of bloody reptile go wangin' everywhere and he's smashed me shed window.'

'I told you to lock that thing up. Who has a pub tortoise?'

'No one anymore. Then a load of coppers turn up because he's feeling "intimidated", and I'll get nicked if I don't calm down and put some clothes on.'

'Clothes?'

'It was early and I'd had a few. I forgot.'

'In the middle of the street? You were lucky.'

'I was hardly waving it at him. I bloody hate the police...'cept you, obviously.'

Anyone else might find this weird, but in the ten years or so I'd been subjected to Keith it was fairly standard stuff. Brought up on a diet of tabloid journalism and the casual bigotry of the pub faithful, he had a calm hatred for just about everyone, happily reeling off the justification for his standpoint as you ignored him with your beer. You could walk off mid-sentence, and unoffended, he'd just carry on the conversation with the next person at the bar, and so on, oblivious to the pained expressions looking back at him.

The pub was far too close to the station in all honesty, and I kept bumping into the wrong people. Like every other regular I would have gone somewhere else if there was somewhere within walking distance. The best we could do was to make sure we spent enough money to get Keith to sod off on holiday every now and again and leave us with the barmaids.

'Jen not joining you tonight?' asked Keith.

'No. Not tonight.'

'Oh, like that, is it?'

Keith had been married seven times, earning him the nickname Liz, after that famous Hollywood polygamist. His first 'I do' echoed off the church walls at the tender age of eighteen, while his most recent – to a Malaysian woman he 'bought' on the internet - was nearly drowned out by the toilet flush in his own bar. He had the place licensed to try and improve business, which certainly worked. What he didn't count on was a function room full of people every month to observe civil partnerships. Maybe it was more discreet, or just that the place was dirt cheap, but there had been several ceremonies in the first few months and plenty more booked.

'We had a load of benders in again the other day,' said Keith, topping up his whisky. 'I don't mind so much 'cause they always drink the expensive stuff, but I prefer the lezzers. At least you've got something to look at, then. I just don't want the place to get a reputation though, you know?'

'Keef! Keef! You must come quickly! Come Quickly!' said Mae Su, appearing behind the bar, soaked from the waist down.

'Now what?'

'Washing machine water all over floor.'

'Well put some towels down.'

'No, is lots of water. Pipe broken.'

'Oh - I knew I should have paid an extra tenner and got your sister.'

Keith chucked his whisky back, making for the stairs and their flat above the pub.

'Hi Kiss!' said Mae Su.

'Hi, Mae Su,' I said. 'You okay?'

'Yeah. Bit wet. I tell him to get a pummer, but he say is too much. Has he not give you cake?'

'Cake?'

'Yeah, I say buy for you.'

She disappeared into the pub kitchen, returning with a little round cake, topped with a solitary candle.

'Happy birfday!'

'Oh, thank you Mae Su. How did you remember?'

'I write on calendar. I would make for you but he did not get me ingredient.'

'No?'

'No. He is asshole.'

'Oi, Ting Tong, are we sorting this out or what?' shouted Keith from upstairs.

'Got to go. See you!'

That poor girl; sex slave for a misogynist, racist homophobe twenty years her senior, and yet that smile never dropped.

No one else knew it was my birthday because I hadn't told them, or more specifically, I hadn't told them on social media. We're such a *social* society, sat about a pub table ignoring each other with smart phones, telling hundreds of people we don't know what a wonderful evening we're having ignoring each other, while the bloke opposite 'likes' it. Along with everyone else in the world I dabbled with it, but as far as I can tell you stay connected for only two reasons; the first is to watch the people you hate get fatter and fatter in their photos, eventually replacing their profile picture with a cat in recognition of their own hideous visage. The second is to look at the people you want to shag wearing bikinis in their holiday snaps, only to find out they're 'in a relationship' with some git you hated from school and they unfriend you. I never understood the games and notifications and 'Geoff stuck a chicken up your arse' stuff you got emails about every five minutes, and after a few weeks I deleted myself. Besides, you're not allowed to have fun in the police. Especially not fun the whole world can see. I'd rather come out into the open air to be around living, breathing people. At least my imaginary friends were real.

I blew out the little candle and reached for my beer, when in the corner of my eye, a light grey suit jacket arm came to rest on the bar. I couldn't see them, but I knew those eyes were fixed on mine.

'Out celebrating with your buddies?' she said, turning the silver base to read the icing on my *Forever Friends* cake.

'Why are you here?' I asked into my pint glass.

'This is my local as well. I don't need your permission.'

'Where's your boyfriend?'

'At the gym.'

'Again? If he's having trouble getting served I could sort him with a fake ID.'

'You're so jealous, aren't you? Is it because he's better looking than you? More sensitive? Taller? Fitter? I could go on.'

'You usually do.'

'Where's Keith?'

'Ordering a new wife.'

Jen moved along the bar to try and alert someone to her presence. I took the opportunity to have a quick glance behind me, and sure enough, Claire snarled back. She was Jen's best friend, or at least pretended to be when she had nothing else to do.

'I take it you put this noise on the jukebox,' said Jen, waving to try and attract Keith's attention.

'T'Pau is not "noise".'

'They did one good song.'

'Which is one more than anyone else manages these days.'

'Sorry, love,' said Keith, returning to the bar. 'Trouble with the staff. What can I get you?'

'Half a Bombadeeay and a soda water with lime, please. We're in the corner.'

I chuckled to myself as she walked off. There always had to be a pretension about everything; "Bombadeeay". I loved the fact she drank real ale, but I must have told her every week it was 'Bombardier' and still she insisted on the French pronunciation. But only a soda water for vegan Claire, of course. I was surprised she had the energy to make it out at all. That growl in my direction must have used up two of her three daily calories.

63

'She's just like my third,' said Keith, pulling at the pump, miffed at having to hand-deliver drinks yet again. 'Did I ever tell you about her?'

'Once or twice.'

I pulled a Garfield in preparation for another half-hour drone. Then Keith's eye was caught by something else.

'Look out,' he said, nodding to the door, 'it's that blonde tart you work with.'

I spun round to see Katya's smile.

'I'd nob that all day,' said Keith under his breath, walking off with the drinks.

Katya had covered half the distance from the door when she turned, obviously waiting for someone to follow her. A short blur behind the frosted glass, I initially thought it was a child, until, almost in slow motion, a man dressed in a police uniform minus the tie and epaulettes emerged, spinning a ridiculously large car key around his finger – Tony Riley.

He sauntered up to Katya, more sideways than forwards, taking hold of her hand as they continued to the bar. My heart stopped and a frown collapsed onto the bridge of my nose. What the *fuck*?

'Chrissy boy,' said the little imp, with a stupid grin on his stupid face.

I could never work out whether or not he thought I liked him. I'd certainly never tried to give that impression.

'I'll have my usual, Kate, I'm just going for a slash,' he said. And off he bowled again, leaving that stupid key on the bar.

'Colin told me about the department,' said Katya, 'I can't believe it.'

'Yeah, it's a real bummer,' I said, watching Tony jig his way to the toilet.

'Are you okay?'

'Me? Yeah, I'm... are you?'

64

'Time will tell. I was amazed. And they're putting us back on zshift.'

'I know... Sorry, Katya, are you and Tony..?'

'Yeah.'

'For how long?'

'Nine months.'

'*Why?*'

'Why not?'

'He doesn't even know your name.'

'Huh. I'm used to that.'

'And he leaves you to buy the drinks?'

'It's my round. He bought the last few. What is it?'

'Nothing, it's...'

'What? We have fun. We laugh. Am I missing out on something elszwhere?'

She looked at me, but not in the way I wanted her to. She was oblivious, and while I could feel the drink egging me on, I knew I had to shut up.

'What's this?' she asked, looking at my cake. 'Is it your birthday?'

'No, it's just a snack. I wouldn't eat anything that didn't have bears on when I was a kid and that's kind of stuck with me.'

She laughed out loud and my spirits rose slightly. Tony reappeared from the toilet, still doing up his fly.

'Having fun?' he said, with a hint of jealousy that he wasn't cracking the jokes.

'You're so funny,' said Katya.

'On your own again, Chris?' asked Tony.

'Not anymore it seems.'

'Ah, well we're only staying for one. I'm driving tonight. I boshed us up in the new M3. You haven't got a M3 have you, Chris?'

'No, I've got a penis.'

Katya roared with laughter, shrinking that little man another couple of inches. Suddenly I was enjoying myself.

'Yeah, well, sorry to hear about your *demotion*,' said Tony, 'but don't drink too much tonight, you don't want to run up *a big bill*.' He snorted to himself, nudging Katya who smiled, but wasn't sure why. Wisely deciding to give up, he peeled away. 'Who've you gotta shag to get a pint 'round here?' he asked.

'Why don't you join us?' asked Katya.

I looked at Tony. 'No. I should go. I'm back in tomorrow.'

'Okay… well, I'll see you at work.'

'Yeah. See you then.'

I finished the last of my beer and scooped my cake off the bar. What a pathetic sight. I didn't want to go home. I nearly stopped and said, 'sod it, I'll have one', if only to piss that elf off some more, but as Katya ordered her drink, Tony started to rub and caress her back and I knew I had to be somewhere else. I watched but she didn't look back.

Jen and Claire only interrupted their conversation long enough to synchronise a brief look of disdain as I walked by, and for once I couldn't even be bothered to smile sarcastically.

Maybe the off-licence was still open.

Happy birthday to me.

11

Colin and I had arranged to borrow one of the pool cars, a decidedly un-fanny-magnetic diesel Astra. Still, at least it didn't smell half as much of stale sick as most of the marked vehicles did, and the sirens meant we wouldn't be late for lunch.

We had an appointment with the manager of a hire car company. Colin took the number plate on the Chrysler at Sammy's, which checked out to a local business. Hopefully they were going to forgo Data Protection issues and tell me who was driving the mobile disco that everyone was so afraid of, or at least give me their payment details and a description.

First we were heading out of town to see a contact, specifically the man that gave us the heads-up on Sammy's new friends. I wouldn't have called this individual a willing source and he wasn't exactly pro-police, but with the correct persuasion his information had proved useful in the past.

As we drove on to our destination the sky seemed to become noticeably darker. Tidy, quiet suburban pads gave way to terraced hutches and tower blocks, until finally, two smouldering cars stood as gateposts to one of the most notorious roads in the town. A couple of minutes more, slaloming around the pot holes, glass and broken bikes, and we were getting close to our man. I asked Colin to slow down and park up. If this guy looked out to see us arrive we'd lose him for a week.

Luckily we were nearer the more respectable end of the street where the graffiti was almost literate, but we knew the car still only had ten minutes before the local idiots stripped it and ate the air freshener. And then came looking for us.

There are some rough places in every town, but the Black Rose Barton estate is the crowning turd peaking up and over the toilet seat, never to be flushed. You were posh in that area if you had both your ears, with maybe one item of genuine jewellery among the quarter of a ton you were wearing. Tracksuits huddled on every corner, drawing on the walls and kicking beer cans into gardens, waiting for someone suitably elderly and unable to jump. Employment just happened somewhere else.

Historically, families from all over Africa and Eastern Europe would have paddled the Channel on inflatable animals for the privilege of living on that estate. Every house and flat was packed, as many as ten to a room in some cases. Illegal extensions had sprung up everywhere, along with tents and makeshift huts in gardens - anything to accommodate just one more person. It looked exactly like what it was; one giant refugee camp, all run by a handful of men perched at the top of the tower blocks, untouchable because no one in authority gave a shit.

Our contact lived in the local pub on the edge of the estate; or rather the over-grown rubble that used to be the local pub. He'd made a little nest for himself, far away enough from the burglary rota everyone else was on to secure whatever money and gear he had in relative safety.

Colin and I edged through the brambles for a boarded window. It only took gentle persuasion to remove the nails from their slots and we propped the moulding plywood against the wall. Satisfied there was no one on the ground floor, we jumped in.

Tiptoeing through the eerie bar area, thick dust danced in the occasional light, settling on tired wooden pumps still connected to long-dry barrels. Behind them, a long mirror rose from a terrace of shelves, home to a few ancient bottles stained brown as the last of the liquid had evaporated. Faded chalk offered us the day's specials with a price you couldn't buy a litre of petrol with nowadays.

Above the bar, engraved tankards bowed from their hooks, surrendered to insurmountable cobwebs, each one carrying the nickname of a man from happier years, long dead or moved far away. In the silence we watched the ghosts of children run through the bar and out onto the rusty slide now choked by undergrowth. It was just visible through a crack in the back door as one more miserable lament to what this area had become.

We avoided crunching as much glass as possible to stop at a door leading to the first floor and the old accommodation area. We were about to ascend when the hinges betrayed us and shrieked a warning. Immediately, hushed, anxious voices were alert to our presence. So began a stalemate of silence as one group tried to figure out who the other was.

It was too risky to climb the stairs. I adjusted the radio on my belt, ready to hit my zero-zero emergency button in case there was a sudden torrent of tracksuits and baseball bats cascading towards us. There was no other way down. The first floor boarding was still intact as protection from the weather and it was too high to jump.

Our car was probably already attracting the wrong attention. I stepped forward and called up the stairs: 'Fitch..? It's Chris...'

No response.

'I just want to talk, that's all.'

Unsuccessful whispers seemed to indicate there were only two of them up there, frightened if anything. Happy we were safe I persisted with more confidence.

'Fitch, get down here, *now*.'

'Me-ooww,' came the pathetic response.

'Seriously? Do I have to come up there?'

A little head sprung out, looking down the stairs at us.

'This is harassment, you know!'

Agitated, he started to limp down the bare, creaking woodwork, a testament to where he was injecting of late. He was in his thirties but looked twice that, with a face so gaunt his cheeks were almost touching inside his mouth. His usual grey sportswear did nothing for the impression that he had somehow been dug up and reanimated. There was nothing but ribs on display between the open halves of his ragged hoody, and those legs wouldn't have stood up to anything more than a gentle breeze.

'You can't prove it was me, I don't care what that dickhead says,' said Fitch. 'I've been here all week, you can ask anyone. Check the CCTV. I bet you haven't done that, have you? No, 'cause it's just easier to blame me.'

'I haven't said anything yet,' I said.

'You don't have to say anyfin. I want a lawyer. And not that twat you gave me for the robbery. If I paid tax I'd be really annoyed.'

'If you paid for anything you wouldn't have been kicked out of the flat you scrounged off the state.'

'That was a computer error.'

'*You're an error*. I'm not here to arrest you.'

'Then I'm not saying nuffin. I'm not getting stitched up again like last time.'

'We're just talking.'

'Yeah, that's how it starts. Then two minutes later I'm the bloke in a balaclava holding up some old bag with a banana. I know how this works. You have to read me my rights.'

'You have the right to shut up – use it. Anything you do say is likely to be bullshit, but we're going to try anyway. Happy? I want to talk about the people you saw at the dock.'

'Do you? Well I told my handler everyfin I know, so why don't you go and speak to him? I've got nuffin else to say.'

Zombie-features can often be found lurking on the dock to buy his gear fresh off the boat - before it gets to the

70

dealers who cut it with anthrax and double the price. However, he became annoyed one day recently when the usual ship pulled up without an ounce on board. Suddenly no one was as friendly, shoeing the little insect away for a day's cold turkey. Nothing gets an addict angrier than missing a hit, so to go some way for petty revenge he told us about the new boys in town.

'Who's up there with you?' asked Colin.

'No one,' said Fitch.

Colin listened in to the first floor for a moment before closing the door at the foot of the staircase, glancing around for any other opportunities for us to be overheard. Satisfied we were as safe as circumstances allowed, he took a surprisingly intimidating stance on Fitch's shoulder.

'This is important,' said Colin. 'Who were the people you saw get off that boat?'

'Oh, important, is it? Sorry, my memory's not what it was.'

'It'll be a lot worse when I hit you with my baton,' I said.

'Ha! Give it your best shot. You can show off in front of your little mate here, but I know you're a pussy. And by the look of your face I'd say someone else knows it, too.'

'Oh, Fitch,' I said, 'that's not the attitude.'

At that point I went into my pocket, and to Colin's shock, pulled out a not inconsiderable bag of lumpy brown powder. Fitch's pupils burst wide with excitement. He was absolutely transfixed, like a cat tracking a mouse, almost slobbering. It wasn't surprising. He'd have to go up town and burgle every house for a mile to afford what I had in my hands. If he was careful with his measures it'd be a full month before he came off the ceiling again.

'Are you serious?' asked Colin.

'I want to know what's going on, don't you?' I replied, holding the bag up and shaking it.

71

Fitch had his hands poised at his chest, ready to snatch the bag when I said he could.

'Right, now that I have your attention – the men on the boat?'

'I never saw 'em before. Five or six blokes from Iraq or sumfin'. They all get off the boat and Sammy's waiting for 'em in a car.'

'What were they talking about?'

'I dunno, it was all in foreign. They got in the car and drove off.'

'You told your handler they'd be meeting at Sammy's. How did you know that?'

'A friend told me.'

'Who?'

'Just some guy who gives me the shippin' details.'

'Lee Carr?'

'Maybe. He said Sammy had plans but he weren't telling anyone nuffin. It ain't drugs though. They were going to his party after they'd been to London.'

'Why were they going to London?'

'I dunno. Sight-seeing? He's sending the crates there.'

'Crates? What crates?'

'Boxes of stuff.'

'Big, small, marked with anything?'

'I weren't looking. They loaded them onto a flatbed and moved them into one of the ware'ouses.'

'On site? Are they still there?'

'Are you gonna hand that stuff over now?'

'I might. Are the crates still there?'

'*I've said enough.* They'll kill me. Hand it over.'

I held up the bag and pulled open the seal, tipping it to the side to allow a fine slither of powder to be taken by the draft. Fitch lurched forward as if he was watching a relative about to jump off a cliff.

'*No!*' he shrieked.

'This is your favourite recipe, my friend, totally pure. But if you don't play nicely it's going to the incinerator where everyone thinks it is.'

I began to tip the bag again.

'Building Twelve!' Fitch stuttered. 'The crates are in Building Twelve.'

'You're sure?'

'Positive. Sammy uses it to stow his stuff.'

'What about Customs?'

'Carr pays 'em to look the other way, no one goes near it.'

'Security?'

'Twenty-four hours, you won't get in... but you might get to watch stuff come out.'

'Yeah? When's that going to happen?'

'Hand over the gear, I'll tell you.'

Colin looked at me, still hoping I was joking.

'Please. I'll help you out,' said Fitch.

I ran my finger and thumb across the top of the bag, resealing it tight. With a last look at my colleague, and admittedly still uncertain myself, I tossed it over. Fitch caught it about his midriff, holding it close to his chest like a new-born baby. Colin tried to pretend he hadn't seen anything.

'So, the crates?' I said.

''ang on.'

Fitch hobbled back to the stairs and opened the door.

'Honey? Can you bring that piece of paper down, please?'

Colin and I exchanged a look. *Honey*?

After a moment, slow, uncertain feet started to strain the stairs on their way down to us.

'It's okay, don't worry,' said Fitch, talking through the doorway at this unseen curiosity. 'Come on. Come out and say hi. Look what we've got.'

Reaching with his left hand, Fitch emerged with what was possibly a woman. She was a good few inches taller than him and at least fifteen times as wide, wearing what was once a lilac velour tracksuit and flip-flops. A small handbag dissected her flab, the strap resting tight under one of two fatty flaps mounted on her chest. Lank dark hair half-disguised a culture of spots about her face and neck, but there was no hiding an expression that looked like a bush baby had jumped on its bicycle only to find the seat missing. She must've been high for a week solid, and wasn't coming down any time soon.

'Officers, this is Marilyn,' said Fitch, as if he was introducing the new girl to a primary school class.

'Hi,' I said, barely hiding my disgust.

'She hasn't got any teeth,' said Colin.

'*I know*,' said Fitch with a dirty smile. 'Where's the piece of paper, honey?'

When the question eventually sank in, Marilyn opened the top of her bag and started to pull things out, holding them up in turn for her boyfriend's approval like a three-year-old learning shapes.

'No, that's a receipt,' said Fitch. 'No, that's a pen... No, that's a tampon – here, why don't you let me help you?'

Marilyn turned to give us a vacant, gummy smile as Fitch rummaged through her bag, wobbling everything across the top half of her body. He stopped to unfold a piece of paper, reading the details for confirmation before handing it over.

'What's this?' I asked.

'Transport details. Those crates start movin' at the end of the week by road.'

It didn't say what they were, but the final destination was somewhere on London's docks – just an address, no person or company name. As a single document it meant absolutely nothing, it was obviously just something that Carr had dashed off so he knew who to expect and when, but the crates were scheduled to move two at a time, no more than six a day. Staggering the transport of goods is a well-known ploy among criminals anxious not to lose an entire shipment if they get stopped for any reason. We'd need a closer look at those things.

I folded the piece of paper back up and put it in my pocket.

'Hey, I didn't say you could keep that.'

'I didn't ask. Come on, Colin.'

'You can't tell anyone where you got that from.'

'We'll see. If you and the Incredible Bulk here can stay out of trouble for five minutes, maybe I'll forget.'

A call came over our radio: *'Delta, Sierra, one-four-two – Sierra Alpha...'*

Colin replied, 'Delta, sierra, one-four-two – go ahead.'

'Colin, can you attend the weir behind Northam's Industrial Estate? A member of the public thinks they've found a body in the river. There's a crowd gathering.'

Colin looked at me and I shook my head.

'Sierra Alpha we have prior commitments this morning, is there another unit that can take it?'

'Negative, one-four-two, all units are tied up at this time.'

I threw my head back. There was always something.

'Received, Sierra Alpha, we'll make on immediate in five.'

Colin shrugged.

'Sorry, Fitch, looks like we can't stay for tea,' I said.

'You promise you won't say anyfin?'

'I promise nothing. Just make sure you stay away from the docks. You tip off anybody I've got these details and I'll make sure you share a cell with Backdoor Barnes, understand?'

Colin had already straddled the window sill and just about managed to land on his feet on the other side, picking brambles from his trousers until the relief of the pavement and open air. I followed him out when Fitch began with his usual distance-acquired bravado.

'You know why he don't bother with you, don't you? Because he knows you're a sad little copper and you can't touch 'im. He's got you lot in his pocket. And if you ever come back here again, you're *dead*. There'll be twenty blokes waiting for you. We'll smash your face in.'

'I think he's calmed down a lot,' I said to Colin as we walked back to the car.

Neither of us was going to give the satisfaction of turning around to acknowledge him, we just kept walking in case someone who really did have a spine came to investigate the commotion.

Hopefully this 'body' would turn out to be the usual plastic bags, or at worst, a dead dog. I wanted to get to the hire car people before I could go back to Straughan and plan the next move – a move closer to proving Special Ops' worth as a team and avoiding that bloody uniform. Those crates could be anything, but they wouldn't be legal. All the same, no one was going to give me a search warrant based on the word of an addict. We were going to have to be inventive.

Arriving at the car, I opened the passenger door just as a board flew off a first floor window on the pub. Fitch leant out, shaking his fists, screaming louder than ever.

'*Rose! This is fuckin' sugar, you fuckin' prick!*'

'Oh, did I get the bags mixed up again? I thought my coffee was very moreish this morning. Oh well – sorry! Love you! Bye!'

Fitch continued with an impressive barrage of filth, even making up some new words I wish I'd written down. I waved out of the window as we passed, and yes, even blew a few kisses.

'We're going to get killed one day,' chuckled Colin, activating the blues and twos.

'Probably,' I agreed.

76

12

Security lifted the barrier to the industrial estate, and as we drove through I was immediately annoyed to see several of our 'tied up' colleagues were already in attendance.

A small group of people had wandered out of their respective warehouses, standing around on the river bank, but it was nothing you needed a megaphone for. However, the crime scene tent had gone up, so it might have been a genuine call for once. Even so, I said to Colin that unless it was a senior royal then we were going to make our excuses and go.

Ross was taking a statement from someone and nodded us towards John nearer the water. We walked over to meet him.

'Alright, boys?' he said.

'Is there enough of us here?' I asked.

'Tell me about it. There're at least five urgent jobs on the box.'

'What's the point?'

'I don't know, but they've been getting excited about something.'

'Have they got the body out?'

'Few minutes ago.'

'Who is he?'

'How d'you know it's a male?'

'I don't, I'm just assuming.'

'Doesn't look like any of our mispers, but then he doesn't look like much at the moment. Must've been floating about for a while.'

'Who found him?' Colin asked.

'Forklift driver Ross is speaking to now.'

'Suicide?' I asked.

'Probably,' said John.

I needed to find out who was in charge and see if we could get away. Ross was taking the only meaningful statement and John could hold an entire army of the press and public at bay with one burp if he needed to.

I stuck my head inside the tent. A junior SOCO in her full protective rig had just finished taking pictures and pulled a sheet over the body. I could see from the contours of the linen it was somewhat bloated, with dark discolouration blotching through the white. There was a musty smell, but nothing worse. He couldn't have been dead that long.

'Hi. Julie, right?' I asked. 'Who's in charge today?'

'I don't know, actually,' said Julie, 'I've never seen him before. He's in the van with one of your guys.'

'Christopher,' said a familiar voice at my shoulder.

I was nudged forward at the base of my back, turning to see DI Martin's gut bursting out of a trench coat. He was followed in by someone I didn't know either; mid-forties, slim, ginger hair, well dressed with a stern look about him.

'Excuse me, what are you doing here?' asked this man.

'I was called here.'

'Well we don't need you, thanks.'

'PC Rose, this is DI Fergus,' said Martin, 'he's the SIO today.'

'Great. So can I go?'

'PC *Rose*,' repeated Fergus, exchanging a look with Martin. 'I've heard a lot about you,' he said, extending his arm.

I didn't know what that meant. Heard what? I hadn't done anything. I worked in a secretive unit that almost no one knew about. Or at least I did. I certainly didn't do anything in my uniform days worthy of attention.

'I deny everything,' I said, accepting the handshake.

78

'No need to be so modest, I'm sure. I understand you've been making progress with McIntyre and his friends.'

'I was,' I said, turning to my inspector, 'but they're closing us down, so I'd expect more trouble if I were you.'

Martin wasn't bothered in the slightest.

'Do what you need to do, Christopher. We've got enough here to handle this.'

'Thank you,' I said.

Without hesitation I left the tent to find my partner, who was with a group of officers intercepting a TV van.

'Come on, we're going,' I said.

Colin ignored me, looking about the scene.

'They must have been moving quickly to beat us here,' he said. 'We only got the call, what, ten minutes ago?'

'They've got nothing else to do. It's a waste of time. Let's go.'

'Who's the victim?'

'I don't know,' I said.

'It's someone important or *he* wouldn't be here.'

Colin nodded at Fergus who had emerged from the tent with Martin. Must have been time for lunch.

I walked back towards the car hoping Colin would follow, but he was transfixed on the scene, clearly suspicious of something.

Martin and Fergus, heavily engaged in conversation, were on their way back to the van. Colin saw this as his opportunity and made for the tent, taking a line out of sight.

'Colin...'

He ignored me and carried on.

'*Colin...*'

He still he ignored me. I couldn't remember a time when he'd been so distracted.

Close to the tent, Colin tip-toed the last few feet and with two fingers, opened the canvass just enough to peek through. One final check the coast was clear and he moved in, completely uninterested as to whether I was following him or not. I jogged to catch up, keeping down-wind of the DIs.

I leant into the tent and whispered: 'What are you doing?'

He *still* ignored me, reading through some of the preliminary notes.

'Colin, what are you looking for?'

'He has to be here for a reason.'

'Who?'

'Fergus. And don't you think it's odd Martin's bothered to leave his desk?'

I might have agreed if it wasn't for the conversation with Straughan - every rank was expected out on the streets, hugging and kissing old ladies, regardless of whether or not they could put two steps together without fear of cardiac arrest.

Colin put down the notes, looking over the mottled death shroud. With thumb and forefinger he gripped the corner of the sheet. He was about to yank it back when Julie reappeared.

'Can I help you, officers?'

'I need a look at the body,' said Colin. 'We might have a match on the misper database.'

That was a lie. Colin never lied. Colin didn't know what a lie was.

Julie obliged, slowly peeling back the sheet with a sickly, sticky noise as it separated from the gelatinous flesh underneath. My expression crumpled in disgust. The bloated face, one eye open, shone in the lamplight. He looked like a giant, mouldy Jelly Baby and the smell of stale canal water tinged with decay made me gag.

Then there was something familiar about him. Something very familiar. In a moment of realisation I almost leaned in too close to the body, tilting my head to take in the features as if he was standing, or rather sitting, upright.

'That's Bingo!' I said.

'What?'

'Bingo Sewell – Eric Sewell. He's one of McIntyre's men.'

'Not anymore,' said Julie.

'What's the cause of death?'

'We don't know yet.'

'Well, has he been shot, stabbed?'

'Like I said, we don't know,' said Julie. 'I would presume suicide.'

'No. Not this one.'

'He must've been in the water for at least twenty-four hours –'

'Closer to forty-eight, actually,' I interrupted. 'He's still wearing the same clothes he had on at the party.'

'Excuse me?' said Julie.

'We had a fight – well, sort of. Have you found his wheelchair?'

'His *wheelchair*? You had a fight with a disabled man?'

'Oh, it's okay, he's a prick. But he wouldn't have wheeled *himself* into the water.'

I caught Colin's eye and he nodded to say, *I knew it.*

This was one of Sammy's big boys. He was heavily involved with the running of the empire and very few people would have been willing to take a target like that on, disabled or not.

'What's going on here?' asked Fergus, swiping back the canvas to re-enter with Martin. 'I thought we dismissed you, PC Rose?'

'Do you know who this is?' I asked.

'We'll confirm his identity with the coroner.'

'This is Eric Sewell. He's one of McIntyre's top men.'

'Like he said, he's going to the coroner,' said Julie, like a temperamental child.

'How do you know him?' asked Fergus.

'There was a time when I arrested him most weeks. We had a… *run-in* the other day.'

'A fight, apparently,' said Julie, who was awarded a stay-out-of-it glare for her trouble.

'Oh? Well it sounds like we might need a chat at some point, doesn't it?' said Fergus.

'Doesn't it?' repeated Julie.

I turned to the skinny lab rat. 'Sorry, don't you have test tubes to polish or something?'

Colin couldn't remove his eyes from those bulbous, gloopy jowls.

'What d'you think happened?' he asked me.

I shook my head.

Martin stepped forward and flicked the sheet back over the body.

'A grass never lasts long, do they?' he said, glaring at Colin and I with accusing eyes. 'It can happen when you let your mouth run away with you.'

I assumed this sudden melodrama was a misdirected barb following yet another official complaint that had been made against him. I didn't know what it was this time, but it wouldn't have been filed by anyone I worked with. My team knew from long experience that there was no point taking Martin through official channels. It could have been anyone with the misfortune to have shared the same county with him for five minutes, but now, as ever, we would all equally bear the brunt of another strop until such time that he was cleared again.

'McIntyre and his men are no longer your concern,' said Martin. 'If this man is who you say he is then we require experienced minds. DI Fergus and I will take it from here, so, you two, out.'

He loved playing the authority figure, especially when there was fresh arse to kiss.

Martin knew nothing of McIntyre or his men. His job was to say yes to the things we were going to do anyway and make sure we had enough Blu-Tack to stick suspect photos to the wall. He'd had countless opportunities to interest himself with our projects over the years and he chose to stay away, attending community dinners and rewriting SOPs no one ever used. If he'd stepped in to keep our department on its feet we might have been able to bring the case unfolding in front of us to a near-satisfactory conclusion. As it was, we may as well have chopped Bingo up and grilled him on a camp fire, taking turns with a verse of Kum Ba Yah. There was no way our CID were even vaguely interested in taking him on. Even if they found the killer had signed his name in bullets on his back, Sewell was going to be written off as a suicide, or at worst, an accident. McIntyre didn't want in-depth investigations into his men whether they were butchered or not.

I really don't mind admitting that I pictured Martin alongside the body on that table. Was there any way I could frame him? Get someone to tie a piano to his ankles and drop him off for a swim? His kids never visited, his wife didn't like him. Would anyone really care?

I shook the anger out of my head as I left the tent and climbed the embankment with Colin. I reminded myself that Martin was absolutely inconsequential. If I wanted to go for McIntyre I would, whether he knew a single thing about it or not. Maybe Bingo was a grisly indication that I was not alone in that aim? Then again, perhaps Sammy got tired of his bullshit and had the pleasure himself, and no doubt, it was a pleasure. Either way, it was a warning that even those who supposedly enjoyed the highest level protection were still vulnerable. Neither Colin nor I enjoyed any such assurances, and anyone could be watching.

13

Colin overdid a laugh to fit in as Keith finally finished slurring his punch line, one of many I could have legitimately arrested him for that night. They clinked glasses and threw their shots back.

Colin was keeping up surprisingly well. His nan, Edith, hadn't allowed alcohol in the house since his granddad died from liver failure around fifteen years ago. The booze was also credited for a string of affairs and a young Colin was a daily witness to some extreme rows. Granddad Burt was from a time when 'binge drinking' was just called 'drinking', and it was almost exclusively by men of a certain age trying to escape the realities of marriage because you weren't allowed to divorce.

Keith necked his seventh chaser and slapped the little glass down onto the woodwork.

'I've got to say,' he said, wobbling on his arms with a smile, or as close as you can get to a smile with six teeth, 'I love the police.'

I frowned. 'No you don't.'

'No, you're right I don't. But if they were all like you two gents, then I would.'

'No you wouldn't.'

'No, you're right, I wouldn't. But at least you're not one of those PCS - esses... PCOFs... PC – '

'PCSOs?' I said.

'That's the buggers.'

It didn't seem likely that the public would ever be entirely convinced about the relatively new phenomenon of the Police Community Support Officer. You can see what the idea was, but sadly, they may as well dress them up in leather gimp suits and write 'Kick me' on their backs. The lesser crooks are very often children and young adults, many of whom have taken the time to carefully develop the attitude and general demeanour of a honey badger. If a PCSO does choose to brave the barrage of insults and low density projectiles, then he or she is only starting with the real problem; namely how to retrieve a bag of cannabis from a feral moron with absolutely no authority to do so. The blue-banded little helper must somehow contain their man long enough for a fully-fledged officer to leave his more serious job, and travel all the way back across town to perform the search, surely negating the entire point.

All the PCSOs I'd met were really nice guys, and many of them use the role as a springboard into the job proper. Perhaps they work at a more rural, small community level, but the general consensus is that if you're going to spend money on training someone, make it an officer who works past midnight and has at least marginally more power than the Liberal MP for Ramsbottom East.

'Right,' said Keith, giving the bar a determined slap, 'we need some real booze'. He called to Mae Su as she arranged flowers at the end of the bar, 'Love, can you go upstairs and grab my scotch?'

'What you say, piss head?'

'My special whisky in the cabinet.'

'You have leg, fuck face. I busy.'

'You can do the flowers later, go and get it.'

'You eat my crack.'

'*Please*.'

Mae Su stuck her bottom out, making a sort of rat-gnawing impression.

'Don't get married, boys, it's just grief. Two secs.'

Keith inhaled what was left of his pint and walked to the stairs, followed all the way by his wife's middle finger.

Mae Su finished putting the last of the flowers together in an ornate vase, and stood back to admire them.

They were completely at odds with the tired woodwork and stained brass, but you had to appreciate the effort.

'They look great, Mae Su,' I said.

'Oh, fank you, Kiss. I grow in garden. I want to make place look nicer, it too dark. How you, Cowin?'

'I'm very well, thank you,' said Colin. 'Those flowers are very pretty - just like you.'

'Oh, don't. You make me go all wed.'

'Mae Su, can I ask you a question?' asked Colin.

'Yeah.'

'Be honest. I don't mind what you say, just as long as it's the truth - do you think I'm attractive?'

'No.'

'...You don't want to think about it?'

'Why I fink about it? You sit there, I see you.'

I stifled a laugh.

Keith reappeared in the bar. 'Oh, now you're finished with the flowers. You can talk to these boys, but you can't be arsed to look after your husband.'

'These boys are nice. You learn. You are wude. No minge for you tonight.'

Colin nearly spat his drink across the bar.

'You look at your dirty magazine you fink I don't know about in the drawer,' Mae Su leant over to Colin and I. 'He like fatty really. His magazine have picture of massive burger-eater.' She held her arms outstretched and simulated munching on giant portions of food. 'Look at me, I am fatty! Keef like me. I am fatty!'

'Go and start the dinner.'

'I see you soon boys. I go to make fatty food now,' and she did another impression right up close to Keith. 'Fatty, fatty titties!'

'Where did you find her?' I asked, laughing into my pint.

'Don't drink and shop on the internet. I was only looking for a cordless drill.'

While Keith was momentarily distracted with another customer I watched Colin. He looked thoughtful, flicking his glass on the bar. He might have been upset not to be thought of as attractive, something particularly tough to take when you've just asked someone married to an elderly goat. Just as likely he was as frustrated as I was that the spectre of shift was a day closer and we had nothing to change that course.

The hire car company were useless. They'd taken an array of fake details and obviously not bothered to check, satisfied enough that the payment cleared, albeit in someone else's name to that on the invoice. The assistant was adamant that it was a white guy who leased the car, but she gave the usual, 'short dark hair, medium build' description that only narrows the field to every man and some women west of Moscow. There was no CCTV in their office, and according to the manager no concerns were raised with him before, during or after the lease. I asked to see the car, but it had gone out again for the week. I was told they clean each one inside and out before the next customer takes it, and nothing unusual had been found in that process. It was a Chrysler alright, but that was as much as we were ever going to know.

Keith returned and poured out three shots of his favourite old whisky. It was good; smooth with just the right bite at the end. Colin almost gagged on his but still forced a short smile before returning his glare to the beermat. There was definitely something on his mind, but before I could ask what it was Keith chimed in again.

'Have you got a girlfriend, Colin?'

'No,' said Colin. 'I work too much. I haven't got time for women.'

We both knew that wasn't true but I wouldn't say anything.

I first met Colin ten years ago when he was fresh out of training. He was assigned to headquarters to look after the technical equipment. He always seemed to be quite popular, though that might have been because nobody knew how to use the photocopier. I'm sure he went out with at least one of the girls from another shift. I have no idea what her name was, but she was pretty and bubbly. He never mentioned anyone else. He was one of those guys you couldn't place with any type of girl that came to mind. He'd be too shy for someone outgoing, too fussy for someone laid back, too hairless for someone who liked the rugged man. And even if he did meet a nice girl they'd have to get through his grandmother – literally. Edith didn't like strangers in the house, particularly women. She'd been looking after Colin ever since his mum died when he was six. His father didn't want to know. He was told from day one he was an accident and I think it's fair to say love never played a part in the family. He was a necessary tax on his relatives until such time that he was adequately employed and the roles reversed. His sister was apparently quite successful, but decided she'd help the family out from afar – Australia - visiting once every decade. And so Colin and Edith were stuck with each other, neither one to allow the other any semblance of a life again.

'Hey, it's the A-Team,' said Tony Riley, appearing on our shoulders at the bar. 'Does your gran know you're out, Colin? Make sure you finish your homework or she'll have you over her knee.'

Colin turned and let out the most enormous fake laugh in Tony's face.

'Good one, Tony,' he said. 'Fucking midget.'

The smirk immediately disappeared from Tony's face. He must have been as shocked as I was, though definitely less amused.

'I find I'm just the right height, actually. Just tall enough to bury my face in Kate's tits. Not that you'd know what that was like.'

'True. I don't want your mum to get jealous.'

'Do you wanna go, you speccy twat?'

88

'Alright, alright,' said Keith, 'You fairies shut-up and tickle each other in someone else's pub. I'm not having it in here.'

Katya appeared at the bar, walking straight into the atmosphere.

'Everyzing okay here?'

'Fine darlin'' said Tony, exaggerating a reach around her waist and grabbing just under her breast. 'Colin was just saying how lucky I am to have you in my life.'

Katya shrugged out of his grip. 'Great. Where's my drink?'

'Go and take a seat, I'll bring it over.'

'Forget it, I'll buy my own.'

'No, no, I'll get it. Grab the comfy chairs in the corner.'

'I said forget it. I want to talk to Chrisz. Go and zsit down.'

'You heard the boss, Tony - sit,' said Colin.

Riley squared up to him and they snarled like dogs in a park. Katya and I had to pull them apart.

'You watch your back, Whyte,' said Tony.

'Oh, go and zsit down, you idiot.'

Colin waved as Tony walked off backwards, keeping his glare fixed. I was impressed and a little unnerved at the same time. Colin downed almost a whole pint in seconds and slid off the stool to go to the toilet.

'I thought he was the quiet one?' said Keith.

'So did I,' I replied.

My attention turned to Katya who had something of her own worried look. She made short work of her half and immediately signalled for another.

'I heard about what you saw at McIntyre's,' she said.

'What did I see?'

'The bomb.'

I hesitated. It was a notion that seemed to be getting more and more ridiculous as time went on and I was beginning to resent that man's power to consume my time.

'I don't know that I saw a bomb.'

'You seem pretty zsure in your statement.'

'Why were you looking at my statement?'

'I'm doing some follow-on from another handler. He zsays that McIntyre may have some contacts up north.'

First I'd heard of that, but if business was slow on the south coast you go where the money is. McIntyre had an expensive lifestyle to fund and a lot of people relying on his decisions.

But at that moment I didn't care, or at least I didn't want to. I was in no state to contemplate what was going on up north, at the docks, with Bingo, or anything else. All the same, Katya said she was impressed with my efforts, and for once it looked like we might be on for a decent conversation, that was until a commotion broke out behind us. Tony had confronted Colin leaving the toilets.

Slightly dizzy, I negotiated several people to stand between the pair.

'Stay out of it, Chris,' said Tony. 'Let him fight his own battles.'

To my shock, Colin lunged in and missed with a punch, tripping and only just staying on his feet. Tony spun round to throw his own and I grabbed his arm in the air. He turned on the spot and swung for me. I ducked and hit him in the stomach before rising again and instinctively throwing my left hand, connecting with the side of his face. He was staggered but still determined. Fuelled with pure adrenalin and about thirty units of alcohol, I threw the biggest right hand of my life, landing with all five knuckles on the other side of his face, knocking him to the floor.

'Zstop! Zstop!' shouted Katya holding her palms to my chest. 'What is it with this macho bullzshit? We're all on the same team.'

90

A surge of pain shot through my fingers and I tried to shake it out. I could see Colin wanted to kick Tony while he was down, but he just about managed to stop himself and walk away.

Tony reached up onto a nearby table and gripped an empty pint glass. Pulling himself up onto his knees he threw it across the room, but missed Colin and hit the back of someone else's head. The heavy-set man looked around like someone had flicked a wet towel at a gorilla's knackers, but he didn't see Tony on the floor, looking past him to someone completely innocent in the corner. He jumped off his bar stool and ran at full-pelt across the room, grabbing his supposed attacker by his hair and dragging him across the table. The victim's girlfriend gripped both hands around the man's huge tattooed bicep, but had no time to explain what had happened before her boyfriend was thrown against the wall.

From that point onwards everyone else in the pub seemed to find an excuse to join in with one side or the other. Two women who were otherwise friends began a slanging match, a group of younger lads picked up a pool queue each and some old sod in the corner was throwing dominoes at anyone in range.

The tattooed man was forced back with a fire poker until he accidentally knocked the vase off the end of the bar. Hearing the smash, Mae Su ran downstairs, instantly becoming enraged at the sight of the damage. She jumped on the big man, wrapping her arms and legs around his body, screaming in his ear and shaking as though she was trying to knock coconuts out of a tree.

In every corner of the bar, punches were landing, tables were breaking and glass was smashing.

'Call the powice, Keef! Call the powice! AHHHHHHHH!'

14

I hadn't been down to custody for ages. Certainly not as a prisoner. It was getting light outside again and I hadn't slept a wink. Every time I managed to drop off a pain somewhere in my body kicked me. I must have broken some more ribs, and re-broken any that may have healed.

Most, if not all, of the others involved in the fight had been processed; fourteen arrests in all, including myself and Tony, but Colin got off. I think he was unconscious on the floor once the first lot of officers waded in with their batons and CS gas. He was taken to hospital by ambulance as a precaution. No wonder he didn't drink if that was the outcome every time.

Mae Su had been de-arrested and left at the scene with Keith. I don't think the sergeant or anyone else could possibly contain that much energy in a pair of mere handcuffs. Fortunately hanging off a man's leg and biting the leather of a Dr Martin never left any lasting marks for a prosecution anyway.

Keith seemed to enjoy it all on reflection. He told one of the officers he was relieved to see a bit of red-blooded action in his pub for a change. New furniture was long overdue anyway. Now he could put some of the money from the civil ceremonies to good use and spruce the place up a bit. Mae Su was in need of a new vase, at least.

I sat upright on the cold, hard mat, looking around the bare room, scratched and smeared by angry, drunken idiots, all of whom would have been additionally arrested for criminal damage. It's something that seems to surprise an entire generation of people brought up to believe it's their right to deface any surface they come into contact with.

Die Pigs said one particularly uninspiring piece of graffiti - you do have a few hours to think about these things, after all. Actually, the term 'Pigs' as slang for the police has an uncertain history. In the nineteenth century, Sir Robert Peel – after whom 'bobbies' are named – apparently used to keep certain breeds of pig, which could be the earliest association. Any American aware of their history will tell you that during the U.S Civil Rights unrest of the 1960s, officers would wear gas masks with an elongated snout, which certainly gave them a swine-esque appearance and lent credence to the label. I think most people today on both sides of the Atlantic and beyond accept the term as a basic insult, and when you've got people like DI Martin clogging up the station, it's hard to shake the image.

Dan waz here, 20/04, 27/4, 04/05, 11/05... stretched another proud scrawl, finishing the night before my arrival. This was the diary of local idiot extraordinaire, Daniel Moss, who, amongst other instances of his constant petty criminality, had recently thrown a BMX through a bus window to 'attract the attention of a friend' on board. At the age of ten some magistrate pronounced that he was destined to become serious trouble owing to his life growing up in a broken home, automatically giving him licence to act up to those expectations with relish. Almost everyone I knew, including myself, was from a broken home, and as far as I knew we'd all been perfectly happy to wait for the bus to stop to talk to our friends.

Next to the toilet bowl it said, *PC Byrne takes it up the arse for free.* I knew that wasn't true. She was very high-maintenance and unlikely to allow that sort of access without at least the promise of some top-end jewellery. However, she was seeing an inspector as far as I knew, so that probably meant he had sufficient funds to claim at least one accident in the sack, if nothing else. I expect he'd need a promotion and at least another eight grand a year if it was to become a regular occurrence, though.

I stood up and stretched; something I immediately regretted with another tug of pain down one side. If I'd already sunk to a career low, the short-to-medium forecast was even worse. Hopefully I could deflect a portion of the flack with the news I gleaned from Fitch.

I also wanted to find out more about Fergus. Colin told me he used to be in charge of Greater Manchester's Murder Squad and they only brought him in for the big jobs. I'd never heard of him one way or the other, but he couldn't be any worse than Martin. Maybe he was the ally we needed to introduce some pace into the proceedings against McIntyre?

I could hear familiar footsteps on their way towards my cell; heavy, annoyed, Scottish footsteps, accompanied by the equally heavy footsteps of Carol, the custody assistant.

The key crunched in the lock. I tried to look as pathetic and injured as possible as the door creaked open. Straughan took a couple of steps into the room, standing over me. I didn't want to look up.

'Thank you, Carol,' he said, and the heavily greased mechanism clicked back into place behind him.

A few seconds passed in silence, each of us apparently waiting for the other to begin. I opened my mouth ready to start making up an explanation but I was shot down straight away.

'Save it,' said Straughan, shaking his head. 'Not now, Christopher, I don't want to know. I'm going to have to waste enough time with this as it is.'

My head dropped again.

He continued: 'I've spoken to the Chief Constable's team and Personnel this morning, and I've managed to cut you a deal. You'll be suspended on full pay, pending a review by CPS...'

I looked up, but Straughan spoke louder to keep me quiet.

'*As yet* there are no formal complaints being made against you specifically, but they will consider the wider public order charges. One way or the other, you are to undergo alcohol counselling... '

You can't be serious, said my expression.

'*starting immediately*. You will be passed fit and dry before you can even consider coming back. Failing that, there may be little else I can do for you. Is that clear?'

'Sir, there's been a development with McIntyre.'

'I really don't care at the moment.'

'I've spoken to one of his contacts. He told me –'

'Did you hear what I just said? You are suspended. I don't give a shit what McIntyre is up to at this present time and neither should you. Do you realise how stupid I looked this morning, trying to explain away your recent antics? It's about time you recognised the consequences of your actions and took your role seriously. Do you hear me?'

'You asked me to tell you –'

'I said *save it*. You are not a rookie, however much you pretend otherwise. I will not go before the Chief Constable again. Understand?'

I was pinned down and my every word was only raising the temperature. I conceded with a gentle nod.

'The words you are looking for are "thank you".'

I nodded again.

'This is it, Christopher, your last chance. You will not make an idiot of me again or you are out the door.'

Straughan turned and tapped on the metal. Carol, who had obviously been listening in, immediately released the door and the chief disappeared up the corridor.

My stare blurred on the concrete floor. Why did it feel like I was the only one for the hairdryer again? I should've shouted back, I thought. I should have stood up to him and said, 'I didn't break these ribs skiing'. Who else is willing to put their lives on the line for this poxy job; a job that punishes industry and endeavour; a job that claims success as a team and isolates the individual in failure? He was right. I shouldn't care about anything. In more than a decade on the worst anti-social shift patterns imaginable I'd done everything that was asked of me, whether I liked it or not. I can't have had more than five days off sick in all that time. I knew people who were taking that every month because of various mythological conditions that only affected them at the weekends. What's the point? I should play the system like everyone else, take my leave, and stay out of anything that carries the threat of returning home even five minutes late.

I wasn't normally an angry person. It's not an emotion that'll achieve you much. I never used to like the cliché, but life really is too short, and when you achieve a certain vintage you understand that. Or do you? What was I doing with that information? I was a single man, couple of quid in my pocket. Was I living life to the full? I certainly wasn't out at all hours partying. I hadn't been to a club in years. I didn't like them. You can't hear anything and they're full of kids.

So what is living for the moment in your thirties? I had recently bought two packets of Hob-Nobs when I only needed one. It was an accident actually, but when I got to the checkout I couldn't be bothered to take them back. That's about as frivolous as it got. I'd never felt the need to acquire a pilot's licence or go bungee jumping naked, strapped to a donkey. I've got some friends that can't sit still for five minutes. They constantly travel around the world, sleep wherever they fall on any given night, no mortgage, no ties... But isn't that just postponing reality? Won't you wake up one day to find you're a leathery sixty-year-old with syphilis and no money?

I'd been in that pokey little cell too long. I couldn't possibly be expected to solve life's mysteries without Keith's help, several pints and a copy of the *Daily Star*.

I really did look pathetic, holding my side as Carol approached me. Her broad, freckled face was as kind as I had ever seen it.

'Are you alright, mate?' she asked.

'Brilliant, Carol. Loving every minute.'

'We've got your stuff at the counter. He said you can go any time.'

'Thank you.'

'I've been asked to pass you this note.'

She held out a piece of folded lined paper.

'What is it?'

'I don't know. Someone dropped it off for you this morning. D'you want a tea before you go?'

'No, I'm fine. Thanks, Carol.'

With a tight-lipped smile, she left, leaving the door ajar. I opened the note, it said, *Sorry. We should meet up. Call me. Katya.*

That was unexpected. It was also very pleasing - exciting even - that she gone to the trouble. But did this mean that we were going to meet up, or *meet up*?

No. It'd be work. I shouldn't read anything into it. I'd call her later and find out what was going on. Still…

Maybe it wouldn't be such a bad day after all? I leapt to my feet - and something crunched, sending a stinging pain across my entire body.

Then again.

15

'This is not a date,' I kept murmuring to myself as I turned into Katya's street. But that hadn't stopped me from analysing every single one of the words in that hand-delivered note, like a schoolboy trying to make sense of the intentions in a love letter. We should meet up it said, not, *Maybe* we'll meet up, or *Perhaps* we will. We *should*. It was a definite statement, positively affirming the requirement for our mutual meeting in person.

Then there were the extra seven words I got in a text when she was too busy to talk at work. She was inviting me over that night. Not *tomorrow*. Not *soon*. Crucially, that short but sweet second correspondence also ended with a kiss. And it was a kiss. Why would you press the X button accidentally? What word could she have been attempting to write that began with, or featured elsewhere, the letter X? My phone was so old it didn't understand those smiley-face things people always send these days; they just come up as squares, like a curious code or hieroglyphic. It wasn't one of those. It was a kiss. Everyone double-checks their texts before they send them. She meant it.

I was surprisingly optimistic for man who was told that morning his job was on the line. By way of reaction to my suspension, I spent a grand total of two minutes looking for alternative employment on the internet, which did nothing for someone with an allergy to the word 'sales'. It wasn't false modesty to suggest I lacked anything approaching a skill. I passed a few exams at school, but I wasn't what you'd call academic. But following that brief examination of what passed as employment beyond the public sector, I wasn't going to fabricate a new CV unless I really had to. The stark truth was that my job was one of the best out there.

We live in a sick world.

I'd known quite a few officers that had been suspended for a variety of reasons, and I half-convinced myself it was inevitable. Once the dust had settled and it was clear there were no complaints worth pursuing, I'd be reinstated. Besides, they need to keep the few experienced officers that remained. In the meantime, I was going to try and enjoy the time I had, I was owed it, starting with that night.

But it wasn't a date. It was business. We were going to talk work. Katya had stumbled across some information and we were going to discuss that. Except we weren't going to discuss it at work, we were going to chat in our own personal time, in our own clothes, at her house.

Considering it wasn't a date, one might question why it had taken me so long to get ready. My usual routine involved three simple steps; get up, grab any shirt that isn't stuck to the floor, leave. I did my washing when I needed to be anywhere important, and I'd always left a tie knotted to the wardrobe handle for special occasions, but that night I'd even used the iron. It was a bit of a relic, coughing up stale fumes with the temperamental steam button, and it did all but ruin my first choice of white shirt, staining it a mixture of rusty brown and orange. I scraped off as much of the gunk as I could from the bottom of the hot plate and tried again with a black shirt. It was tighter than I remembered, but the cut was still just about more flatter than flab. I left the top two buttons undone for a cheeky hint of chest hair, pulling a couple of greys out.

Aftershave was another thing I couldn't normally be bothered with, but I'd blown the dust off the trusty bottle I'd kept on standby for the last few years. It was the cologne I was wearing when I first started going out with Jen and it seemed to work.

But it wasn't a date.

I parked up outside Katya's house, an impressive new-build with views out over the sea. Her car was on the drive, and the first lights had gone on downstairs as the sun began to set.

I took the wine from the passenger seat and locked the car. I was standing at the foot of her front garden when a thought occurred: *why* did I bring wine? I didn't even know if she liked wine.

Ah, every woman likes wine.

But what type did she like?

It was only a bottle I'd had lying around that Jen and I were supposed to have one night, but now it seemed suggestive.

I walked up the driveway looking for somewhere to hide it when Katya saw me at the window. She waved from behind the net curtain and came to let me in.

'Hi,' she said, swinging the door open with a pleasing amount of enthusiasm.

'Good evening,' I said, in a random, breathy drawl, even mustering a sub-George Clooney head wobble from somewhere.

'Perfect timing. Come in.'

I stepped through the door and she looked down at the pavement behind me. 'Is that yours?' she asked.

'What?'

'The wine.'

'Wine?'

She pointed. 'Yes, there.'

I looked over the whole garden before my gaze finally settled on the obvious, lone bottle.

'Oh, yes. I like to let it chill for a bit first.'

'Red wine?'

'… Yes.'

'Well I have a fridge inszide.'

'Oh, do you? Yeah, let's do that then.'

I picked up the bottle and brushed past Katya into the hallway, mentally slapping myself across the face and swearing.

'Have you been painting?' she asked, wrinkling her nose.

'Painting?'

The aftershave.

'Oh, yeah. Little bit. I always get the brushes out after I've had a kicking. Helps me relax.'

She laughed.

That stuff was going straight in the bin when I got back. I knew Jen had olfactory problems. I could eat a full Chinese with beers and still creep one out on the sofa without so much as a twitch of a suspicious nostril.

Katya's place was pristine and inviting, with a large white corner sofa in the open-plan lounge and dining room, positioned to make the most of the view. The TV was just a quiet trinket in the background, almost hidden in the shadow created by a variety of Scandinavian-style designer lamps. However, there were no books on the coffee table, no sign of any pets, no family photos. It could almost have been a show home, giving away little of its owner.

She seemed vaguely impressed with the choice of wine as we walked into the kitchen, a room which maintained the same anonymous theme. It was light and enjoyed that spectacular view again, but there was still nothing of a character evident. Everything was hidden behind brand new, glossy-white cupboards, with only the essentials left out on the sideboards. No washing up left to be done. The sink was gleaming. She couldn't have been home that much.

There was something about the atmosphere in that house that almost made me feel like I was on holiday. I didn't live a million miles away, but I certainly didn't enjoy anything like as much luxury. My place was a bit of a shit hole to be honest, and I was glad I didn't invite her over as I was considering at one point.

I looked over her body as she reached for glasses in a cupboard. She wore a light t-shirt that flapped open slightly at the cleavage, and tight jeans that could have been sprayed on. She allowed her hair to fall about her shoulders, and hadn't bothered with shoes or socks. No nail varnish. She was all natural with no obvious effort, nigh-on perfect. And I really had to start thinking about something else.

She gestured to the wine. 'Are we going to have zsome now, or..?'

'Sure.'

The deep claret glugged into proper red wine glasses, almost big enough to handle a bottle each.

'I've already eaten,' she said, 'but if you're hungry I have zsome –'

'No, no, I'm fine, thank you. I whipped up a little something before I came over.'

Her eyes flicked up with interest. 'Do you cook?'

'I dabble. I like to throw a few ingredients together and experiment a bit.'

I opted not to disclose that the ingredients I had 'thrown together' that evening were a chicken and mushroom Pot Noodle and a Mars Bar.

'Me too. It doesn't have to be hard, does it? Tony can't cook to save his life.'

I smiled politely. I'd almost forgotten about him.

Katya handed me a glass, we clinked, and I followed her into the living room.

To my relief there was no sign of Tony in co-habitation. The shoes and coats in the entrance hall all belonged to a woman, and I noticed there were no pint glasses when Katya opened the cupboard. You have to have pint glasses in the house as a man, even if you're small enough to drown in them.

I sat down, completely contented with the surprisingly good alcohol and allowed the soft cushions to engorge me at all sides. Material sofas are so much more comfortable than leather ones. We definitely had things in common. Katya tucked one leg under the other on the opposite side of the L-shape, and for a moment we just looked out the window, soaking in the last of the sun.

'So, where is Tony tonight?' I asked, hoping for any combination of the words 'abroad', 'accident' or 'dead' in the reply.

'He's on nightsz.'

'Does he live here with you, or..?'

'No. He has a place across town.'

'This is beautiful. Will he join you at some point, d'you think?'

'I don't know. I haven't really zought much about it. I doubt it.'

Good.

'I'm zsorry about last night,' she said. 'Tony was out of line. He's lucky they're so zshort-staffed. He should be zsuspended too.'

I held my hand up. 'You've got nothing to apologise for. I shouldn't have reacted the way I did, it was stupid.'

'You were only protecting a friend, I underzstand. What did Straughan say to you?'

I shook my head. 'Nothing unexpected. I just need to take some time out for a while. I'll do this pointless bloody alcohol counselling and hopefully things will go back to normal.'

'Oh, I'm so zsorry. I should have offered you a zsoft drink. Let me take that.'

'Don't you dare,' I said, stopping Katya from getting to her feet. 'I'm not an alcoholic. Straughan has to look like he's taking action, that's all. I'm fine. There's no problem.'

'Are you zsure?'

'Very sure.'

'Well I'm glad you could make it. I didn't think we'd ever meet up, what with work. Cheersz.'

From then on we relaxed into the conversation, and the wine, finishing the bottle well within the hour and quickly moving onto another two more.

Interestingly, the contact Katya had been looking at seemed to corroborate the notion that McIntyre's drugs had dried up completely. All the same boats were arriving but there was nothing on them, and none of the dealers knew why. Where was the money being invested instead? It was well-known Sammy held legitimate shares in several FTSE companies via sham businesses and the charities he'd set up years ago, but that didn't guarantee the sort of returns he needed to keep up with his living costs. He supported a criminal network too large to suddenly go straight, and even if he tried, someone was always going to fancy themselves as No.2.

And then there was poor Bingo, and the infamous bomb sighting that wasn't.

Sewell could have been an early warning for lost money, but who did Sammy owe these days that was big enough to admit to something like that? Between us we could think of a few people who'd love to raise their profile, but that was a risky way of going about it. Bingo was nothing as an individual. He had to be a message. How would Sammy respond?

Katya was most interested in the penguin files, however, or rather the half a side of A4 we had to explain the night, most of which concerned the wanton violence I enjoyed. Her research again seemed to confirm some kind of Middle-East interest, possibly linked to British nationals in the Midlands, but that was about it, there were no specifics. She thought I might know more, and I was somewhat embarrassed to say that I didn't.

In all truth, Sammy was far from the only concern I had in the office. In fact, in spite of recent events, he was rarely a concern at all. Stumbling across a new piece of information every now and again, there was a brief rush of excitement that we had the missing piece; we had enough to put him away. But in the back of your mind you knew that even if we could get past his moles and through his lawyers, he wasn't going anywhere; too many people wanted him to win. So you turn your attention to something easier that's going to secure you a detection. McIntyre becomes another face on the board until you're ready to get back on the merry-go-round again the following year, or the year after.

With hindsight, that 'bomb' could have been more to do with the beer than I wanted to admit. Perhaps that's what I wanted to see. McIntyre had run his operation for years with meticulous attention to detail; no emails, personal phone calls only – definitely no guns or explosives. He was the most invisible, high-profile, extrovert criminal I'd ever heard of, and it was working perfectly. Why risk all that, and in the most dramatic way possible? I had also started to wonder how far the talk of men from the 'Middle-East' was helping to obscure my opinion. In the absence of any concrete evidence it could come off as borderline racism. Those guys probably weren't legit and knew exactly who they were dealing with, but terrorists?

The more I thought about it, the less I cared. It was effortless listening to Katya speak about where she grew up in Poland, her family, and the incredible rise to where she was. I couldn't imagine enjoying my time like that with anyone else. I was exactly where I wanted to be and work really didn't matter. I could feel what was left of the urgency drain away from me with every sip of wine, laughing and talking into the early hours.

'Zso why do you do it?' asked Katya, starting to look glassy eyed. 'Why the police?'

I paused. What had I concluded in the cell that morning? A tiny voice whispered in my ear, 'to help people', but fewer and fewer of the public seemed interested in our services. We just took their drugs away and locked up their relatives for no reason. It was just a job, marginally less awful than anything else out there.

'Haven't you ever been tempted to lead a life of crime and dezception?' she asked.

'No.'

'I think it's zsexy in a way.'

'Well, there was this one time –'

She laughed, almost spitting her wine back into the glass. I think it was becoming obvious that I was dancing to her tune, and she could play on that at her whim. I laughed with her and decided to drop the act.

'No,' I said again, looking into the last of my drink. 'That station couldn't function without me. Who else is going to dress up and taking a beating, and still have enough energy for a pub fight? Can you imagine John or Ross doing that? Or Travis?'

'Oh, Travisz. He's a pretty man. Such a waste.'

'How'd you mean?'

'Well, he could have any woman he wanted. Not me, you undersztand – I don't want to have to fight for my moisturiser – but still.'

I was confused. 'What d'you mean?'

'Travisz.'

'Yeah?'

'He's gay.'

I scrunched my face up. 'Travis? The tall bloke from traffic?'

'I don't know anyone else with that name, do you? Don't tell me you didn't know.'

'No,' I said, quickly sobering up. 'I didn't know that.'

'I zought it was common knowledge. Perhaps he is not official at work.'

Or in his home life. It was certainly possible the more I mulled it over, but that was taking aside the one glaring fact that he was playing happy heteros with my ex.

So he must be bi-sexual?

'*No,*' said Katya. 'A friend of mine asked him once; I think zshe was hoping. He was quite offended. I get the impreszion he doesn't like women much.'

And he was using Jen to change that opinion? That's like going to Scunthorpe to prove Britain isn't a shit place to holiday. It didn't make a lot of sense, but I wasn't going to press the matter any further. It was probably the usual office slander that had got out of hand, although Katya seemed pretty certain.

'How about you? Do you live with a wife or a girlfriend?' she asked.

'No.'

'Boyfriend?'

'*No.*'

'Family? Children?'

I found it hard to gauge a woman's interest in kids, and going in with how I dismiss *Children in Need* as propaganda has, historically, proved a difficult position to recover from, so I stuck to the facts. I told her about Jen – skipping over the identity of her new boyfriend - and made it perfectly clear how we were finished. As for family... I patted both my trouser pockets and pulled out my wallet.

'I've never shown anyone this before,' I said, handing over the old photograph.

'Who is this? Is this you?'

'Yeah.'

'Aww, so cute. Who are you with?'

'That's my mum and my sister. We're in Dawlish there, on the Devon coast. We never had any money to go abroad, but every now and again mum would pawn off some of her old jewellery, or sell some books so we could take the train to the beach.'

'How old were you?'

'Nine or ten. Emily would have been about six. It's a special photo because we even had ice-creams.'

'It looks beautiful. Where are they now?'

'Mum died a few years ago.'

'Oh, I'm so zsorry. And your sister?'

'She's gone, too.'

'My god... father?'

I shook my head.

Katya was almost tearful. I explained how it was a happier childhood than I had any right to. It might have been very different. If I had one regret it's that I could never repay my mother in the end, not in any meaningful way, and losing Emily clouded her last few years. She never got over that. That picture was almost all I had left of them. Two smiles increasingly lost to a sepia mist.

'It's just you,' said Katya, a sad smile breaking across her face.

I nodded. 'Despite my best efforts, yes.'

'I have a child,' said Katya. She got up from her seat and crashed down again right next to me, almost spilling her wine, 'back in Poland.'

I have to say my heart sank at that news, but as she leant forward to open a silver locket around her neck to show me a picture of a *dog*, it soon got going again.

I have absolutely no idea what she said for the following minute or so, and I couldn't tell you what breed of dog it was to save my life. All I saw was seventy-to-eighty percent of the two most perfect breasts in the history of womankind. Above them, expelling that gentle foreign husk, her moist lips glistened with whatever it is that women put on their lips to make them look like that. I looked up to take in her face and we were inches apart. If it wasn't for the Travis revelations I may well have just dived on her there and then, mid-sentence, but I had rediscovered some restraint. In the moody lamplight, those wide pupils were threatening to suck me in regardless, though, and I had to move.

There was a break in the conversation as she closed the locket and I got to my feet to go to the toilet. As I left the room I noticed she didn't move back to her original spot on the sofa, reaching for the wine and topping us both up again. We were sitting together.

In the bathroom the mirror was quick to remind me how little sleep I'd had. From under one side of my shirt collar, the white of the considerable bandaging across my torso was peeking out. Getting naked, however much encouragement I was getting from my trousers, was not going to be a good idea, if it was an idea at all. After all, she was just as tipsy and hadn't made any move. But then she's Polish, so doesn't the culture dictate that the man has to instigate everything? Is *that* racist? Or sexist? For all I knew she could have given me a full list of her favourite positions while I was wallowing in her cleavage. Perhaps I missed the sign and now she thinks I'm not interested?

This was ridiculous. If something was going to happen, it was going to happen, but not that night. I needed to make my excuses and go. I certainly couldn't stay in the bog any longer or she'd think I was taking a dump. I flushed the empty toilet and used the sound to cover gargling with water, washing away the excess sting of alcohol. Just in case.

Composing myself again, I was about to walk into the lounge when I noticed Katya had my phone in her hand. I leant forward and squinted. It was definitely my phone. She seemed to be browsing through the menu, and turned it over a few times looking at the case. Adding a new mobile number? I thought. Perhaps a cheeky message for me to discover later?

Then I remembered I wasn't fourteen.

Katya jumped as I appeared on her shoulder.

'Your phone made a noisz,' she said. 'I think you have a message.'

'Ah, it's probably the battery.'

I picked it up. There was no indication that was the case.

'You need to upgrade. It's a bit old, iszn't it?'

'I know. I don't plug it in anymore, I have to cover its buttons with a blanket and give it a Horlicks.'

She bent over with laughter again. I could listen that all night. She looked at me standing.

'Aren't you going to zsit down?'

I didn't, and against all logic made the excuse that I should go and try to rest, if for no other reason than to be fresh for the start of counselling the next day. She offered to call me a taxi, but I said I'd walk, it wasn't far and it was a nice night. It was actually about three miles and my side was killing having got up.

I finished the last of my wine and Katya saw me to the door. We agreed it was great to chat properly without Martin standing over us, and we should do it again. We waffled other such awkward pleasantries until our eyes locked. After a few moments I leant in and kissed her on the cheek, near to her mouth. She returned the gesture, making sure she connected with both lips.

I turned to start down the path, looking back with a wink – I don't know why, I never normally do that either. She smiled, and I watched as she closed the door. Two locks clicked into place and the chain slid across. If Tony decided he wanted to come round after his shift, he wasn't getting in, and that made me smile.

I had a pleasant, just-drunk-enough feeling as I walked the quiet, empty streets back towards town. That was the best night I'd had for a while.

Then a burst of laughter came from nowhere, making my sides ache.

I shook my head. 'What the hell are you doing, Jen?'

16

The old community centre used to be something of a mecca for those with, shall we say, no agenda, but when the government announced that they were sinking more money into councils that provided for addicts, the cash-strapped local authority suddenly farted and half a million quid fell out. The centre was completely refurbished and hosted everything from jazz nights to these counselling sessions.

For two hours every week for six weeks, I had to sit on a little plastic chair and tell everyone why I liked beer and hated people, in particular myself. In my group, however, I had a head start. We may all allegedly have been alcoholics, but there would be nothing anonymous about our meetings. I don't know if it was deliberate or not, but at least half of the twelve people sat in a miserable circle knew exactly who I was. Whispered conversations provoked slow nods and the narrowing of eyes all around me. That's right; I arrested you. I poured your beer away. I threw you in jail. And now here we are, all criminals together trying to dry out.

The counsellor was Jez. With a Z. Because if you tell drunks your name is Jeremy they beat you up and steal your wallet. He was a bit younger than me, plainly dressed with no labels, never giving away any emotion one way or the other on an expressionless face. It was like a job interview. You'd never know how you'd done until the report came back the following week to explain your progress.

At the start of the meeting, two or three people would explain their stories to the rest of the group, or what they'd been up to in the week. As it was my first day, it would be my turn, along with a schoolgirl of just fifteen.

After a good ten minutes wasted on pre-session gossiping, Jez began: 'We have two new people to welcome to the session this week. I'd like you to meet Vicky.'

All nodded and smiled at the girl, some giving away more of their thoughts than they had intended, almost drooling. I felt uncomfortable for her immediately.

My welcome was slightly less warm, largely intense glares and bile bubbling gently behind gritted teeth. I stretched a toothless smile to acknowledge that, yes, I remember you too.

'Vicky, would you like to start for us, please?' asked Jez.

Vicky fidgeted in her seat. She looked more annoyed than I did to be there.

'Do I have to?' she asked.

'Only if you're comfortable,' said Jez.

She rolled her eyes. Clearly you were never going to be comfortable in that scenario, but you were going to have to speak eventually, one way or the other.

She shrugged. 'What d'you wanna know?'

'Just tell us a bit about yourself, and why you think you're here.'

She pulled her slight legs up onto the chair and clasped her hands about her shins.

'My name's Vicky, and I'm here because they said I have to be.'

'Who's 'they'?' asked Jez.

'The police.'

Great. Another fan.

'Why d'you think they wanted you to come and talk to us?'

'I dunno. Stop me drinking, I s'pose.'

'You get into trouble when you drink?'

'Sometimes.'

'How does that make you feel?'

'Annoyed.'

I was hoping he could keep her talking, because when it came to me I'd be lucky if there were no weapons involved. Jake Spurrier was watching me intently, his hand in his jacket as though he was twirling something in the inside pocket. He'd been involved in more bar fights than a Tombstone cowboy with ADHD, and on every occasion we'd found something on him, usually a knife. There was about ten feet between us and I got the feeling he was waiting for the right time to lunge at me. I made sure I kept an eye on him, without giving away the fact I was keeping an eye on him. I wasn't going to get any help if he did kick off. They'd all sit back and watch. Maybe one or two would join in while I was down and couldn't identify where the kicks were coming from. Jez would only follow Health and Safety and call 999. He looked like a vegetarian anyway. Vicky was probably the toughest prospect in that room, but with everyone in a brawl she'd most likely walk off to the park with the bottle of vodka I'd noticed in her shabby handbag.

'Why do you turn to alcohol, do you think?' continued Jez.

Vicky shrugged.

'What does your dad think?'

Another shrug.

'Does he have a job?'

'Stealing.'

'Does he drink?'

'All the time.'

Jez nodded knowingly, thanking Vicky for being brave. He explained how her story was very similar to that of a lot of other people he'd known. She obviously didn't care much for compliments and I caught her eyes flicking towards her bag time and again. She couldn't get out of there quick enough, and when she was free, she was going to hit that bottle hard and stay on it. She wouldn't remember where the meeting was the next week even if she did try and turn up. She could make up anything she wanted for her probation officer, but there was no need to worry about that any time soon. The Youth Justice Department had enough to think about, and little girls annoyed at daddy tend to lose priority to the bigger criminals. Another forgotten file.

Then all eyes turned to me. I was so preoccupied with my old friend opposite I'd forgotten to make something up as I had planned. But who cares? I thought. I didn't need to be there, I didn't want to be there. I could pretty much say anything as long as Jez signed the form to say I'd attended the course each week. Why not have some fun with it?

'Welcome,' Jez smiled at me. 'Tell us a bit about yourself.'

'Okay, well my name's Chris. I enjoy long walks in the country, drinking, and religious hypocrisy. I'm very catholic. You can ask my husband. When he's finished his homework.'

I feigned a little laugh. No one else did.

'Why do you think you're here?' asked Jez, absolutely unmoved.

'Well, Jeremy, much like this young lady, I have been asked to attend this group by the police, who have decided that you should never stand up for your friends.'

'Do you recognise you have a problem?'

'I do – he's a short, wide-boy problem called Tony, who has somehow acquired the most amazing woman I know.'

'So, in your case, the alcohol exacerbates feelings of jealousy, or inadequacy?'

'I just think, from time to time, what's wrong with punching someone you don't like? Can't two people have it out without charges and being sued for once?'

Now that *was* hypocrisy, and looking around the room at all the vicious creatures I'd dealt with in the past, it wasn't clever to fuel the fire.

Jez still wouldn't judge me. Not outwardly, at least. He just nodded every now and again and leapt in with new questions to keep the discussion going. It felt surprisingly good, sitting there talking crap, almost as if we were all friends. I could be who I wanted to be in that room. Some of the tension started to ease, even drawing the odd laugh here and there.

The first hour was up and Jez gave us fifteen minutes for a tea break. There was free stuff at one end of the room and a few of us made our way over. Spurrier was watching me again. I kept glancing over my shoulder to make sure he didn't follow me. Fortunately Jez engaged him about something and I was safe for that interval, at least.

Vicky walked up to the table and took an empty plastic cup. She didn't fill it with anything and went out into the hallway. As she disappeared behind the door flapping on its hinges I was sure I glimpsed something. Looking around again to check everyone was suitably preoccupied, I finished making a tea and followed her out.

Facing away from me, she was shaking slightly, pouring neat vodka into the cup and throwing it back. As she bent down to put the bottle back in her bag my suspicions were confirmed. There was bruising all across the back of her neck and the top of her shoulders. It was a mixture of brown, purple and yellow. Someone had grabbed and held her in that spot repeatedly over a period of months, and with some force. Her wispy top lifted slightly to reveal the same pattern across her lower back, one that I imagined continued around onto her front and down her legs.

'Mind if I join you?' I asked.

She jumped forward, almost tripping over her bag.

'I'm just going to the toilet,' she said.

'Toilets are down that other corridor,' I said, pointing in the opposite direction. I swished my drink about in the cup. 'I hate this tea.' I opened a small window in the corridor

115

and threw it out into the garden. 'I need a proper drink. Would you mind?'

She obviously did mind, but she still yanked the bottle out of her bag and gave me a half-decent measure.

'Cheers,' I said, raising my cup, and back it went.

It was obviously the cheapest stuff on the shelf, but that meant she was buying rather than stealing it.

'Did you hurt yourself?' I asked, gesturing to her neck.

'No.'

She filled her cup to the top this time.

'Looks nasty. Must ache,' I said.

'Sorry, but aren't you gay?'

'What?'

'Your husband doing his homework.'

'Oh. No, I'm giving that up. Makes my eyes water.'

'Well look, mate, I'm not interested, okay?'

'That's not exactly what I had in mind.'

'So, what are you? A doctor?'

'No.'

'Well we've already got one counsellor in here, so you can leave it, thanks.'

'Hey, I'm just making conversation.'

She sucked up the vodka, tilting her head back before stretching a palm to the wall to steady herself. Her shoulders scrunched tight about her neck with sudden pain.

'Is it your dad?' I asked, but she'd had enough, and shouldering her bag she brushed past me and disappeared into the main hall.

I really didn't know why I cared. I'd seen hundreds of kids just like her in the parks and outside shops, swearing at anyone who walked by, puking all over the pavement and fighting with each other. Most of them couldn't even claim to be from a broken home, they were just showing off in front of their friends, emboldened because no one ever challenged them. That's how people like McIntyre start.

116

Perhaps the stories that day had inspired me, and despite all the conflicting evidence and my outward reservations to the contrary, I was still naïve enough to think I could help someone. You can take the officer out of the police…

That wasn't too bad a morning, I thought, turning into my road. My ribs were starting to ache like hell again, but the tablets always did their job. If I could remember where I'd put them.

I'd have a celebratory drink to mark the first day at alcohol counselling, and sausage and mash later for tea; loads of gravy, of course, and a token helping of peas. There must have been some slowly dying at the back of the freezer somewhere. And I'll send Katya a text, I thought. Thank her for a wonderful evening again. Maybe I could sort out another non-date? I might even get another kiss.

Then I saw my driveway, or rather the police car sat on it. As I got closer it wasn't Trev helping Jen strip my house of the last of the fixtures and fittings, but a standard marked panda.

Two officers got out as my handbrake went up. I didn't know either of them, they were from a different shift.

'Christopher Rose?' asked one.

'Yes?'

'I'm arresting you on suspicion of the murder of Eric Sewell…'

17

Custody tea is awful. The little grey bag on a string looked like a dead man's bollock and probably tasted twice as bad. Add that to the lime scale-infused water and no amount of sugar was going to recover it. I made no attempt to hide my disgust from the officer sat opposite me; a short, dumpy blonde thing, no more than twenty-five, but the lack of make-up and scraped-back hair gave her at least another ten years. She kept catching my eye and looking away again. Obviously we didn't know each other. Murder suspects aren't supposed to talk to anyone except their solicitors. Not that I was going to bother with one of those.

They were taking their time and I was getting fidgety. I was annoyed more than anything, but I wasn't surprised. You need to cover every possible base with murder, however unlikely the scenario. I just had to keep saying to myself: you haven't done anything wrong. Answer the questions they put to you, and then you'll be allowed to leave. There was no other outcome.

I slouched with my arm across the back of the chair, still struggling on with the tea for something to do. I tried to raise a smile from the officer with a ridiculous toothy grin, but she just took her phone from her pocket and pretended to look through it.

Admittedly, there's nothing else in the room of interest. A table, four chairs, cameras in the corners of the room to record the DVD of the interview, the old tape recording system built into the wall. I pressed a couple of buttons to see if it still worked. Pressing forward and rewind set off two different squeals. I flicked between the directions, trying to make a tune of sorts. The officer held a stare at me. She still wouldn't smile. Quite the opposite, actually.

I looked up at the cameras. How am I going to look on TV? I wondered. They were positioned to get four people into the picture, but where I was sitting was too far forward, surely? The angle would decapitate the people opposite me. They could be pulling faces or anything, and I'd have no defence for why I laughed through the interview. I put my tea down and gripped the laminated chipboard either side of me. Gently pulling the table back provoked a sustained shriek as the metal legs braced against the stone floor. I wriggled my seat back and checked my position with the camera. I was nearly there and repeated the process, trying to be quicker this time but the screech was worse. The officer glared at me as if to say, *Finished?*

It was then I noticed I'd spilt some of the tea. Tut. I didn't have any sleeves so I pulled at the base of my t-shirt, trying to get it up and onto the table without exposing myself. I couldn't do it sitting down, but you get in trouble if you stand up, so I pushed my gut forward, poking a finger through the material as far as I could. No good. I leant over to see if I could use my shoulder. Still couldn't reach. I didn't want to put my legs on the table. My hair was too short to use my head. Then I saw the officer's note pad and ripped off the top half of one of the pages, patting it flat with the palm of my hand onto the wet patch and wiping it around. Unfortunately I only seemed to be spreading the problem, splashing both of us with little grey droplets. The officer looked down at her lap and back at me with raised eyebrows. I half held up my hand in apology, scrunching the paper up and placing it to one side next to the wall.

Where were they? All they had to do was retrieve a few notes. It's not like I actually had a criminal record, or at least not one I'd disclosed during my application. Maybe that's what the delay was. They'd finally realised I'd nicked a succession of Nestle Crunches on my way home from school when I was twelve, and expert profiling had determined the killer must have a history in petty confectionary theft. Then there was the graffiti on my music teacher's shed; but as it turns out he *was* a Nazi. And, okay, I'll come clean, that was me ordering pizzas, taxis and strippers to go to my old boss, but even that was a favour to start with, the uptight bastard. If he'd heard of 1471 I might have stopped after the first three months.

I balanced on the two rear legs of my chair, swinging backwards and forwards. I was staring at the officer and she knew it, but she refused to remove her eyes from the phone.

'Who are you texting?' I asked. 'Boyfriend...? Girlfriend..?'

She gave me a look. It wasn't girlfriend.

Rocking gently on my chair, I began to 'sing': *'There was an old lady who swallowed a fly... I don't know why she swallowed a fly, let's give her the benefit of the doubt and assume she didn't know it went in her mouth...There was an old lady who swallowed a spider, that wriggled and wriggled and tickled inside her... She swallowed the spider to catch the fly, I don't know why, she swallowed the fly, perhaps she's an ex-copper and had her pension slashed by the government so she hasn't got any food...There was an old lady –'*

'Oh, for *fuck's sake*,' said the officer, just as Fergus opened the door.

'Haha!' I said, pointing at her.

'Is everything okay in here?' asked Fergus.

'We're fine,' I said. 'Don't be hard on her - *boyfriend trouble.'*

Fergus gestured at the door and the officer got up to leave, but not before giving me a look of concentrated evil.

'Sorry to have kept you, PC Rose,' said Fergus. He took a seat, laying paperwork out on the table. 'This is DC Turner, he'll be observing this interview.'

I turned to see a young man in the doorway; late twenties, smart suit, clean-shaven. He was obviously CID's latest recruit, learning how to give a suspect a good grilling.

The training is more advanced once you're clear of uniform, owing to the inherently more sinister people you come up against. I'd only conducted a couple of such interviews myself, but it can be daunting. You need to maintain your train of thought when the guy opposite could throw absolutely anything at you. His lawyer will interject at every opportunity, noting where your allegations don't correspond with the arrest, or where your questioning is leading or discriminatory and will be disregarded in court. You have all the evidence you need, but suddenly you can't remember what order events took place in and you pause, sifting through papers for a statement from someone whose name you can't remember. Now your case looks weak and ill-prepared, even unprofessional. The clock on the wall ticks louder with every second, a constant reminder that you may only have the next twenty minutes to cover every base and at least secure bail before your suspect walks free to terrorise people all over again. And if he does, then that's only ever going to be one person's fault.

Turner closed the door and pulled up a chair. Fergus finished neatly placing his paperwork and engaged the DVD system. We all announced who we were and he officially cautioned me.

'You've waived your right to legal representation, is that correct?' asked Fergus.

'It is,' I replied.

'I'll remind you that you are entitled to free representation if you need it.'

'I know.'

'You wish to refuse that offer as well?'

'Shall we just get on with it?'

Fergus obliged: 'Where were you on the night of the tenth of June, between the hours of approximately ten-PM and one-thirty the next morning?'

'You know where I was.'

'For the benefit of the recording, please.'

'I was on an operation.'

'At the residence of Samuel Richard McIntyre?'

'That's correct.'

'And on this operation, did you encounter a gentleman by the name of Eric Sewell, a known associate of Mr McIntyre?'

'Do you seriously think I killed Bingo?'

'Answer the question, please.'

'A house full of known criminals, thugs and druggies and you've dragged *me* in here first.'

'Answer the question, please.'

I sighed. 'He's not a *gentleman*, but yes, we said hello.'

'What did you talk about?'

'We didn't really talk.'

'But you ended up in a fight?'

'I wouldn't call it a fight.'

'What would you call it?'

'As per my statement, he tried to attack me and I defended myself.'

Fergus picked up one of his sheets of paper. 'Medical records show that Mr Sewell has been wheelchair bound for more than ten years and suffers with a number of conditions; type-one diabetes, osteoporosis, a congenital heart condition...'

'It's the least he deserves,' I said.

'I beg your pardon?'

'He's a convicted paedophile, and that's still one of his better traits. It was only thanks to a bent parole board he got out when he did.'

Fergus' eyes nearly burned through mine and out the back of my head.

'He made you angry, didn't he?' he said. 'Never more so than when he drove your little sister into a wall at high-speed.'

The cold detachment of that statement was almost delivered in mirth. The pleasantries were officially long gone. This man really wanted to get at me. It might work.

He continued: 'She was an addict, wasn't she? Your sister. You kept that quiet when you joined the force; that a member of your immediate family was a user, and regularly associated with known criminals.'

'She wasn't a user. She didn't know what she was getting into.'

'Oh, come on. She was nearly twenty. I'm sure she had a rough idea who her friends were.'

'It wasn't her fault. That night she was going to come home.'

'So they forced her into that car, did they?'

'Perhaps.'

'Would it be fair to say you're happy Mr Sewell's dead?'

'I'm *delighted* he's dead, but as anyone with half a brain can work out, I didn't kill him. There are witnesses, as per my statement.'

Fergus plucked another sheet from the table. 'The pre-autopsy report on Mr Sewell's body indicates massive chest trauma, consistent with a heavy punch or kick. Do you concede, *as per your statement*, that you are responsible for these injuries?'

I was struck with unexpected nerves. I felt my face flush and tingle. Had I kicked him hard enough to kill him? That had never entered my mind. I was preoccupied with trying to get out of that garden, I never looked back. I replayed the incident in my mind, or as much as I could remember.

No. I can't have. They wouldn't have just left him. And how did he get in the river?

I watched the corner of Fergus' mouth lift slightly into a pre-smile of sorts.

And then I realised. Why didn't I twig before?

Who was this man? How can it be that someone I've never heard of is suddenly assigned to a murder case for one of McIntyre's men? He'd never worked on our patch before, I was certain. And yet, here he was, blaming me for a murder based on speculation before they've even bothered to cut the little bastard open.

Now the plan was clear. Guilty or not, my name is 'accidentally' leaked to the press, along with a detailed history of every wrong turn I'd ever taken, and I'm shit smeared up the wall; disgraced, never to work undercover again. Maybe I'd be frozen out altogether until I eventually resigned or tripped up one final time. You don't risk killing a police officer if he's getting too close; someone takes out the sort of prick Sewell was and your inside man points the finger. Good thinking, Sammy. But who else knew about this?

I didn't start out with many friends and they were getting fewer, but while Fergus was playing by the rules I had some time. He didn't have enough to charge me, not without an autopsy report. He was trying to get me to cough up enough to remand me in custody for the time being. I had to get out of there. I needed to find out what really happened to Bingo before the post-mortem result was adjusted accordingly and everyone was paid to keep quiet.

I looked up at Fergus, disgust pulling my lip into a curl.

'How much is he paying you?' I asked.

'Sorry?'

'He gave a couple of PCs at least ten grand a piece not so long ago, so a Detective Inspector, you've got to be worth, what, five times that? Ten times for a successful case?'

'If you don't mind, I'll ask the questions. Now again, do you – '

'This interview is over.'

'Do you accept you were responsible for those injuries?'

'I said this interview is over.'

'I have a number of things to get through with you today, PC Rose, and it will certainly help your defence if you answer my questions. Do you concede you were responsible for Mr Sewell's injuries?'

I leant forward. 'Fuck off and sort my bail out. Now.'

He almost smiled as he looked down to gather some composure, reading a few more notes. Turner was still blank and awkward. He didn't know what was going on.

Fergus wasn't ready to concede. He tried another tack: 'Have you had a drink today, PC Rose? You're currently on suspension pending an alcohol counselling review. You assaulted another police officer, and according to your own statement, you were drunk on the operation during which time Mr Sewell was killed.'

I refused to answer. I turned my attention to the newbie.

'You're not bent, are you, Turner?' I asked.

'The alcohol makes you aggressive, doesn't it?' said Fergus.

I ignored him and continued with Turner: 'It's just that they'll ask you at some point. They'll want to know whose side you're on.'

'You'd had a skin full at McIntyre's, hadn't you?' asked Fergus.

'If you're lucky you might even get offered a job by the big man himself,' I said.

'And when you were gifted the opportunity, you killed a defenceless, disabled man over a long-standing grudge.'

I glared at the new man. 'Whose side are you going to be on?'

It was certainly a lot more than Turner bargained for in the interview and he was worried. He should be. I'd have said he was a quiet family man with a lot to lose; Sammy's favourite prey. He didn't know enough about either of us to decide who to trust, but he was going to go away and think about it. Maybe I'd saved one, if only one.

Fergus still wanted my confession so badly, scowling at me as I ignored him after several more attempts to incriminate me. Eventually he hit the stop button, telling Turner the interview was suspended. The new guy was quick to leave the room. If he hadn't transferred out of that unit within the month I'd have been amazed.

Fergus got up and walked around to me. With one hand on the back of my chair and the other on the table he spoke close to my ear.

'Don't think this is over,' he said. 'I know all about you, and quite frankly you're a disgrace.'

'If you're going to lean over me like that can you at least clean your teeth?'

'You can get used to it. I'm going to be breathing down your neck every day.'

'Down my neck's fine, just not in my face.'

'Make sure your passport's across that front counter. You're not going anywhere.'

He peeled away from my seat and wrenched the door open, leaving it to slam shut on its own behind him.

The adrenalin started to catch up with me and I felt a shiver in my chest. I had to get to the hospital immediately, but that's a move they would have anticipated. Someone would be waiting for me.

18

Predictably, Jen wasn't answering her phone and wasn't going to respond to the five voicemails I had left, no matter how urgent I made them sound.

I tried Colin again. This time he answered almost straight away.

'*Hello?*'

'Colin, where are you?'

He could hear the anxiety in my voice.

'*In the office. What's going on?*'

'They're trying to fit me up. You were right.'

'*Right? What? Where are you?*'

'On my way to the hospital. Get Straughan to authorise a search on that warehouse. Sammy's got something. He's trying to take us out of the picture.'

'*Hang on, slow down. What's going on?*'

'Fergus is working for McIntyre. They're going to say I killed Bingo to keep me out of the way. Has anyone spoken to you?'

'*No.*'

'Don't say anything. If they ask, stick to your statement. We need Straughan to set us up at the docks, tonight.'

'*There's no way he'll do that.*'

'Just tell him to call me, I'll explain.'

'*Alright, I'll go up now. Are you okay?*'

'I'm fine. We need to meet up. I'll call you when I'm finished here. Just keep your head down.'

I felt slightly better for the conversation, however brief.

I'd brought along a pair of lens-less glasses I'd used on an undercover job a little while back. It's amazing how something so simple can throw people, even if they think you look familiar. Finding a lab coat wasn't going to be too hard; perhaps a clipboard, too. No one bothers anyone moving at a suitable pace with a clipboard, and having something to look down at would help disguise my face. Only a few of Sammy's inner circle should know what I looked like anyway. A flash of my warrant card ought to keep anyone else at bay for time enough to secure the genuine autopsy notes.

This all hinged on acquiring a key card from Jen, however, who could conceivably raise the alarm and have me thrown out immediately. She worked in the physiotherapy suite on the far side of the complex. Hopefully she was still there, just about to finish.

I walked through reception, unobstructed, striding purposefully so everyone could see I knew where I was going, and no, I didn't need any help, thanks. I had been to the hospital a good few times on official business in the past, but that was usually about three in the morning and across the way at A&E, trying to keep a puke-stained moron at arm's length as we nicked him for Drunk and Disorderly.

In the communal courtyard I passed through the lingering fumes from several tarred wrecks, smoking the last of their lives away in wheelchairs. Nurses stood dutifully behind them, punctuating barely audible tales of 'in my day' with unlikely pleasantries and forced smiles. The smoke wrestled with the thick, plastic smell of steamed hospital food; still the ultimate reason to avoid all but the most essential treatment. Young South-East Asian nurses skated the wards, jabbing, injecting and drawing every type of fluid, struggling with their duty-free trolleys, overflowing with medicines.

The garden ended at the tinted windows of the physio gym and I pressed my face against the glass. There she was, putting away equipment as a man hobbled out on crutches. I held the door for him and as he thanked me, Jen turned to see who it was. Her smile dropped instantly.

'What the hell are you doing here?'

'Did you get my messages? I've been trying to call you for the last hour.'

'I don't have my phone with me when I'm working. And I'm not finished yet, so can you get out now before I call security?'

'I need to borrow your pass.'

'I beg your pardon?'

'Just for ten minutes.'

'What?'

'I'm in trouble, Jen. I'm being stitched up. I need to see a body.'

'You need to see a psychiatrist.'

'I just need to run down to the basement.'

'You can't run around the hospital with my pass. You'll get me fired.'

'I'll be two minutes.'

'You said ten a moment ago.'

'I won't be long.'

'No.'

'Jen, I haven't got time to argue.'

'Good, 'cause I haven't got time to listen.'

'Give it to me, please.'

'I said no.'

'*Jen.*'

'*No.*'

I swiped a small barbell from its rack next to me and shook it in anger between us.

'They're trying to fit me up with murder, do you understand? *Do I look like a murderer to you?*'

Another door on the far side of the room opened and an anxious trainee appeared.

'Is everything okay in here?' he asked.

'Get out or die,' I said, still gripping the barbell tightly.

Jen held her hand up to allay any concern. 'It's okay,' she said.

The trainee gave an unconvinced nod but backed out all the same, understandably reluctant to become involved.

Jen put her hands on her hips, frowning at my wild eyes. She knew I was usually calm and placid and, quite frankly, lazy. Something was wrong, and there might have been the tiniest hint of concern behind that thick wall of disdain.

'I know you've been suspended,' she said. 'Claire's boyfriend got knocked out in that brawl. His jaw is broken in two places. He can only eat soup.'

'He only eats soup anyway. I've eaten sandwiches that weigh more than him.'

Then I recalled the conversation with Katya.

'I suppose your boyfriend told you that?'

'That's right.'

'Your *boyfriend*. He's such a *man*, isn't he? Not gay at all.'

'Just because he shaves more than once a fortnight doesn't make him gay.'

'No, it's *what* he shaves that makes him gay. Does he have any unusual habits? Make you wear a false beard? Get you to dress up like a rugby player?'

'The jealousy is eating you, isn't it?'

'And what's eating you? Not him, is it?'

'Get out.'

'Is it really just a game to get at me? Was it Claire's idea?'

'I don't know what you're talking about.'

'Trouble with an ex or something? Pesky bloke won't go away, so you do each other a favour; he pretends to go straight and you get someone to go shopping with.'

130

For once she didn't even try to shout me down, even though I found myself pausing out of habit for a sharp response. There was a lot going on in those eyes. They were alive with thoughts, but she wasn't going to tell me what they were. Maybe she really was only just piecing two and two together. I might normally have pushed things further, but it wasn't the time and I was getting nowhere. I allowed the last of the frustration to subside and spoke softly.

'Look, I wouldn't be here if this wasn't serious. Do this one last thing for me and you'll never see me again, I promise.'

She stood there defiantly, stubbornly. Pride had run off with her words, but the silence was all she needed to make things impossible for me yet again.

I shook my head, more at me than her. It was always going to be a long-shot. It was time to initiate Plan B and steal a card from somewhere.

I placed the barbell back on its rack and went for the door when Jen said: 'My pass is in the office... wait here.'

I turned around, watching her slink off in that tight gear.

Was that why we could never make it work? It was too easy for her? I should have been more aggressive? She never lost an argument, or at least she'd never admit to it. I was always the one to back down. But that made an even greater mockery of this alleged relationship with Trev. He was no match for her, unless by some highly unlikely quirk he was one of the quiet ones that transform behind locked doors, coming home to slap a weasel on the table and shout, 'Make a casserole out of that, bitch!' More likely this was just a rebound for them both. Two people who happened to be on the same page, trying to figure out what they really wanted; friendship, stability, a shorn scrotum.

Jen returned and moved in close to me, holding the sharp plastic of the key card against my chest.

'If anyone finds you with this, I'm going to say you stole it. Understand?'

'I'm only going – '

'I don't want to know, Chris. But this won't get you into the mortuary, if that's what you want. You'll have to find another card downstairs.'

I nodded. 'Thank you… Look, I'm –

'Do what you have to and put the card back in my desk drawer. I don't want to see you here again.'

I took the card, inadvertently rubbing my fingers gently on hers. It had been a while since I'd felt her skin. She used to like holding hands, and I didn't mind it. We both could have said plenty more – we probably needed to - but it'd only end up as another argument. For once, I thought, let's enjoy the silence and part-company as relative friends.

19

In the main building I used Jen's card to access another corridor, looking into the wards that branched off as I passed. It wasn't manically busy but there were enough people that I could only give fleeting glances here and there, I didn't want any questions.

I came across a small staff room with the door open. On one of the pegs was a non-descript white coat. Checking around me, I shrugged into it, adding the glasses from my pocket. My clipboard was on a desk with a blank form attached. But no key cards for the lower levels. They were all hanging around the appropriate necks. Still, I was leaving for the basement as Doctor Rose. I could just knock.

The mortuary was usually quiet and largely empty of the living. As far as I could make out, looking through the little window in the door, there was only the one junior assistant with her back to me. The room was freezing, with a strong smell of chemicals permeating the secure doors. There were several bodies lying in various states. I didn't know if I'd recognise Sewell if I saw him, but then, in the far corner, protruding from under a sheet, there he was. Bingo. Literally.

I tried Jen's key card a couple of times, but sure enough the LED stubbornly refused to move from red. Clearing my throat, I pushed the glasses back up onto my nose. I'd almost knocked for the assistant's attention when a huge man appeared in an office window overlooking the body and I ducked. Rising to look again I could see he was tired and bored, sipping from a polystyrene cup, staring at nothing. He must have arrived with Sewell and been there ever since. I needed him moved.

Fortunately I still had one bar of signal on my phone. I dialled, watching the big lug as I waited for an answer.

'*Hello, switchboard,*' said a friendly lady.

'Hi, it's Doctor Rose. Could I have the mortuary, please?'

'*One moment, sir…*'

I heard the phone ring in the office and the man went straight for it.

'*'Ello?*'

I put on a suitably authentic voice. 'We've 'ad an update from McIntyre. Meet me on the top floor of the Baker building, across the gardens. Now.'

'*Who is this?*'

I hung up. The man looked at the handset for a moment before downing his drink and leaving the room. I smiled and held the door as he barged past me, jogging up the stairs. Too easy.

Keeping my back to the assistant, I approached what was left of Sewell. I searched around him for the paperwork at arm's length, trying to ignore that black face and an open skull with several chunks of brain missing. There should have been a checklist showing what stage they were at with the autopsy and the findings so far. I looked over the neighbouring instrument table, home to all kinds of sinister implements, then under the body on a shelf, but I couldn't find anything.

'On the wall, sir,' said a young female voice behind me.

The lab junior was approaching.

'Thank you, I've got them,' I said, turning slightly, trying to halt her in her tracks. But as I picked the notes from the wall she was right behind me and I could feel her eyes.

'I finished most of the toxicology myself. And I helped with the organ work,' she said.

'Well done,' I said, looking down at the single sheet of paper.

134

As far as I could tell Bingo was ready for the oven. Every test had a result marked and signed. I kept my eyes fixed on the notes, hoping the assistant would lose interest and wander off, but even after several moments silence she was still on my shoulder.

'Would you like me to talk you through the procedures so far?' she asked.

I turned, gripping the rim of my glasses with my thumb and forefinger to help obscure my face. She looked like a friendly little thing, slight with long red hair tied back in a ponytail. She wore an almost constant look of anticipation, peering over thick but fashionable lenses. She was pretty in an I-understand-complicated-textbooks kind of way.

'Oh, sorry professor, I thought you were Doctor Wells,' she said.

'Professor? No, I'm not a professor. I'm just here to collect the notes for the…' I put my hand over my mouth to help muffle the word, '*hontolocology* department.'

She pointed at my chest. 'But your badge..?'

Sure enough I was a professor, according to the nameless plastic tag I hadn't noticed pinned to my chest. I looked at it for a few seconds, trying to think, before raising my eyes.

'Good. Very good. Dr. Bells tells me you are one of his smartest.'

'Wells.'

'Yes. But I loathe formality. It's Colin, Colin Smith. You must be..?'

'Penny.'

'Penny. How lovely to meet you finally. Where's the coroner today?'

'He's still in London, sir. I don't think the case finishes until next week.'

'Ah. Of course.'

135

'Have you seen Dr. Wells? Are we completing this subject today?'

'Yes, yes you will be. He's just in the canteen for a spot of dinner. They're doing some lovely beef at the moment.'

'He's vegetarian, isn't he?'

'Yes, and he's complaining about all that lovely beef, and asking why there isn't more salad, and, and fish. He's a very passionate man.'

'He always seems quiet to me.'

'Quietly passionate. You don't always recognise it straight away, but it's there. D'you know he petrol-bombed a fast-food joint in his youth?'

'*No*. How old was he?'

'Oh... how old would you say he is now?'

'Early sixties.'

'Early twenties. Student protest. Anyway, why don't you tell me what you've been doing here?'

'Oh, would you mind?'

'Not at all. Please.'

Penny whipped the sheet from Bingo's body to reveal a wide, fleshy cavity with most of the organs removed. I tried not contort my face too much, but I had to hide all but my eyes behind the clipboard while she described in detail the various parts of the body and their chemical properties at the time of death. I snuck a look at my watch, narrowing my eyes as I considered how long the security would wander the hospital looking for his phantom friend.

Through the complicated talk of samples and procedures, there was no mention at all of my alleged contribution to Bingo's demise. I took the opportunity to cement my authenticity, but at the mention of 'severe chest trauma' Penny was dismissive and uninterested. If there was a kick, she said, it was not the cause of his death, going on to say – I felt superfluously, and possibly owing to her inexperience – that the kick was 'feeble', and could have been inflicted by an 'average girl'.

Regardless, it was only going to take a few grand and a carefully forged document to convince a court that I had in fact struck him with all the force of a truck and killed him instantly. Penny would suddenly find herself gifted the opportunity to work abroad – in the arctic – and no one would be any the wiser. How did he actually die, and how would I prove it?

Penny looked around.

'There was hardly any water in the lungs,' she said. 'Dr Wells is surprisingly resistant to acknowledge it, but he had a lot of Class A drugs in his system. It looks to me like he suffered a cardiac embolism. I'm sure he was dead before he came into contact with the water.'

'An overdose?'

'The drugs may be a factor. But there was something on the skin swabs.'

'What?'

'I don't know.' Penny looked around again. 'I hope you don't mind, sir, but I've asked the lab to run a couple of extra tests. We should have the first batch of results in the next couple of days.'

'What caused the embolism, do you think?'

'It could simply have been high cholesterol. Perhaps there was some air in his bloodstream. But that doesn't explain where he was found.' Penny nodded at the office. Her voice dropped to a whisper. 'Who is that man? He hasn't moved from that room once in two days. Doctor Wells says he's a policeman, but I've never seen him in uniform. I'm really worried something's going on.'

Penny was tenacious and reluctant to be fobbed off. Even someone like me could tell she was brilliant, with a huge career in front of her. She was the key in determining the truth surrounding Bingo's murder and someone I could trust, all of which instantly put her in extreme danger.

Unfortunately, it was obvious her boss was already on the payroll, or at least buying into the misdirection of those who were.

I took Penny by the shoulders. 'Look, I can't go into details now, but you're right, something is going on here. Don't talk to anyone about this case. If you get any trouble from that big guy or anyone else, run out of the building and call the police.'

'Oh my God, professor, what is it?'

'It's better you don't know. When you have the results back from the tests, take copies and hide them somewhere safe, and in different places. In the meantime act normal, do everything you're asked and carry on with your usual work.'

'Right. Okay. Safe. Different places.'

'Try not to worry. No one's interested in you – well, I don't mean no one's interested in you, you're a lovely girl, I mean – you know what I mean.'

'Will you write a report for me? Let them know I had nothing to do with this.'

'Of course. I need to disappear for now, but I'll be in touch in the next few days.'

Heavy footsteps approached the main doors.

'Get back to your post,' I said.

Penny scurried across the room. I backed up against the wall as the huge man walked in. Before the door shut again I swept out behind him into the corridor.

'Has anyone been 'ere looking for me?' he asked Penny.

Penny shook her head, pretending to read some notes.

The man looked confused but clearly didn't care one way or the other. He walked back to the office, yawning and scratching his arse.

Penny looked over to give me an exaggerated wink. I returned the gesture and ran up the stairs.

20

Daylight was fading fast. I stood at the window, looking out over the dock. No sign of life at Building Twelve or anywhere near it since the last shift of workers had clocked off at six-thirty. It was nearly ten. I scanned across the yard and up the derricks with my binoculars. Gulls sat quietly on the tattered metal with nothing to spook them. There was only the occasional creak of shipping crates contracting as they cooled.

The hot day had given way to the coldest possible night. We didn't have any heating and neither of us had brought a decent coat.

'I can't feel my feet,' stammered Colin.

'Just keep moving on the spot.'

'I can't feel my legs.'

'Move quicker.'

'I can't feel my bum.'

'You aren't supposed to be able to feel your bum, Colin, that's for your girlfriend to do if you ever get one.'

It wasn't easy to convince Straughan to authorise this. I was, after all, suspended and on bail. But I think he knew what I was going to do, authority or not. He also had to concede that Fergus' involvement was suspicious at best, and to that end he would be making his own discreet enquiries. The chief knew I was a lot of things, but none of them was a murderer.

It was agreed that we'd never secure a search warrant based exclusively on Fitch's account. In light of the days' events as a whole, Straughan unofficially sanctioned a stakeout on McIntyre's building. It was strictly observations-only. We were not to enter the premises or engage with the suspects. Only the three of us would ever know we were there. Sammy was already cupping the constabulary's balls, and bomb or no bomb, he'd have the ammunition he needed to grab, twist and pull if he found out about another illegal operation.

We made a couple of calls to secure a neighbouring warehouse, positioned at ninety degrees to Building Twelve. We didn't dare whisper the word police. Instead, our story was that we were Environmental Health officers with a legal obligation to carry out pest control in the area. The warehouse and its offices needed to be inspected from top to bottom, but to save any embarrassment to the owning company we'd only begin after everyone had left, working through the night. Straughan faked the requisite faxes and suitably attired, Colin picked up the keys on our way.

We set up camp in an office that protruded from the sloping roof. It was an ideal vantage point and we were almost invisible at that height. No one was going to arrive without us knowing about it. McIntyre's place was a carbon copy of our own. There were few places to hide, and even if someone tried, we should still know exactly where they were.

Colin was excited because he could bring some of his gadgets along. Aside from the high-powered binoculars and the telescopic lens for the camera, we had highly sensitive sound equipment. Pointing a small satellite dish in any direction, we could hear a mouse fart at two thousand feet, and digitally record up to a week's worth of conversation. We sat it on a tripod, angled at the main entrance so we wouldn't miss a second.

I took the note from Fitch out of my overalls pocket and read it again. Closer inspection had seemed to reveal a possible bonus for us that evening in the shape of an old friend. Underneath the day's shipping times, Carr had scrawled, *Jones boys.*

We took 'Jones' in this context to mean Arthur Jones, another self-made criminal working predominantly out of

140

London. That may have explained the destination for the crates – old friends working together again. Except for one thing; they weren't friends.

McIntyre had something of an apprenticeship under Jones in his early days, before leaving to set up the empire. The old man had always maintained a gang of considerable size, but he sorely lacked Sammy's business acumen. Where McIntyre had his people offer everything but a signed invoice for every transaction, Jones was more a traditionalist. Owing to his high-visibility methods, at least half his people were in prison at any one time, but he was never going to change. He loved the theatre and the fame that went with it, literally drilling fear into people in order to keep them onside and punctual. However, he'd largely made the transition from drugs to loan sharking, an enterprise increasingly problematic for the modern criminal seeing as it was now advertised on TV as a legitimate service. Business was bound to have been affected.

So, had he given up and started working for Sammy? No chance. You couldn't fit both those egos in that warehouse and still expect to be able to close the door. They only ever met to discuss new business, and whatever it was, I was sure the terms were still open to fraught negotiation.

I loved this type of policing; stealing a march on your suspect and lying in wait. A few weeks later and it gets better. There's nothing sweeter than watching smug faces drop into despair when everything they've denied is played for the jury in crystal-clear Dolby. You never get to do that in uniform.

Three hours later and several flasks of coffee were just about maintaining basic neurological functions.

'You want a jelly baby?' asked Colin.

'No thanks.'

'Milk bottle?'

'No thanks.'

'Drumstick?'

'No.'

'I haven't got any Parma Violets left. Love heart?'

'I don't want anything, thanks Colin.'

'… Do you want to hear a joke?'

'No.'

'Knock-knock…'

'Go away.'

'Who's there..?'

'Nobody.'

'Lettuce. Lettuce who? Just shut up and *lettuce in*. I made that up when I was at school. Okay, how many blondes does it take to screw a light bulb? No... How do you unscrew - hang on…'

I was losing all sense of guilt for never socialising with Colin for more than a few hours at a time. The inane, chirpy bollocks after he'd had any significant caffeine was unbearable.

I forced myself up and out of my seat to pace the windows, watching the lone security guard complete another lap of the buildings. He'd arrived at ten, aimlessly wandering the yard, shouting and laughing into his mobile phone. It didn't seem likely he was in on anything. There had been only one other minor development.

Since just before midnight, at roughly twenty-minute intervals, the main doors to Building Twelve would creak ever-so-slightly open and two men would appear to chat and smoke; Steve and Ben, apparently. They were big guys, most likely two from the house the other day. Following them back inside with my binoculars, it looked like they were living on site. They'd set up a small folding table, littered with cards and beer bottles. A portable TV was plugged into the corner. There were sleeping bags on roll mats. But the conversation wasn't worth recording. It was just mindless, everyday chat. I got the impression they didn't know why they were staying there. All the same,

Colin took several shots, and we had our first glimpse into the warehouse proper. Unfortunately, everything else bar a forklift was obscured by heavy dust sheets.

Another hour passed and there they were in the doorway again. This time around, however, they flattened their cigarettes out on the floor, locked-up and got into a nearby car, driving off towards town.

'Have you seen the site guard lately?' I asked.

Colin was slouched in his chair, fiddling with the recorder.

'No. He's probably asleep. Why?'

'The two guys have gone. I'm going to take a look inside.'

Colin jumped to his feet. '*You can't*. What happens if they catch you? There might be more of them.'

'We need something tonight. If Jones is a no-show and nothing moves we've wasted our time again.'

Colin looked down at the warehouse. 'The door's padlocked shut. You can't get in.'

I pointed across to the office on the roof, identical to ours. 'I'm sure that window's open. I can make the jump.'

'Are you *mental*?'

'We're looking into it. Give me the earpiece and the mike. If you see anyone approach I'll come back.'

'And what am I supposed to do if you get caught again?'

'Bag up all the non-essential stuff in case we need to move quickly.'

I poked the earpiece in and clipped the mike wire to my overalls. I pushed the window open and listened for a moment.

Colin huffed. 'What call-signs are we using?'

'No bloody stupid names. I'm only going over the road. How loud is this thing?'

'Testing, testing –'

'AH! That's far too loud.' I adjusted the volume on the receiver. 'Go again.'

'Testing, testing.'

'That's better.'

I pocketed a small digital camera and gripped the window frame. One leg steadily over, then the next. I bobbed up and down on the corrugated metal to check my footing.

'Keep your eyes open,' I said.

Colin reluctantly took position behind our equipment.

I looked like a cat on thin ice, placing each foot carefully to avoid slipping on the condensation, leaning into the slope. I was around fifty feet from the ground, illuminated in patches by lights attached to the derricks. Thankfully there wasn't a breath of air, but as I neared the edge of the roof my confidence started to drain. The gap between buildings was much wider than I had anticipated - eight or nine feet. That'd be fine if I could take a run up, but in the dark, across the ridges, I could trap my foot and face-plant into the concrete below.

Colin was scanning the area with the binoculars.

'It's still clear,' he said in my ear. *'Whatever you're going to do, do it now.'*

That was a shot through my system. Suddenly I was twelve again and all my friends were shouting at me to jump. I had to do it.

I took several steps back and spring-loaded my thighs. I ran, pushing as hard as I could from the edge, launching into the black air. My legs bicycled underneath me, but as the lights in the distance disappeared with my descent I still couldn't feel anything solid.

Then I clattered into the edge of the other roof. Stretching and clawing, I tried desperately for purchase on the smooth, wet surface, but I kept sliding backwards. I couldn't stop until I hit the guttering, when the brittle metal immediately began to snap with my weight. I swung an arm up and clawed the rusting edges of a large strut bolt, just as a chunk of the gully full of moss fell away into the black.

'*Pull yourself up,*' said Colin. '*The guard's on his way over.*'

I leant back to look past my shoulder. I could see the intermittent flash of a high-vis jacket working its way towards me in the floodlights, but I couldn't tell how fast he was moving, or if he had seen me. Looking down my body there was nothing to save me; no ledges or window sills; just a straight drop onto the tarmac. I needed to hook my boot on the roof and I swung for momentum.

'*Quickly,*' Colin whispered, '*he's getting closer.*'

I thrust my leg up and over another bolt, scratching my calf on the sharp edges as I tried to hold it there, but it wouldn't stay and I ripped some more guttering out. The security guard definitely heard that. He was running.

'*Quickly,*' repeated Colin, as if I needed the encouragement.

I gnashed my teeth for one more swing and this time the heel of my boot held. My hamstring pulled tight, reeling my body upwards and across the roof. I rolled onto my back, splaying my fingers out at either side of me to hold position, but I was already slipping towards the edge again. A beam of torchlight shined up, scanning over the damage.

'*Keep still. He's right below you.*'

I couldn't keep still. And my top half was sliding faster than the bottom. I was going to fall head-first. I found a bolt at my side and gripped it as hard as I could, holding myself parallel with the edge, only just out of sight. The curious light still looked over the damage. I had five seconds before my wrist snapped with my weight and the security guard and I were going to get seriously acquainted. I wanted to shout. The tendons were ready to burst from my arm. I was nearly visible when a couple of gulls squawked and flew inches over my head. I could hear the guard murmur complaints to himself, kicking pieces of the guttering to one side.

Finally he cut the torchlight.

'*Okay, I think he's going,*' said Colin. '*… He's checking the padlock on the door… yeah, he's going. You're clear.*'

I spun onto my front and brought my knees up underneath me. My heart thumped as I tried to keep my breathing quiet. My wrist was killing. My ribs burned.

If there was any rush to leave I was in serious trouble, but there was no turning back now.

21

I crept up to the office and crouched. There was light from the warehouse under the door but otherwise the room was in darkness. I pulled open the window and vaulted inside – to land right next to a man sleeping on an old mattress. It took everything to withhold a shriek and I backed against the wall on the other side of the room, ducking behind a desk.

'There's someone asleep in here,' I whispered.

'Who is it?'

'I don't know. I'm not going to ask him. Asian male.'

'Just one?'

I looked up from the desk and around the room. 'Looks like it.'

'Come back.'

'No. I'm going into the main warehouse.'

I edged out from behind the desk and tip-toed over to the office door. The man was snoring peacefully. He didn't look like one of those I'd seen at Sammy's. He was around thirty-five, forty, with a neat, trimmed goatee beard. He was of thin build with thick glasses folded next to him on a chair. At least that was one fight I might win if the alarm was raised. Looking closer at his surrounds there was a laptop on a filing cabinet and a neat grey suit hanging from a hook behind the door. It was as though he'd finished at a banking conference and all the hotels were full.

I snuck out onto the metal gantry above the main warehouse store, pulling the door to. I could see the corners of several boxes protruding from under the sheets below me.

'Hello?' said Colin.

'Yeah?'

'I'm at work... I know what time it is... Because I have to sometimes...'

Colin was on the phone to his nan. I don't know if he knew that the mike was still open or not, but Edith was obviously concerned her grandson was out way past his bed time. I tried not to snort, running like a roadie across the gantry to the staircase.

'... I'll put it in the microwave when I get back... I do appreciate it, I'm sure it'll be lovely... No, you don't need to send it to the kids in Ethiopia...'

There were at least twenty boxes in the main storage area piled on top of one another, roughly a metre cubed. I lifted the edge of the nearest sheet, kicking up plumes of dust. They were wholly unremarkable wooden containers, the kind of thing you might expect bananas to be transported in.

'... I'll get some milk tomorrow... Well why do you always get up at five? You're eighty-seven years old. What are you going to be late for..?'

The boxes were nailed shut. No obvious labels. I pulled another sheet away for more of the same - bare, splintered wood. They were customs-stamped in Arabic, but that was it. I climbed on top of the first row and swiped away the next sheet. I found myself looking at some kind of symbol.

'... They're not there now, are they..? Kids are supposed to play in the park... How would you know what crack cocaine looks like..?'

There was a marking on every lid; a red three-pronged symbol on a green background. I was sure I had seen that somewhere before. I took the camera out from my pocket and clicked several snaps, looking up at the office after every flash.

'... You should bloody well go to sleep... I can swear... You won't smack my legs... You won't smack my legs. I only have

to run up five stairs and you can't get me, you dalek... Maybe the new ones can, but you can't. I'm going now, bye.'

'Trouble at home?' I asked, checking through the angles I had on the camera.

'Did you hear that? She's lucky I don't give her a sedative and take her to Dignitas. Where are you?'

'Main warehouse. I'm with the boxes. What does a –'

'Hang on... movement. White van. No sign writing... One occupant in the front... I think it's Carr. He's coming in.'

I slapped the camera into my back pocket and jumped off the boxes. I was about to run back across the room when I heard the jangle of keys at the main doors. Even if I could get up the stairs in time I would still be exposed on the gantry above. I ran around the boxes and found a gap between them, flicking the sheet back over my head.

'Two more people approaching from the rear. Man and a woman. Carr's going to speak with them. Don't move.'

I used the momentary delay to peek around the wood and look for another escape. There was an emergency exit behind the forklift on the other side of the warehouse, but that may well set an alarm off. There was nowhere else to go. I was trapped.

'I don't believe it.'

'What?'

'Did you tell anyone we were here tonight?'

'No. Why?'

'...It's definitely her...'

'Who?'

'Katya. With Tony Riley.'

'What?'

'They're talking to Carr now.'

'It can't be.'

'I can see his BMW parked up in the distance. I've got it on camera.'

'Did you say anything to anyone?'

'No. Me, you and Straughan, that's it. There're more coming. Several cars... It's Jones. Looks like he's got a few people with him... Oh my...'

'What?'

'Machetes and bats... McIntyre's here. They're at the main entrance now. Stay down.'

The chain rumbled off the metal and dropped to the floor. I forced myself as tightly as possible between the boxes, sanding my face. I could just see the doors through a gap.

The warehouse flooded with Jones' men. They were all in black – the unofficial uniform – and every single one of them had a weapon to hand, very deliberately on show.

Jones still sported the handlebar moustache he'd first donned in the seventies, though like his long, slicked-back hair, it was more grey now than black. He was hairier than a French porn star, with a couple of naff, faded tattoos up his forearms, just visible through a tangle of curls.

'Jonesy!' said McIntyre, entering with his arms outstretched. 'It's been a while. How are we doing?'

'You're behind with your rent, Sammy.'

'I know. We'll talk about that. How's your mother?'

'Dead.'

'Oh. Well, never mind. She was fucking ugly anyway.'

'These the boxes?'

'They are.'

'Where's the money?'

'Coming.'

'You're going to have to do better than that,' said Jones. 'Why have you stopped paying your suppliers?'

'I don't need 'em anymore.'

'You're sure about that? I know a lot of very unhappy people.'

'Well, you will keep getting married.'

'Where's the money?'

'What's the matter, Jonesy? D'you miss a gas bill or summink? What's with all the tools?'

McIntyre was only feet away from me now, allowing his fingers to run along the splintered wood, smiling at Jones' thugs as he passed.

'I had a meeting with some of your dealers the other day,' said Jones.

'A meeting? That's very adult of you, Arthur.'

'Every one of them said the same thing to me...'

'Well don't listen to 'em, your 'tache is lovely.'

'They want you out. Now, I'm here to collect. Have you got cash on site or not?'

'Cash? What, d'you think I'm fucking stupid? They have banks these days, old man. Look, don't get me wrong, I think you and your anonymous friends are really brave to have a load of big lads gang up on me with bats, but I'll remind you that you're *here* because I invited you. What d'you say we stick to the plan, eh? It's late, and I really can't be bothered to dump a load of bodies.'

Several of McIntyre's men appeared in the doorway, variously armed with bats, knives and lengths of chain. Each of them found a space on the crowded floor, looking to size up their opposite number.

At that, Jones nodded to one of his men who produced a sub-machine gun from his jacket and trained it on Sammy. I was directly behind him. Firing at the hip, I'd be lucky if I was only hit ten times.

'Oh. Could you only afford the one gun?' asked McIntyre.

'You think you can snap your fingers and everyone'll come running, don't you?'

'Not everyone, Arthur, just you.'

'Who *dumped* Bingo? I heard he left it late to learn how to swim.'

'It's not nice to mock the disabled. But yeah, sad day. I have faith the police will find his killer, though.'

151

'I'm sure you do. I'm gonna need that money now.'

Jones nodded again and his man took a thick palm to the top of the gun to cock it.

McIntyre sighed. 'A word of caution about firearms in this building, gentlemen; one stray bullet and none of us will land for a week.'

He slapped the box he was leaning on and every pair of eyes was drawn to the mountain of wood.

Jones hesitated, trying to work out whether Sammy was serious or not, inadvertently staring straight at me.

I held my breath.

Sammy looked at the man with the gun. 'Can you fly, big man?'

'What the hell are you playing at?' asked Jones.

'You don't wanna know. Just give me the time I've asked for and make sure there's someone at your end to let us in. After that, this shithole's all yours again. You and your fucking spineless mates can ski down the gear.'

The man with the gun looked back for instructions.

'This is your retirement, Arthur,' said McIntyre. 'Trust me.'

There was no such thing as trust between those men. Jones didn't like being left in the dark. Such was the nature of his business that he wanted to watch his investments like a jealous boyfriend. Nonetheless, he gave the nod for his man to stand down and to my relief that gun barrel dropped.

'Just two boxes tonight,' said Sammy. '*Carefully*. And stick to the route we agreed. Key's in the forklift.'

Jones followed his men as they began to filter out, dragging his reluctant pride with him. Carr opened the main doors to reveal the van waiting outside. Scooping up the first box with the forklift accidentally pulled the sheet from over my head. I was exposed and I couldn't duck down any further. One of my feet was poking out.

152

McIntyre was uncomfortably close as he beckoned my supposed colleagues over.

'Can you believe that guy?' he said. 'Guns. Should I call the police?'

Tony let out a burst of fake laughter. McIntyre half-feigned a grin in return.

'What's the latest with your lot?'

'We're clear,' said Katya. 'Everyone is behaving.'

'What about Rose?'

'He doesn't know anyzhing.'

'You're sure about that?'

'He doesn't know shit,' said Tony. 'We're ready when you are. Call the missus and get your flights booked. You're going on holiday, my friend.'

McIntyre moved in close to Tony. 'I'm not your friend, little man, and let me make it clear that if there are any problems, they will be your fault. Consequences apply accordingly.'

'Sammy, Sammy, Sammy, ease up, mate,' said Tony. 'Haven't we delivered so far?'

'Piss off, the pair of you. I don't want to see either of you until next week.'

They didn't need telling twice.

Then McIntyre saw something on the gantry above us. It was the Asian man I nearly stood on. All he had to do was look down through the grating and he could see me, plain as day.

'Sorry to wake you up, Ashane,' said McIntyre. 'We're just leaving. Try and get some sleep. I'll pick you up for lunch tomorrow, my treat.'

Fortunately the bleary-eyed man was too tired for a conversation, whether he understood what was being said or not. He yawned and shuffled back into the office.

McIntyre turned to Carr. 'Keep these things covered. I don't want that bloke on the gate asking questions.'

He tossed the sheet into the air and it came to rest over my head.

22

In the hospital waiting room my leg shook like I was awaiting biopsy results.

I'd deliberately chosen a seat with my back against the wall, a vantage point where I had a clear view of everyone and no one could sneak up on us.

We were seen leaving the docks. That morning a man followed us to the hospital, staying three cars behind at all times. He stopped when we stopped. He drove quickly when we sped up. He was on the phone when Colin and I parked the car, confirming my location. I didn't glimpse his face, but I knew he was one of the men in that room. If I got up from my seat I'd be followed. Five minutes more and everyone might have had to canoe out of that waiting room, but I couldn't risk the toilet. It was too easy a trap.

Then I saw him. In the corner. Dark jacket. Our eyes met as he finished reading a text. The order had been given. He was going to kill me.

That was bollocks of course. He was just some bloke who happened to be going to the hospital as well, using the same route Colin and I had taken like hundreds of other people. But it felt real. I was struggling to steady my mind. I knew too much.

We had already been to Straughan's house. Meeting on-site at the station was no longer an option. The chief listened to the recording - a marked improvement on the last one it was noted - and I didn't have to say anything else. Behind the scenes he would apply to the court for a warrant, but absolutely no one could know what it was for. Officers for the search would be drafted in from another force, and even they wouldn't be told what was going on until the very last minute. We arranged to meet at Colin's place later in the day to set everything in stone, until then, Sammy's rules applied; no calls, emails, texts, nothing. Silence. No risks. This was too great a chance to compromise.

All the same, the chief rightly insisted we otherwise maintained normality. Suspicion may arise if anything suddenly changed in our programmes, especially as our worst fears had been confirmed and at least one of the team had been identified as an insider.

Colin would lose himself in as many broken photocopiers, computers and tangled wires as he could find, preferably in the bowels of headquarters, out of everyone's way. He drove me to the hospital under the pretence that my injuries were worsening, which wasn't far from the truth after my exploits on the roof. Any excuse would do to stay out of the Special Ops office for as long as possible. DI Martin would never check. He didn't care. All our cases were already in the process of being transferred to CID. It wasn't like we could fall behind with anything.

I should have been absolutely ecstatic, but I certainly didn't feel like a winner. In fact I was furious when I wasn't nervous. A few coppers would give into some easy cash in exchange for a story here and there, I'd long accepted that, but back-handers to ignore what looked like terrorism?

I'd felt stupid at times during my professional career, but that night at Katya's house just added the can-I-eat-these-or-not? silver beads to the cherries to the icing to the marzipan on the cake. She sang her 'zsexy' song and I danced like a ten-pinter at closing time. It's only fortunate that I really didn't know anything. I should have seen it coming; if it seems too good to be true, then it's probably Samuel Richard McIntyre. Or one of those microwavable cheeseburgers.

I'd rarely confided in anyone like that before. Not even Jen knew I had that photograph. I bet the picture of that bloody dog was cut out of a magazine while I was on my way over, a deliberate ploy to hypnotise me with those breasts; two gently wobbling weapons; warheads of mass distraction. On the one hand I was pleased with myself for ultimately showing restraint, on the other, I was slightly annoyed that I didn't just dive in. I wasn't going to get another chance. But that's the thing with hindsight; we'd all sleep with attractive terror suspects before it became morally reprehensible if we knew.

'Are you alright?' asked Colin, dropping a copy of *Woman's Own* to his lap.

'Yeah.'

'Why are you sticking your tongue out like that?'

'I'm just thinking.'

'About what?'

'About Katya's… involvement.'

Colin frowned, but returned to his problem page.

It was no wonder McIntyre wasn't paying his suppliers anymore. The sums to acquire materials, manpower and secure protection must have been enormous. But what the hell could you blow up, or threaten to blow up, in order to recoup those costs? Sammy was no extremist. He had to be funding a plan for someone else that guaranteed enormous returns.

What of those alleged friends in the north Katya mentioned? Was she checking what I knew of genuine contacts, or was it a red herring; another distraction in case I got clear of the Bingo charge earlier than expected? Perhaps the new guys had gone to meet them? They might even be related to a home-grown terror cell. Sadly I was in no position to find out one way or the other. It was all wild speculation until we kicked the doors through on McIntyre's warehouse.

My legs continued to bounce up and down of their own accord. It was a busy morning for Outpatients and my X-rays were clearly a long way down the list of priorities. I don't like to bother busy nurses, but I had the feeling I might be forgotten altogether if I didn't say anything. I needed to get up anyway. If I kept disturbing Colin he wasn't going to learn a thing about why his breasts weren't developing.

Someone certainly wasn't happy in one of the examination cubicles, thrashing about like a cornered cat every time the doctor tried to step in. I was on my way over to speak with Reception when the source of the noise tore open the curtain and ran for the exit, nearly knocking over several people and tripping on a chair leg.

I recognised her.

'Vicky?'

She looked back. It was definitely her - the girl from my counselling group. Half her face was freshly bruised and she seemed to lean uncomfortably to that same side.

'*Vicky*,' I shouted, but she was already running through the car park towards the main road and out of sight.

I was still looking out the window when a heavy-set nurse appeared at my side.

'Excuse me, are you Vicky's father?' she asked.

'No, I'm a police officer.'

The nurse gestured down the hall to speak in private. Colin looked round at me and I asked for a moment with my index finger.

I was led into a small office a short way down the corridor. The nurse closed the door behind us and snapped off her rubber gloves.

'Are you familiar with Vicky's case?' she asked.

'No. No, I'm not.'

'Do you have your ID?'

I handed over my warrant card.

'I'm Gerry, the ward matron. I've known Vicky for some years. I've been working with a colleague of yours in the Child Protection Team.'

'What's her situation?'

'Well, we haven't seen her in a few months, but when we do she's almost always drunk and usually injured.'

'I can believe that.'

'To cut a long story short, she's a repeat victim of aggressive sexual abuse. Now, she's been bleeding heavily again today. I believe she's miscarried.'

'She was pregnant?'

'She's had at least two terminations with us in the past. The first was when she was only twelve. She's never confirmed it to me personally, but your colleague and I both suspect she's working as a prostitute, possibly under duress from her step-father. I can recover her file if you'd like it?'

It would be at this point that I should reveal the fact that I'm suspended, or if I found that too embarrassing, that I didn't want to step on any toes at Child Protection. It would have been the easiest thing in the world to shirk responsibility and just tell Gerry I'd give the officer in charge a call. But when she handed me the file I only needed to read three lines of Vicky's profile before I knew where and when she would die, with a margin for error no greater than a few months.

'We'd like to have her back with us, at least overnight,' said Gerry, 'but every time we've tried to hold onto her she always runs away. I don't suppose it would be any different this time.'

It was clear that we were well beyond standard procedure and meaningless bits of paper. A PPO was never going to work and we couldn't force her back. She'd tear the place apart trying to escape and end up arrested again, or worse, at home. Either way, she'd be on the streets within hours and more vulnerable than ever. The CPT had clearly tried everything within their legal power, but like so many cases involving teenagers they had run out of legal clout. Gerry explained that Vicky had run away within hours of being placed with several foster families, threatening them with anything sharp that came to hand if they tried to stand in her way. At fifteen she wanted her independence. She was old enough to make her own decisions, but too young and far too drunk to account for them.

Perhaps it was residual excitement from the night before. Maybe I just thought I was going to be bored on my suspension. Either way, I was going to investigate.

'Where does she hide?' I asked.

23

'Why are we doing this?' asked Colin.

'Because no one else will,' I said.

'Don't you think there's a reason for that? Chris, we haven't got the time.'

'We've got loads of time. We're not meeting Straughan for another two hours.'

We'd checked just about every street corner in the area, stooping to look under hoods and following every teen-packed hatchback. I couldn't remember what colours Vicky was wearing, only that she was carrying the shabby handbag she'd had at counselling. She couldn't have gotten far. Not in that state. She'd need a drink. She'd be out somewhere.

I flicked through her file again. I wasn't familiar with her surname – Maynard. The step-father had given a different ID every time he arrived and could have been anyone. He'd stopped bringing Vicky in once the staff began asking questions. There were no known blood-relatives.

We crawled along the park perimeter for another forty minutes, stopping every now and again to look over various groups. I had to concede it was looking like a lost cause when I saw a girl outside the corner shop. She was waiting for someone. A few moments later and a slightly older teen emerged from the shop to hand over a single bottle, taking cash in exchange.

'That's her,' I said.

'Are you sure?'

'Certain.'

Vicky stuffed the bottle into that familiar bag. It bounced off her pathetic frame as she scurried towards a secluded wood, unaware she was being watched.

'Park here,' I said.

'I can't, it's disabled.'

'So pull a face. I want to go to that shop.'

'We're shopping now?'

'Are you missing a hair appointment or something? I won't be long.'

Colin pulled into one of a number of empty spaces. I knew exactly what I wanted and I was in and out of the shop within thirty seconds, jogging for the wood.

The tangle of trees and general refuse eventually gave way to a small clearing and a stagnant pond. On an old bench with most of the slats missing, Vicky was gulping back her vodka. She wiped some excess from her mouth and bent forward holding her stomach, rocking gently on her toes. Deep, almost permanent bruises daubed her lilywhite skin for every centimetre it was exposed. She straightened again just enough to take another glug. And then she noticed me.

'Hey,' I said.

She turned like a squirrel, forgetting her injuries, ready to run if I made another move.

'What the fuck do you want? I said I'm not interested.'

'And I said it's not like that.'

'Piss off.'

'Give me a chance.'

Vicky screwed the top back onto her bottle and forced it into her bag. She stood, trying not to let the pain show, wiping a tear from her eye.

'Wait,' I said, 'I'm not here to take you back. I just want to talk.'

'So phone the Samaritans.'

'I can't, I'm banned.'

'Is that a joke?'

'Look, if you don't like what I have to say then you can leave, or I will. I promise.'

She considered me for a few moments. In the end it was probably more her injuries and a simple lack of alternative than anything else, but she fell back onto the bench and pulled her vodka free from the tatty leather. I asked if I could sit down, at which I was offered a now trademark shrug.

I looked over the putrid water, the bow of the ubiquitous sunken trolley collecting gently floating debris.

'Nice view,' I said, trying not to breathe in too many midgies. 'I like the smell, too.'

'You don't have to stay.'

'Don't get me wrong, I can see why you come here. Beautiful brambles. All the animals… floating upside down in the water. If you need a Rizzla or a condom it's on the floor here somewhere.'

There was almost a smile as Vicky carefully licked alcohol from her swollen lip.

'Here,' I said, handing over the plastic bag I was carrying.

She looked inside and pulled out a much more expensive bottle of vodka than she was used to.

'What's this?'

'What does it look like?'

'Why?'

'Keep drinking that cheap stuff and you'll shit your innards out.'

She looked at me again. 'What do you want?'

'I told you, I just want to talk.'

'I thought the police were supposed to take alcohol off kids, not give it to them.'

'How d'you know I'm a copper?'

'I heard them talking in our group. What happened to your face?'

'A big guy's fist happened to it. How about you? Step-dad?'

She nodded

163

Once you'd climbed the initial wall of attitude, Vicky was surprisingly open to conversation. In fact she was brutally honest and direct, assisted in part by the litre of neat vodka we were sharing. But she didn't slur. She didn't giggle like a typical teenager. This was a fully-fledged young woman, trapped in a frail girl's body – and a sick man's house.

Mark Hudson – nothing like any of the names he'd given to the hospital - had been in prison at some point during every one of the ten years Vicky had known him. He used to have a family of his own; a wife, several kids. Then one day he came home from a rare day at work to find they had gone. It was an escape plan that must have been gestating for months, if not years. He would never see them again.

Mark latched onto Vicky's mother at her most vulnerable, newly divorced and un-employed with a young mouth to feed. Almost immediately he wanted to start a new family to get the benefits flowing, but when complications arose with cancer, a hysterectomy put paid to that. Mark was forced to consider something else.

'She's beautiful,' people would remark of Vicky, playing in the street with her friends.

Yes she is, Mark thought.

The first time was two weeks before her eleventh birthday. Mark had promised Vicky a new bike. It was going to be expensive, but he knew a man who could get them a good deal. He just needed Vicky to do something for him first. In fact, for just a few secret little favours she could have anything she wanted. Sure enough, on her birthday, a bike was propped against the lounge wall, but it wasn't the one she wanted. It was a boy's bike, rusting with broken gears. Not that she could sit on it for a week anyway.

Vicky wasn't sure when her mum first found out. She thinks she feigned ignorance while planning how to leave Mark, just as his wife had done. Her cleaning jobs throughout the day and night meant she never really saw the full extent of what was going on, and Vicky was warned to keep her mouth shut. Confronting Mark directly was only going to make things worse for both of them. Their only hope was to convince the authorities that he needed to go away and stay away. In his absence, perhaps the state could organise another house elsewhere in the country and they could hide. But the inevitable delay in organising the evidence brought new danger. Mark would kill Vicky. He'd hide the body and never tell her mother where it was for as long as he lived. Frustrated with a lack of cooperation, the CPT variously charged him with a number of lesser offences. Sadly, this meant months rather than years of incarceration and did nothing to improve his mood. It worsened further when he found the pair of them at a women's refuge.

Probably owing to the increasing stress, Vicky's mother's health began to deteriorate rapidly. The cancer was spreading and the operations did nothing to halt its progress. Still she worked to bring in every last penny until she collapsed hoovering an office. While visiting her mother in hospital Vicky was handed a building society book. The account contained almost every penny her mother had earned.

'Don't tell Mark,' she was told.

Vicky's mother died the next day.

It was almost like talking with someone disgruntled with a desk job. There wasn't a hint of self-pity. No want for help. No blame. Even the crying was only a subconscious reaction to the physical pain.

'It's not always bad,' said Vicky, her watery eyes lost somewhere in the pond. 'Last year, there was this guy... he would talk to me, buy me stuff.'

'Like a boyfriend?'

'They all think they're my boyfriend. He was just nice.'

'What happened to him?'

165

'I think his wife found out. Never said anything. Just stopped coming one day.' Vicky looked over the bruises on her arms. 'He thinks it's my fault when they don't come back... when I get pregnant...'

Finally the emotional dam cracked. Vicky turned away from me, almost embarrassed. I wouldn't step in to try and comfort her. The last thing she wanted was another man's arms around her. I let her cough up the tears until she could hold still again and control the pain.

'There's nothing you lot can do,' she said. 'He knows how it works. He's all nice and helpful until the front door closes again.'

I knew exactly what she meant. I'd attended countless addresses, thick with atmosphere and distress. I've looked into eyes that screamed at me for help, but fear had stolen the words. A smile fools no one as a shaking hand signs the statement to say everything's fine. And there's absolutely nothing you can do about it.

There was a future for Vicky. She'd been running for the horizon for years, but the alcohol was a hurdle, not a barrier. At worst it provoked a few fights with her peers. Fights she would generally win. Drinking was simple pain relief. It was forgetting. It wasn't essential. Within a year she could be dry and legally self-sufficient. She could have a tutor and prospects.

'Vicky, I have a place,' I said, 'across town, big spare room. I'm never there. You can treat it as your own. It'll give you time to think.'

'About what?'

'About what *you* want to do. Mark's not your dad. He's no one. If we can't keep him in prison we'll at least keep him away.'

She shook her head. 'He'll find me.'

'You don't need to be afraid of him. He's just a man.'

The tears welled again. 'You're not a perv?'

I laughed. 'Part-time. But not in your category, I promise.'

She'd had enough crying. Feeling sorry for herself was a weakness. She dried her eyes with her sleeve and stood, shouldering her handbag.

'I can pay you,' she said.

'Why don't you use the money to buy yourself a new bag?'

She cradled the mangy leather tight to her side.

'It was my mum's. It's all I have left.'

I introduced Vicky to my cupboards, the microwave and a whole raft of medical supplies. She seemed to be feeling a lot better, even if she didn't look it, smiling then crying to herself on the silent car journey. There was no plan yet, only a determination to seek a life beyond that estate, and I was going to help her in any way that I could. Lastly I gave her the TV remote and warned her explicitly not to answer the door to anyone except me and to make absolutely sure it was me.

'How will I know it's you?' she asked. 'You could be anyone in the dark. What's the passphrase?'

'Passphrase?'

'Yeah, something that only we'll know.'

'You can just look through the letterbox.'

'No, come on, you're the police, this will be fun. How about you knock five times and say... "It's me, the stallion. I'm going to jump the bush".'

'You really have to stop drinking.'

'Ooh, good point. Where d'you keep your booze?'

With any luck she'd still be there when I got back.

24

Colin and I pulled up outside his house. Straughan was waiting, sat in his car. Behind him, a short way off in a block of garages was Colin's nan. As usual she was standing in the garage doorway with her mobile IV stand, smoking endless cigarettes. She had a face like a bulldog licking piss off a nettle, though that was only when she was happy.

As Edith lacked mobility, other than the fleet of foot to get her out to the garage and back, the downstairs of the house was all hers. The dining room had been converted into her bedroom and there were handrails every few steps. Little brown pots of pills littered every surface and in more than one spot it smelt ever so slightly of stale urine. The knackered old cat hissed at us from the back of an armchair as we passed towards the stairs. Colin stamped his foot and it cowered under an antique cabinet, watching us resentfully as we ascended.

The first floor was another, altogether more modern, world. Colin slept in the smaller of two bedrooms, while the larger was kitted out with a giant TV, stereo, games consoles, gadgets, magazines – all apparently lower shelf – and a black leather sofa and matching lazy-boy armchairs. Very impressive. It really was just me behind with my furnishings. I'd have to get a catalogue or something.

Straughan checked all the windows were shut tight and closed the door behind us. I tried out one of the lazy-boys, pulling the lever to stretch out into a gloriously comfortable position. I could have gone to sleep instantly and stayed there for hours.

'Tea, sir?' asked Colin, going to a window sill that was home to a kettle.

'Haven't you got any beers?' asked Straughan.

'Not in this house,' I said.

'Actually, that's not strictly true,' said Colin. He reached down behind his sofa and I could hear a small fridge opening. 'Lager or bitter?' he asked, holding up two cans.

Straughan took the latter.

'Chris?'

'I'll have a ...'

The chief was looking at me.

'...Tea, please, Colin.'

I had to at least pretend. Colin flicked the kettle on and snapped open the lager for himself.

There were prints of the photos we had taken from the docks on a coffee table. Straughan picked them up and began to thumb through them, sipping his beer. We went over everything that I'd seen again; the guards, the Asian man, Carr, McIntyre. The chief recognised Jones immediately, and half his men. There was a furious glare at the excellent shots Colin had taken of Tony Riley and his car – the number plate was as clear as day - but the biggest sigh and a shake of the head that seemed to go on forever was reserved for Katya. Again, there was no doubting her identity. The focus was so good we could almost see individual hair follicles. The beautiful traitor.

Straughan asked about the boxes and Colin realised he hadn't printed off the shots I'd taken *inside* the building. Where I wasn't supposed to be.

'Have you ever followed an order in your life?' the chief asked me.

I thought about that. There had to have been one.

Colin went to his computer to start printing while Straughan spoke: 'We've got the go-ahead for the warrant tonight, midnight. Seeing as he's already moving those things I don't want to delay any longer. I've got twenty officers from next door. We'll secure the warehouse and arrest McIntyre. If he's true to his boast, we should have enough to remand him this time, but this has to run like clockwork. We're already on thin ice. If we miss anything his lawyers will snap us in two.'

Colin handed me a tea and gave the new photos to the chief. Anticipation started tingling through my body as I thought about how close we were, and what could go wrong. The nerves forced my fingers into an involuntary tap-dance on the leather.

Straughan was struck by something. He looked at a second photo, then a third in quick succession, holding them up and squinting.

'Were all the boxes marked like this?' he asked, turning the photo to show me the unknown symbol.

'Yeah, I think so,' I replied. 'I meant to Google that. D'you know what it is?'

'I haven't seen it since my military days.'

I looked at Colin. 'So, what is it?' I asked.

'Some years ago I was in charge of a small unit on operation in Iraq. We were following a militia convoy when it left the road for the mountains. I was told to break off and return to base, but I didn't like it. I knew they had something. We tracked them to a camp where several other vehicles were waiting to swap cargo. Going one way were crates piled high with U.S dollars, millions upon millions. Going the other were boxes marked with this symbol.'

He held up another of the photos.

'I don't think I've seen it first-hand before,' I said.

'I should hope not. It denotes a chemical weapon.'

Silence.

McIntyre was orchestrating a chemical attack? On who? Where? Was he going to try for a ransom? Surely the world wasn't big enough to hide once you'd thrown that hand down? You'd be found. They might even reintroduce hanging for something like that.

'How do you get chemical weapons into the country?' I asked.

'You can't,' replied Straughan. 'Not unless you've paid a truly spectacular sum of money to secure their safe passage. These might just be components. He could have a buyer somewhere.'

Or he was acting as the broker for six Middle-Eastern men – six bona fide terrorists - who may or may not be hiding somewhere up north.

'I need to speak with Counter-Terror before we go in tonight,' said Straughan. 'Only governments are supposed to deal in these things.'

'What did you do with that camp in Iraq?' asked Colin.

'The only sensible thing you can do. We radio-d in an airstrike and incinerated the place.'

'That must have been fun.'

'No. It wasn't.' The chief was somewhere else for a moment. 'On our way back to base, my corporal, a good friend of mine, was on point. In the excitement we'd neglected to consider our route – *I* had neglected to consider our route. As far as possible, you come back the way you arrived, single file, to minimise the risk of mines. We were on unfamiliar territory, and… the explosion knocked all six of us to the ground. Only five of us got up again.'

'He died?' asked Colin.

Straughan nodded. 'Worst day of my life.'

'You could never have known. It wasn't your fault,' said Colin.

'Oh, I assure you, it was. That man was my responsibility. If I'd done what I should we'd all be here today.' Anyone else might fish for more words of consolation, but the chief wouldn't allow himself to be caught in his thoughts again. 'I want you both to understand the gravity of what we're dealing with here. This has just got a lot more serious. McIntyre will have everything he has tied up in this plan. He will expect it to work.'

171

Another prolonged silence was broken by an elderly shriek.

'Colin..! *Colin..!*'

'Oh, not now. *What* nan?'

'Come down these stairs, boy.'

Colin asked for a minute but Straughan was already leaving, throwing his beer back and gathering up the photos.

'I'll see you at the RV point,' I said.

'No chance,' said Straughan. 'You're staying well away. You can attend the station once the results are in.'

'This is my case.'

'*Was* your case. You're suspended, remember? If his lawyers get a sniff you were at the scene the whole thing flies out the window.'

'You need people you can trust.'

'And unfortunately for me, no such people exist.'

I would have argued with that if it wasn't for the roll-call of cock-ups casually jogging through my mind. The penguin, fighting, disobeying orders; the ground was far too shaky to mount a case for my defence. I was still a liability in his eyes and I had work to do yet before I could turn that opinion around.

Straughan was on his way down the stairs when he remembered something.

'Oh, but I've been doing some digging on your friend, Fergus,' he said.

'Who is he?' I asked.

'He's a Detective Inspector with the homicide unit. Nothing untoward on his record. Several people vouch for him. Clean as a cat's arse.'

'So why's he after me?'

'He must think you're a murderer.'

The chief pulled his eyes from mine and continued on his way. Apparently Fergus might not be alone in his thoughts. I had a *lot* of work to do.

I left Colin to reassure his grandmother about yet another group of youths that had congregated nearby – a 'youth' being the modern-day derogatory term for anyone under the age of ninety-seven that doesn't live in a Neighbourhood Watch co-ordinator's road, and therefore, clearly up to no good. The mob of ten and eleven-year-olds were once again viciously minding their own business in the park, designated for their use.

Walking to the car I checked my mobile. To my great surprise I had missed two calls from Jen. She'd left a voicemail, barely above a whisper: '*Chris, it's me. I can't talk now, he's here. I'm coming over to yours, I need to see you. If you get this, don't phone me back, I'll be there soon…Okay, mum, yeah, I know. Well, love to dad and I'll talk to you at the weekend. Bye.*'

The line dropped.

25

Jen was waiting on my drive when I arrived, clutching a large handbag about her waist. She looked anxious, fidgeting like a dealer on a street corner. I got out of the car and met her at my front door.

'I'm sorry, I didn't know what to do,' she said.

'What is it?'

She opened the bag and produced a small leather-bound diary. My diary.

'I've been looking for that,' I said.

She opened the bag again to hand me an A4 envelope. Inside were details on several cases I'd worked on in the past, along with my personal information and photographs. It was largely stuff acquired through the Freedom of Information Act, but at the very end were specifics on my minor criminal history. That wasn't easy to come by. I had to make sure of that before I applied for Special Ops.

'I thought he'd picked up by mistake at first. But every time I got in the shower, or he had five minutes alone, I'd catch him reading through it all.'

'Travis?'

She nodded. 'The other day when you were passed out, he must have been going through your drawers. He's obsessed with you.'

Was there a single person at my station who wasn't bent? That may have explained how I was caught out at Sammy's place. I never write specifics, but double-checking the entry on that date I had alluded to the location.

Nothing was surprising anymore. Everyone was to be treated as hostile unless there was cast-iron proof to the contrary.

I closed the diary. 'He's not obsessed with me. He's working for someone I'm investigating.'

'Then how do you explain these?'

Jen reached into her bag again and pulled out a pair of white underpants. They were almost a thong with a posing pouch.

'Those aren't mine,' I said.

Jen pulled a face and her hand started shaking as if she was holding a slippery fish. She turned in disgust and threw the pants into my neighbour's garden, wiping her hands on my shirt. She gagged with her tongue poking out, shivering with disgust.

'Come on. We'll talk inside,' I said.

I twisted the key in the lock but the door wouldn't open. It was dead-bolted from the other side. I'd completely forgotten about Vicky.

I knocked. The letterbox sprung open at my groin.

'Yes?'

'Open the door please, Vicky.'

'Vicky? Who's Vicky?' asked Jen. 'Have you got some girl living with you already?'

'No, I'll explain in a minute. Vicky...'

'What's the passphrase?'

'Vicky, it's me. Please open the door.'

'Sorry, but I've been given strict instructions. You could be anyone that looks and sounds like Chris. And who's that?'

'Who's *that*?' said Jen. 'Who are *you*?'

'He locked me in here.'

'*Vicky...*'

'I haven't eaten in three days. It's just endless sex. Then he beats me.'

Jen looked horrified.

'She's on my counselling course,' I said. 'She thinks she's clever. Vicky, open the door, now.'

'Passphrase.'

175

'I'll kick it through.'

'I'll call the police.'

'Vicky – '

'I've got the phone in my hand. Dialling now…'

I checked around to see if anyone was watching. I leant down to the letterbox to speak quietly.

'It's me, the stallion – '

'What? Can't hear you.'

'It's me, the stallion, I'm here –'

'Still can't hear you.'

I stood upright and shouted at the door, 'It's me, the stallion. I'm here to jump over the hedge!'

'Bush.'

'Bush! I'm going to jump the bush. Open the door.'

The locks clicked and I pushed the door open.

'It is you, Chris,' said Vicky. 'That's a relief. I wasn't sure.'

'Vicky, this is Jen, a friend of mine. Jen, this is Vicky, a fifteen-year-old-alcoholic who obviously doesn't get beaten enough.'

'Friend, eh?' said Vicky. 'I see. I'll go for a little stroll while you *talk*, shall I?'

'Does anyone know you're here?' I asked.

'No,' replied Vicky.

'Take the house phone upstairs. Talk to a friend you can trust. Let them know where you are.'

'I haven't really got any friends like that.'

'Then call your social worker. We need a meeting.'

'She doesn't like me.'

'I can see why. Go on'

Vicky jogged upstairs as Jen searched the lounge for a clean spot to sit, eventually settling on the armchair. She perched solemnly on the edge of the cushion like we were at a wake. I felt my ribs start to ache again as I lowered myself onto the sofa like a pregnant woman.

'Fifteen-years-old?' said Jen.

176

'I'm not shagging her.'

'*Liar,*' shouted Vicky.

'*Shut up.*'

The spare bedroom door closed.

'How'd she get all those bruises?'

'Her step-dad. He gets drunk and they fight. I said she could stay here while we sort something out.'

Jen was uncharacteristically subdued. She kept her hands and legs tight together. Her face was almost all obscured by her hair; her friendly hair. No tight ponytails today. For the first time in a long while she was also just wearing jeans and a t-shirt.

'What's going on, Chris? What was all that at the hospital? Why is Travis so interested in you?'

'Nobody's interested in me. They just want me out of the way. Did he say anything to you? Ask you anything?'

'No. He denied everything. Hid your diary. I found it when I was cleaning, then the file, then... the pants. He was so enthusiastic. It was his idea we should move in together, but every time we went to... there was always some excuse.'

'Does he know you have these?'

'No. I don't know what he'll do. I'm scared to go back.'

Whatever her motives for getting together with Travis, Jen clearly regretted ever setting eyes on him. In truth, I was no better a boyfriend. I never listened. Over time I'd learned to filter our conversation for key words - fire, sex, lasagne.

I'd always fancied Jen, especially after a few beers, but I could never maintain the feelings to a degree I'd class as love and I thought the feeling was mutual. But what is a relationship if not two people who talk to each other more than anyone else and have sex at the end of the day? Just because we didn't have seventeen kids or write poetry to each other in our own blood, that didn't mean that what we had was any less valid. She could have gone to any one of her friends for comfort and advice, but she came back to me.

'You don't have to go back,' I said.

I gestured for her to sit with me on the sofa. At first she was hesitant, but as I lifted my arm, hers slotted into place and she came to rest on my chest. I couldn't remember when we'd been that close. At that moment it felt like it happened every day. I leant in to smell her hair and I nearly kissed her head.

'You knew,' she said.

I nodded.

'Why aren't you laughing at me?'

'Oh, I did laugh at first… to be honest, I didn't think it was true.'

'How long have you known?'

'Few days.'

'How?'

'Katya.'

'Oh, well there's a surprise. Bit of pillow talk, was it?'

'Hey, excuse me. You're the one pretending to have a relationship just to spite me.'

Jen pulled back. 'I never pretended anything. Are you pretending to be with her?'

'No, I never have. Admit it, you're paranoid.'

'Admit you're an idiot.'

'I've never denied that.'

'You can't.'

'I won't.'She paused for a moment. 'Don't you ever think about me?' 'Sometimes, if I have too much cheese before I go to bed.'

'You miss me.'

'I'm too busy to miss anyone.'

'You're lonely'

'I'm not. I have Keith, and he loves me very much.'

'He's just after your money.'

'Now you're jealous. You obviously missed me.'

178

'Don't flatter yourself.'

'No one else is going to.'

'Are you going to kiss me?' she asked.

'I might.'

'Come on, then.'

'Okay.'

She jumped onto my lap, and I pulled her into me. She cleaned my mouth out with her tongue, holding my face before her hands slid down my body. I sucked some air through my teeth and she stopped.

'God, it's nice to kiss someone who doesn't smell of coconut,' she said. 'Are you okay?'

'I'm getting there. The ribs are still a bit sore.'

Reluctantly she climbed off, cuddling into me with her legs at ninety degrees across mine. She settled and we found ourselves caught in our thoughts.

'What will you do?' she asked.

'We're working on it. There's something important coming up tonight.'

'Is it dangerous?'

'Could be. Look, stay here. I could use someone to look after Vicky.'

'I'm not a babysitter.'

'You don't have to be. Just talk to her. You heard yourself she hasn't got any friends. I'm no good to her, but I bet she'd love some female company.'

'Is she… okay?'

'All things considered. She acts tough, but she's good as gold really.'

Then the doorbell went.

I opened the door to find a man in a baseball cap struggling to look around an entire column of flat, square boxes.

'Did you order pizza?' he asked, trying to keep his balance.

'No,' I replied.

Then a skinny old man ran into the doorway, wearing a suit too large for him and clutching a bible about his chest.

'Hello. I came as fast as I could,' he said.

'*Vicky.*'

26

It was just after one in the morning. I was on the sofa with Jen asleep across my lap when the phone rang: *'We've got him,'* said Colin.

I'd never known the station to have such a buzz about it. It felt amazing. The atmosphere was aided in a large part by officers we'd brought in from the next force. They had so much energy, laughing and joking with us. Every single one of them seemed to get on. I was obviously working in the wrong place, but then, I knew that.

I was reminded of when I started with the force. In an instant you transform from a mere civilian into a demi-god with the power to control life and death and issue an £80 fine for pissing in the street. That naïve optimism was flowing through those young coppers, and long may they hang onto it.

I finished stirring the teas and handed one to Colin. We clinked cups.

'No hitches?' I asked.

'No. Everything just as we left it. You should have seen the look on that security guard's face when we all marched towards him, he shat himself. Same two at the warehouse door and the Asian male upstairs. They're looking at his laptop now.'

There was no trace of anyone from the Middle-East, and a whole truck-load of henchmen would still need bringing in, but they could wait. We'd secured the night's star prize. Just down the hall, sat in black silk pyjamas and looking a beautiful shade of annoyed was the great man himself.

He refused to speak until he had his lawyer present, a particularly haughty sort by the name of Giles Sloane. One of the Cambridge set, Sloane probably could have got Jack the Ripper community service, provided Mr Ripper could have afforded him. According to the last lot of court papers I'd seen, Sloane was claiming nearly two grand an hour for his reliable services. No surprise then, that if McIntyre clicked his fingers, Sloane did up his fly mid-piss and ran from London.

The chief was going to lead the interview. Unfortunately, I couldn't be gifted the pleasure with my status, so DI Martin would be at his side. As my supervisor he was otherwise the man most closely associated with the case, roughly in the same way that billionaires are associated with their Premiership football clubs.

There was another hour pacing the corridor before Sloane finally arrived. He parked his Mercedes at an angle across two bays and kept everyone at arm's length with thoroughbred disdain as he was led into our biggest interview suite. Everyone wanted to watch. Bodies crammed in tight around Colin and I in the observation room as though a new blockbuster film was about to start.

McIntyre slouched at the table, exaggerating yawns. If he felt under pressure he'd never show it. He watched Martin dump himself in the chair opposite.

'You're up late, Dave. You're gonna miss the kebab van.'

Sammy looked over the mirrored glass. His gaze passed straight through me. He knew he had an audience. He knew I was there. But he didn't know what was coming.

Formalities completed, DVD engaged, Straughan dived straight in: 'Mr McIntyre, are you familiar with a warehouse on the commercial docks, specifically designated Building Twelve?'

'No.'

'You don't lease any such building?'

182

'No.'

'But you own some property under that roof?'

'No.'

'Oh. You're sure of that?'

'I think my client has made it perfectly clear that he has no interest in this building, Chief Superintendent.'

'Well it's very late, Mr Sloane, a lack of sleep can play havoc with the mind. Perhaps these photos will help jog your memory?' Straughan took my pictures out of an envelope and placed them in front of McIntyre. 'Recognise these?'

He certainly did. The smile lost something of its shape. How did someone get that close? But he would concede no ground.

'No,' he said again.

'Well that *is* strange, because you have been observed and recorded in their presence inside that very building, even alluding to their contents.'

'Don't respond to that,' said Sloane. 'Chief Superintendent, if there has been an operation that I have not been made aware of, then I will expect leave to study the information before this interview continues.'

'Forgive me, Mr Sloane, but you will understand we must move quickly on matters of terrorism.'

'*Terrorism?*' Sloane turned to McIntyre. 'Has anyone asked you about this prior to my arrival?'

Sammy shook his head.

'On what possible grounds can you accuse my client of engaging in terrorist activities?'

'On the grounds that your client is suspected to have in his custody, articles for the preparation and execution of such offences, believed to involve chemical weapons, or components thereof, the trade in which is illegal, the profiteering abhorrent, and the consequences potentially fatal to thousands.'

'I request leave immediately to examine this allegation.'

Straughan slid the photos further under Sammy's nose.

'These are yours aren't they, Mr McIntyre?'

'Don't answer him.'

'They arrived with your new friends, didn't they?'

'Chief Superintendent…'

'You've paid out a *lot* of money. What's the plan? The plan in *London* that is? Hold the city to ransom? Drugs not paying what they used to?'

'*Chief Superintendent*. I must insist this interview is stopped immediately. Furthermore, if I discover that there has been an illegal operation –'

The door opened and one of the sergeants poked his head in.

'Sorry, sir. Senior CT to see you. Urgent.'

Straughan called a temporary suspension to the interview. Martin remained in his place, while Sloane and McIntyre began their own whispered conversation behind his open briefcase.

The chief led our top counter-terror man into the observation room.

'What have you found, Jack?' asked Straughan.

'That's just it, Barry – nothing, I'm afraid.'

'What d'you mean?'

'All the boxes are empty.'

'Empty? You're sure?'

'We're still doing some chemical-radioactive checks now, but it doesn't look like there was anything in them to start with. Nothing that would kill you, anyway.'

'What about the markings?' I asked.

'That's the other thing. The customs stamp appears genuine, but the hazard warnings were rubbing off on our hands. I shouldn't be able to sand them off.'

Straughan shook his head. 'What does that indicate?'

184

'The symbols are fake. They were painted on. To be honest they didn't look like standard markings anyway. They could just as well be a company logo of some sort.'

'What about the guy hiding out in the office upstairs?' I asked.

The sergeant stepped forward: 'He claims his English isn't great, so we're waiting on an interpreter to complete his statement. According to the papers he has on him he works for an IT company in Sri-Lanka.'

'IT?' said Straughan.

'They have a contract in London. He's got photo ID.'

We all looked through the window at McIntyre, who was in the middle of some more vaguely insulting banter with Martin.

'What have the Met said about Jones' place?' asked Straughan.

'If your address is correct it's on Essex's patch,' said the sergeant. 'Had a call from them half an hour ago – nothing. And no trace yet on Riley or Lisicki. They've disappeared.'

The chief leant forward onto the table, his eyes closed.

'Jack, is there a single charge I can level at this man, before he walks free yet again?'

The silence said everything.

'He's got the stuff at his place,' I said.

The chief almost head-butted the table in frustration, swearing with clenched fists at his temples.

'We need to search his house,' I said.

Straughan ignored me and walked out. I followed him.

'Sir, we have to search the house tonight. Get Martin to delay him. We'll be in and out within the hour.' He still ignored me. I grabbed his arm just as he was about to open the interview room door. 'Sir, we have to do this, *now*.'

The chief looked at my grip on his arm.

'Do you mind?' he said. 'Get back in that room before he sees you and we get stiffed for that as well.'

'We can't let him go.'

'You heard the man.'

'Oh, come on. If you bail him he'll disappear.'

'What would I bail him for? Not colouring between the lines?'

'He knew we were coming.'

'Just because I write Claudia Schiffer on the door, doesn't mean she's in here.'

'Who the fuck pretends to have chemical weapons?'

'The kind of man that wants to lead you on a merry dance, I imagine.'

'What's he doing, then?'

'Drugs, people smuggling - who knows?'

'There won't be this chance again.'

'Maybe not. But I can't change that tonight.'

'Get a warrant signed for his address –'

'*We tried*, Christopher. We have lost.'

He held a look at me for a moment, a look that said *I'd* lost. There was no 'we' about it. I was the only one driving it forward, and in the fullness of time management was bound to make sure it only blew up in my face.

The force wasn't going to risk another failed search attempt, not with a solicitor like Sloane tearing loopholes in everything. Tony and Katya could have walked through that door there and then, it wouldn't have mattered. Without the evidence to anchor them down the recording was useless. They'd be investigated, maybe even fired, but that would be a long time after McIntyre had run free, and at what cost? I felt sick.

The chief took his seat again next to Martin. Sammy wore the biggest grin he could manage.

'Problems?' he asked.

I didn't hear what Straughan said next. I didn't want to. Everyone filtered back out of the obs room as the news

186

was passed on. No one seemed to care that much, but then they wouldn't. It wasn't their station, their case, their life. Colin didn't know what to say. He gave me a consoling tap on the shoulder as I leant against the table looking at the floor.

I had the rope around his neck. Yet again, he'd escaped before I could get the trap door open. That's what he did. I lose.

Then I heard my name.

'You in there, Rose?' asked McIntyre, being escorted to the door. 'What did you do to poor old Bingo?' He looked over the mirror, through me and past me. 'If there's a killer 'round here I reckon it's you, wouldn't you say?'

Sloane tried to discourage him but McIntyre held his hand up to keep him quiet. Straughan and Martin ignored it all and gathered their papers ready to leave.

'Did it feel good?' McIntyre continued. 'I bet it felt great, just for a moment. Doesn't bring her back though, does it? Good try tonight.'

Colin and I said nothing to one another on the way back to my place. The car did its best to bob me back to calm in the passenger seat, but all consolation was lost in the darkness. That journey could have been ten minutes or ten hours. There was no one and nothing until the solitary bulb on my porch coughed faint orange light through the dust and cobwebs.

At the foot of my drive we were about to exchange goodbyes when Jen ran from my front door.

'Chris! He's taken her!'

'What?'

'I've been trying to call you. He's taken Vicky! She's gone!'

'Who?'

'Her step-father, I think. He bundled her into a car. I couldn't stop him.'

187

27

The house was prime Black Rose Barton; the top half rotting, off-white wood, the bottom moulding brickwork. Tall grass fought with weeds for custody of some abandoned white goods in the small front garden while a side gate led to a jungle at the rear.

'Stay with the car,' I said.

'What are you going to do?' asked Colin.

'… I don't know.'

Even so late at night, I could already feel several pairs of eyes permeate shabby net curtains from windows either side of the decaying house. I tried to ignore my ribs and walk upright. It was unwise to show any sign of weakness to the animals in that area.

I decided against the front door, opting for the relative seclusion of the back garden. If things got exciting I'd have time to run before the neighbours saw what was going on and wanted to join in.

I followed a trail of cigarette butts to a deck chair on the shattered rear patio and an overflowing ash tray. An explosion of aluminium glinted across the lawn and throughout a mob of angry, overgrown raspberry bushes. Most of the fence had passed out into the neighbours' gardens, leaving the odd splintered wooden post jutting from the sodden earth.

The advanced neglect reminded me of the last house we shared with my father. The back garden was my retreat. I'd carefully engineered a tunnel through the thorns, large enough to crawl through but small enough to dissuade any adult from following. In my mind all the cans disappeared and I remembered the toys I had hidden in the clearing next to the fence. Most of the time no one knew I was there. If I was called in for tea, I'd wait until no one was watching before I re-emerged.

Then I recalled the sound of mum and dad arguing; physical, violent. Things being thrown...

I leant to look into the kitchen window. I tried the handle on the back door and it opened.

Whoever lived there obviously didn't have a pot to piss in, which might explain why the carpets were so sticky. In the dirty, barren lounge, and consistent with Vicky's description during counselling, a big, black holdall lay empty on the lounge floor, lined with foil. A small pair of wire cutters sat on a variously stained armchair. It was a thief's house. Then in the corner I noticed an emaciated Staffordshire terrier, nervously backing away from me. I reached down to offer a comforting hand when my father barged past me in the doorway and kicked the dog – our dog. There was a single high-pitched yelp and Barney fell lifelessly at the fireplace. He never got up again. Dad couldn't find what he was looking for and swiped me out of the way to leave the room and run upstairs. He didn't acknowledge me. He never did unless I'd done something bad...

Despite my best efforts every stair moaned as I ascended to the first floor, but at the landing I was more or less convinced that no one was home. I needed some ID; maybe a picture or a stray letter. Passing the disgusting bathroom, I searched the first bedroom, trying to ignore the screams of my parents in the next room. There was a mirror and some low-budget female grooming accessories, but nothing that told me who the owner was.

Something smashed near the door. On the landing I see my young self crying outside the next bedroom. It's dark inside. The curtains are closed. Mum runs from the room but he has her, gripping her throat, leaning her over the frail bannister. He holds a receipt to her face. Why did she buy the wine? Where is it? There's been another man here. He knows that's not true but anger has reason and the slaps become punches. The neighbours must hear but they're tired and don't even bother to call the police anymore. They just wanted to move. I couldn't run downstairs and dial 999 quick enough. I still had the lump on the side of my head from last time. I couldn't stop him hitting her, bursting her eardrum to leave her partially deaf for the rest of her life. I was too small.

Mum saw me. She pulled dad's fingers away enough to wheeze, '*Chris, run!*' I jumped down the stairs in three strides, bursting into the front garden. I covered my ears, waiting for the noise to stop. But it never stopped…

I could hear someone in difficulty. I pushed open the next bedroom door to find Vicky, face-down and gagged on the bed. Her hands and legs were tied together with bungee ropes. She panicked, trying to look over her shoulders to see who it was.

'Vicky, it's okay, it's me. Let me take this off.'

I undid the gag and she gasped for air.

'Chris, he'll be back in a minute. Please, just go. He'll kill me.'

'Does he always do this?'

'When he goes out. He's gone to the garage for fags. Just go.'

Vicky jumped as someone appeared in the doorway.

'Hey! Who the fuck are you?'

It was a grubby man of around forty, receding hair, caked in blurred ink. He carried a transparent bag full of rolling tobacco and Rizzla papers. He hardly filled the doorframe. There was probably only one person in the world he could physically overpower, but by the look of the scratches on his arms and face, even she was more of a match than he'd like.

'Mark? Mark Hudson?' I asked.

'If you want a go on her you phone me like everyone else. You don't get a discount for just turning up.'

'Thanks for the tip. I'm a police officer. Just want to ask a few questions.'

Mark dropped the plastic bag and ran. I shot out after him. On his way down the stairs I reached over the bannister to grab a fist full of his hair, pulling him screaming to the landing again. I dragged him into the bedroom and threw him against the wardrobe, smashing a mirror on the door. I untied Vicky and she jumped off the bed for the safety of the hallway. I picked Mark off the floor and secured him in Vicky's place.

'Got anything you shouldn't have on you?' I asked, patting him down.

'Fuck off. I'll fucking kill you.'

'There's no need to be polite with me, I'm just doing my job.'

'Vicky, get help, love. We'll sue their fucking arses off.'

Happy he was tied tight, I sat on the side of the bed, waiting for him to stop wriggling.

'Vicky, call the police you stupid little bitch! HELP! HEL-!'

'No, no, no, Mark, we don't want you disturbing the peace as well.'

I tied the gag tightly around his head, noticing it was a bath robe belt that had been cut in half for the purpose.

I allowed him to expend the last of his energy while I studied our dire surrounds. Dark green climbed every wall. The air was thick with damp and anything other than gentle breathing drew spores of mould into the lungs. Small paper bags littered the bare floorboards, each one half filled with the pathetic snacks Vicky was permitted between shifts. Spiders, sat on deep webs, watched us from every corner.

191

Vicky stood in the doorway. Fear had given way somewhat to intrigue. Her swollen face was streaked clean with saltwater.

Finally Mark lay still. He looked at me with a pronounced frown, trying to work out what I was going to do.

'I had a violent father,' I said. 'To be fair I don't think he was quite as bad as you. Certainly tidier. Wonderful singing voice. I haven't seen him for twenty years. To be honest, I don't know if he's still alive… I often wonder what I'd do if I ever saw him again. If he were tied up, powerless… what would I do?'

I smiled. Mark looked at me like I was insane, struggling to breathe.

With a clap, I snapped out of the drama. 'Okay, Mark, quick game: I ask you a question and you either nod for yes or shake your head for no. Now, it's important to be honest here and not to hesitate, or there will be a forfeit. Kind of like Mallet's Mallet, but more violent. Okay, first question: is it just the two of you living here?'

Mark tried to spit filth.

'What's that? Fuck off? It's not what I've got on the card I'm afraid.'

I turned him around on the bare mattress and forced his head through the metal bedstead. He looked like a child stuck between fence railings. Then I turned to his step-daughter.

'Okay, Vicky – kick him.'

'What?'

'Kick him.'

'Why?'

'Because I'm not allowed to.'

To her credit she really wasn't going to. Mark glared a warning whilst trying to articulate what he was going to do to her when he was free. There was no doubt he meant every word. He snapped like a tethered dog, until, in one hate-

192

filled moment of determination, Vicky took two steps forward and launched her foot into his face. Mark screamed behind the gag, sucking it deeper and deeper into his mouth as he tried desperately for more air.

Vicky liked it. She *loved* it.

'Okay, now we're better acquainted with the rules, let's try that one again. Is it just you two here?'

He thrashed harder than ever, trying to back his head out from the railings. I drew his hands up further behind his back and hooked the end of the bungee rope onto the top of the bedstead before giving Vicky the nod. His nose crunched this time and blood began to drip in great blobs to the floor. He was trying to eat through the gag, screaming and swearing like he was in labour.

'And again, Mark: is it just the two of you?'

He nodded furiously this time.

'Do you *manage* Vicky with anyone else?'

He shook his head.

'Are there any other family members anywhere?'

Another shake of the head.

'Is that true?' I asked Vicky.

She nodded.

'Okay... Mark, I want you to say goodbye to your step-daughter. You won't see her again. But before we go, I'd like to give you this opportunity to apologise to her.'

Whatever he said, it wasn't sorry, and I didn't need to extend another invitation. Vicky lunged in and gripped Mark's face with her nails, screaming and clawing stinging, red streaks into his skin. The emotion consumed her. She slapped and kicked him again and again and again until I had to pull her away.

Mark was gasping, crying, pleading, overcome with a wave of intense pain every few seconds, the only thing that prevented him from passing out.

'Well, I'm glad we could all talk about this,' I said. 'I really think we've made progress today.'

I knelt at the end of the bed waiting for Mark's breathing to slow. I wanted his full attention.

'There, there,' I said, patting his head. 'Look, I know you're not afraid of the police, so let me explain what's going to happen. I'm going to be watching you very closely. The next time you put a foot wrong and you get sent down again, I'm going to pay someone to rape you for every single hour you're inside. I don't care if you just nicked a Mars bar. I know some very big, very willing men who aren't getting out any time soon. You will bleed permanently. And if I ever hear you've come within two miles of this girl again, or any other, you will beg me to kill you. Do you understand?'

Tears streaming from his eyes, he nodded.

Message received. Time would tell if it was understood. I'd be only too happy to go over anything once more.

Outside, Colin was standing at the front door.

'You guys okay?' he asked.

'Fine. Let's get out of here,' I said.

'Who else is in there?'

As we walked away from the house I looked back up at the bedroom window to see my father crying, helpless as he watched us leave for the last time.

'No one,' I said.

194

28

I was absolutely wankered.

The pub didn't open until midday, but I was at the door from half-nine that morning. Keith perceptibly came to the conclusion that I'd had the odd one or two prior even to that. In fact, I'd started at about four in the morning when I got home, and I wasn't going to stop.

I'd had some shit days in the police – most of them, in fact – but watching McIntyre saunter back out of that building and then dealing with filth like Hudson was the final straw. What was the point? What do the police really do, apart from bend over for the wigs and make endless apologies in the press for doing our jobs?

I unloaded the last of my change into the jukebox. There was now £24.50 of non-stop, uninterrupted eighties goodness to follow, and everybody that busy afternoon was absolutely delighted, albeit choosing to express that delight with a number of swearwords.

I collapsed into a chair at one of the little tables, interrupting a conversation between two young professional types. They turned to me as though I'd scraped myself off a bench and asked for money.

'You look like two intelligent gentlemen,' I said. 'Here's one for you: should crime be legal? Discuss. It's just that every time I try to do anything I get shot down.'

Both lads looked at me awkwardly, glancing over at Keith every now and again.

'No? No thoughts? Come on, you're young, you're funky, you're in t-shirts with a plunging neck line. Aren't you supposed to have boobs for tops like that? Anyway, you'll need to make these decisions soon. You're the future.'

'Can I have a word, mate?' asked Keith, appearing at the table.

'You can have several, Keith,' I said, and turned back to my reluctant audience. 'My supervisor always says that. He's fat.'

'Come on, mate,' said Keith. 'Come and sit at the bar with me.'

'But these boys need my help. They're wearing women's clothes.'

'Come on. Fancy a chat.'

I slapped the table. 'Got to go, lads. But it's been a pleasure.' I extended my hand. They both limply obliged and forced toothless smiles. 'And don't worry; the body hair *will* come. But you'll have to buy the tits.'

I staggered back over to the bar and tried to climb onto a stool. After several failed attempts to get a leg over it crashed to the floor. As did the next two.

'I'll stand, I think,' I said.

'Are you alright, mate?' asked Keith.

'Yeah, yeah, yep, yeppee, yepson, a-ffirmative. Why?'

'You're not holding your drink quite as well as normal, that's all.'

'Really?' I picked my pint off the counter and immediately dropped it on the floor, smashing it everywhere. 'You might be right, you know.'

I was attracting a lot of attention. I waved and everyone turned back to each other again.

'Jen!' said Keith, as I heard the door open behind me. He frantically waved her over.

'Uh-oh,' I said.

I pulled a goofy smile. She was casually dressed again, making the most of her figure in a tight-fitting jumper.

'How long's he been here?' asked Jen, looking me over.

'Six hours. He was pissed when he turned up. I've never seen him like this.'

'What has he said?'

'Nothing. He just keeps drinking and talking crap. He's had The Bangles on a loop for an hour.'

'I am here, you know,' I said.

'No, I don't think you are actually, mate.'

I took Jen by the waist and turned her to face the crowd.

'I want you to meet some of my new friends,' I said. 'Hey everybody, this is Jen.'

'*Chris…*'

'This lovely lady used to be my girlfriend, but she doesn't really like me anymore. A lesser man might put this down to hor-mones,' fingers as inverted commas, 'but I'm a policeman, and I've picked out the subtleties in our conversations. Just last week, for example, she said, "Chris, I hate you." Added to a number of other such cryptic clues, and I realised all was not what you might call peachy.'

'Sorry everyone,' said Jen, trying to smile.

'Still, it looks like she's going to use me for sex again until somebody better comes along. But don't be too hard on her. She's just found out her last man parks the pink pony in the back stable.'

'Okay, time to go.'

'Go? The night is young. Come on everybody - *Woooaaah, we're half-way there-ere, woooaaaaOOOAAAH, livin' on a pra-* you lot are no fun.'

'What happened last night?' asked Jen.

I shook my head. 'Nothing much. Vicky shouldn't have any more trouble with her step-father. If she does I'll kill him. I'm not joking.'

'And at work?'

'…They let him go, Jen. They just let him go.'

'Who?'

'McIntyre. He's free. They don't care.'

'Come on, I've got the car.'

'No. I don't want to.'

'Let's go.'

'*No.*'

'Why are you doing this?'

'Why? *Why*? I seem to get asked that question a lot lately. Is it really just me? *Why*?'

'You're not impressing anyone in here.'

'I'm not *looking* to impress anyone. What do you want, Jen? Why did you come back? I'm boring, remember? I've got no ambition, and I refuse to spend thirty quid a week on pro-biotic yoghurt, whatever *Cosmopolitan* says about it.'

An older man huffed at the nearest table, annoyed at my interrupting his conversation with a colleague.

'For God's sake,' he murmured under his breath.

I glared at him. 'Hey. I'm a murder suspect. Bear that in mind.'

The whole pub was looking at me again, many in confusion, some in pity, more with disdain.

I took a step forward to address them all: 'You lot need to make a choice. You can't complain you're all victims and moan when someone tries to do something about it. The police aren't your personal whipping boys when you get annoyed with a neighbour whose name you never bothered to ask. Don't look a gift horse in the mouth. Don't look at a gift horse at all. Just close your eyes, hold out your hands, and accept his gift without whinging for once... what was the question again?'

As I stood there wobbling, Jen's hand came to rest on the base of my back. A tingle shot up my spine, the first that wasn't pain in some time.

She spoke softly to my ear: 'Come home with me. Please.'

Keith sat a pint of water on the bar and I took it down in one go. I thanked him, wiping my mouth with my sleeve, trying to bring everything back into focus in front of me. Fortunately, everyone else was returning to their own conversations. I was becoming self-conscious again and slightly embarrassed to look around.

And then it happened - Jennifer Rush.

Everyone watched as I ran across the room to grip the edges of the jukebox.

'Sing to me, you sexy, big-haired bitch,' I said.

I absorbed the music, slowly gyrating my arse around, just above the fish and chips on a table in front of a young couple. As the song went on I cuddled the machine, taking in the warmth from the lights.

By the first chorus I was asleep.

I woke up on the sofa. It was quiet. Light swirled in a glass of water left for me on the coffee table with two paracetamols. The place was tidy – clean, even.

Jen and Vicky were talking and giggling upstairs. It was nearly ten. Ten *PM* I had to remind myself, remembering what had happened. I was still drunk, but I was thinking clearly. In fact, my thinking was clearer than ever.

I grabbed my car keys from the table and left.

29

There were no lights on, inside or out, as I drove up to McIntyre's house.

I dumped the car awkwardly on a piece of lawn between the perimeter hedge and the road, crushing some flowers. It took me a good five seconds fiddling with the handle to get the door open. I nearly fell out as it gave way.

Gripping the cold, black iron of the automated gates I confirmed there was no sign of life; not at the front of the house at least. The windows were all dark. No curtains.

The side gate was locked. I certainly couldn't negotiate the barbed wire on the walls, but next to the main entrance some roots had lifted from the soil under the thick hedge. With a bit of persuasion I could just about squeeze through.

On the other side I brushed myself down and scampered for the first cover among black roses. I looked across at the nearest neighbour's house. All dark there, too.

Colin and I had worked out that the CCTV could see anything within a thirty metre range. To be sure I kept myself tight against the hedge as I made for the back gardens, past the door I'd used to get in first time around.

The lounge that had hosted the party was eerily silent. I could see through one window and out the next on the far side. Looking again I was almost certain that the furniture was gone. All of it. I walked back a few steps to check another reception room. That was bare, too.

Maybe he didn't use that side of the house when he wasn't hosting guests?

Or maybe he was gone?

I stood upright from my sneaky crouch and double-checked my bearings. I was definitely at the right house. I could see the distinctive swimming pool, covered up with a plastic sheet. In the other direction was the silhouette of a giant penis.

I crept towards the house, constantly checking left and right, half-expecting someone to come running out, or an alarm to shriek. But with my hands finally on the coarse brickwork, everything remained still.

It was empty, the entire place. Circles in the dust marked where the furniture had been taken. The walls were naked.

I began a jog to the back gardens. Near the rear gates one of the triple-garage doors was open. I stayed on the lawn and off the gravel to approach, but inside the garage there was only cold bare stone disappearing into shadow. The other two doors were locked shut. I turned with my hands on my hips to take in the whole house.

And then I heard the growl.

I'd forgotten about the dogs.

I turned to find a massive Rottweiler giving me a look at every one of its teeth. It stepped out of the garage, matching my pace as I backed away. It wasn't on a lead. There were no sticks. I had nothing on me. There'd certainly be no pissed idiots falling out to door to help me this time. There was no way I could out-run it.

'Oh, bollocks.'

The growling stopped.

Hang on.

'Bollocks.'

The dog's ears lifted and he tilted his head.

'Bollocks? He's actually named you Bollocks?' The dog's tail started to wag and he came over to me. 'Oh, thank God it's you,' I said, slapping his sturdy back and rubbing behind his ears. 'Are you out here all on your own? Where's daddy?'

'*Hello?*' said a hushed voice from behind me.

I froze. Bollocks started to growl again.

'Chris?'

It was Colin.

'What the hell are you doing here?' I asked.

'What am *I* doing here? What are you do - there's a really big dog behind you.'

'It's okay, it's Bollocks.'

Colin frowned. 'Jen called and said you'd disappeared, she's worried. She's out looking for you. I thought you might be here. Come on, let's go.'

'Not yet. I haven't finished looking around.'

'What are you expecting to find?'

'Whatever was in those boxes. They've probably been empty since the party. Why else would you leave two idiots on guard at the warehouse? He bluffed Jones.'

'So why did he get him to take empty boxes? I think the chief's right, he's winding us up. The place is empty.'

'There's only one way to find out.'

'What are you going to do? Break in?' Colin looked like he might cry as he studied my expression. 'Oh, you've got to be joking this time. Please.'

The dog was growling again. Someone else was approaching.

We scampered into the back of the garage. An angry rumble reverberated through my entire body as I tried to hold onto that thick, furry chest. The pitch rose as footsteps crunched the gravel, closer and closer. The person was coming straight for us, just a few metres away.

The dog broke free of my grip, ran and jumped. The shriek was instantly recognisable.

'Bollocks, *no!*' I said, pulling him off the man on the floor – the chief. 'Sit!'

Straughan picked himself up and shouted a whisper: *'What the hell are you two doing here?'*

Before either of us could answer a light flicked on in the house, somewhere on the first floor.

'Quick, inside,' I said.

All three of us and the dog huddled tightly together in the black of the garage, watching the window. A figure appeared momentarily, looking out over the back gardens. It was too far away to make out who it was.

'What are you idiots doing now?' whispered Straughan.

'What are you doing here?' I asked.

The chief nodded at Colin. 'He called me.'

'I think he's leaving, sir,' I said.

'Who?'

'McIntyre. All the furniture's gone.'

'Good, then hopefully he's someone else's problem.'

'We can't just let him go.'

'Christopher, we're going, now. You're in enough trouble as it is. You stink of booze. I should have you for drink-driving.'

'You guys go. Let me take the flack. I'll go to prison, I don't care. I have to do this.'

The figure appeared in the window again. Everyone ducked.

'I was speaking to an area sergeant earlier,' said Straughan. 'Little incident on the Black Rose Barton estate. You wouldn't happen to know anything about that, would you?'

'Maybe,' I replied.

'Why did you use bungee ropes to interrogate someone?'

I shrugged. 'I didn't have any nails.'

'Christopher, are you *trying* to get fired?'

'I'm *trying* to help a rape victim.'

'She should be under the care of the CPT.'

'She is, and look where that got her.'

'You could have started a riot in an area like that.'

'Well it's been a week, they're due another one.'

'If that man makes a complaint, I can't –'

'If he says anything I'll get him bent over on the nonce wing every day for the rest of his fucking life. I *dare* him.'

'We're *going*,' said Straughan.

'I'll see you later.'

'I will arrest you if I have to.'

'What would have happened if you turned back in Iraq?'

'This is not the same thing.'

'*Yes it is*. How many would have died? You had a hunch and you were right. I know I'm right.'

A slow hot huff percolated that thick moustache.

'Remind me not to tell you any more stories.' The chief ran his fingers through his hair and pulled at his face with his fingertips. 'Chris, this isn't Iraq, there are rules.'

'McIntyre *owns* the rules. There is nothing we will ever legally be able to do to nail him. *Nothing*. He's got his hand up our arse. You might as well bring him in on your meetings.'

Another burst of air momentarily plumped those thick bristles. He looked at Colin.

'What have you got to say about this?'

'Since when does anyone listen to me?' said Colin.

'Sir,' I said, 'we're the last ones left.'

Straughan looked to the sky, shaking his head. He knew I was right. He trusted me that far. But he also knew that there were going to be reprisals, whether McIntyre was home or not. In the silence I could hear the river that carried Bingo's body away. Even my enthusiasm may have dulled if the chief hadn't begun to speak.

'I'm supposed to retire this year. I should be in a country pub, planning a fishing trip... But no, I'm going to shag a hornet's nest instead.'

We all looked at each other. The chief had to stifle a laugh. I smiled. Colin tried to do the same. The dog farted.

We needed to get out of that garage.

It was impossible to tell how many people were home. It could just have been that dippy bint he was married to, spraying her fake, leathery body a new shade of orange. It might have been several bruisers. In any case we decided to split up. If one or even two of us were cornered, there was still someone free to move and raise the alarm if needs be. But there were no radios. We'd have to listen out for each other.

30

We'd try the doors first. No sense making this any more complicated than it needed to be. Colin went to one side of the house, I went to the other and the chief had the back.

If everything was locked up tight and all the windows were closed, I had my trusty emergency exit hammer. I liberated it from a bus when I started undercover. All the savvy criminals use them for break-ins; they make next to no noise on impact, and they're designed so that the glass falls, rather than shatters, perfect for avoiding those stray shards when a SOCO is looking at your clothing.

The dog insisted on following me. I tried to get him to stay, but he was a surprisingly sociable thing and probably thought I was going to get him a biscuit. There was a metal water bowl in the garage, but I didn't notice that any food had been left out.

The door I'd used to get into the party was locked tight. Through the windows I could see the chief was having no luck either, looking up and about him for another way in. No sign of Colin on his side of the house.

I was running my fingers along the window frames to the lounge when Bollocks walked over to the conservatory and sat by a UPVC door. Sure enough, it opened and he happily jogged inside towards the kitchen. I waved my arms to attract the chief's attention.

'Where's Colin?' Straughan whispered, carefully closing the conservatory door behind him.

'Haven't seen him. He might have made it in on the other side.'

'D'you know where you're going?'

'Sort of.'

'Can't we secure that thing?'

'He's hungry. He won't stay.'

We climbed the stairs and the dog ran past us to wait patiently on the landing. Now I could see light from under one of the doors at the far end of the corridor, near to McIntyre's office. I told Straughan we should duck into the neighbouring room. The walls were thin enough that we could make out any conversation and plan our attack from there. At the very least we should have an idea about how many people we were dealing with.

Along the corridor almost every single door was open. The rooms were empty. It was surreal to be in a place that large with nothing in it. We had to step carefully as our movement echoed and amplified off the walls.

As we got closer it was clear there were at least two people; foreigners. Before I could grab him, the dog pushed past us to wait outside the door. I tried to call him back but he just sat there proudly, as if to say, *this is the place.*

We were nearly on the neighbouring room, when, from behind us: *'Guys...'*

Straughan and I jumped. Our backs hit opposite walls and the thud reverberated up the corridor. That was heard. The men were coming out to investigate.

We bundled Colin into the next room and hid behind the open door. At the crack between hinges I watched light spread across Bollocks' wide, solid head, then the loom of a man-shaped shadow. I didn't have a clue what they were saying, but there was obviously some amusement and curiosity as to how the dog got in.

We held our collective breath as one of the men, with noticeably heavier footsteps than his companion, walked the dog back along the corridor and downstairs. The second man stayed behind, packing something.

'There's a load of stuff by a door downstairs,' whispered Colin. 'Metal cases.'

Straughan peeked around the door. 'Okay, so there's only two of them. Chris, stay up here. Watch - don't engage.

207

Colin and I will secure downstairs and we'll come back to assist with his friend.'

'Be careful,' I said.

'When we've got them pinned down I'll call in the troops. Come on, Colin.'

Straughan stuck his head round the door again and with impressive fleet of foot for a man his age and size, ran down the hallway almost completely silently. Colin followed like a fawn with a limp.

In the next room, zips were opened and closed, but I couldn't see what was being packed. I nudged the door with my knuckle and it gently swung into the room a few inches more. This guy was definitely one of the late arrivals at the party, smartly dressed in a dark suit and an open black shirt. He only seemed to have clothes on the bed next to the suitcase. I leant into the room as he pulled more things from a wardrobe with his back to me. There was a passport on the bed, but I couldn't tell which country it was from.

Then the single worst scream I have ever heard stunned me cold.

It was deep, agonising pain. For a few moments I forgot myself, looking down the corridor, when a dark blur in the corner of my eye quickly became a man and I was thrown against the wall. A fist crunched into my face and I was on the floor, watching my assailant run down the corridor, clutching his suitcase.

An engine started. Metal cases squealed as they were thrown on top of each other, and a boot slammed shut. At the bottom of the stairs the dog was barking at the kitchen door as wheels spun on the loose gravel outside. Through the window I could see Colin run to his car just beyond the rear gates to give chase. I was about to follow him when I saw the figure lying on the kitchen floor.

'Chief! Are you alright?'

I knelt down and he flinched with my touch. His shirt was soaking. I found the light switch and turned to find him covered in blood from a wound to his chest.

I spun around, looking for something to use. There were no towels or clothing. The place had been completely emptied. I yanked my t-shirt off my head.

'Colin!' I shouted out of the open door, but he was already in his car.

The two men smashed through the rear gate onto the road. I ran into the doorway.

'Colin!'

He was gone. Within moments both cars had disappeared behind the trees.

The wound was wide and deep. The knife had been twisted so it wouldn't close. I pressed hard and Straughan moaned with the pain. My t-shirt was quickly heavy with blood. I patted myself down but I knew I'd left my mobile at home. I slapped the chief's pockets and found his job mobile.

'999 emergency. Which service do you require?'

'Ambulance, please, quickly.'

'Transferring you now. One moment…'

With every unanswered ring the chief passed further beyond help. Blood seeped through my fingers as I tried to maintain pressure. Looking over his broad frame I couldn't think of a way I could pick him up. I'd never get him to my car on the other side of the gates, he was too heavy. There was no time.

I stood to have one more look out of the window. Colin wasn't coming back.

The chief swallowed hard, gulping for air. He was determined to speak.

'Chris, it's not your fault. You were right.' He began to choke. Blood streaked his cheeks as it pooled in his mouth. 'He always wins. But he doesn't have to… I'm proud of you, son.'

I dropped to my knees and the phone fell to my lap. The chief extended his hand and I took it to my chest.

'*Ambulance emergency,*' said a tiny voice. '*Hello..?*'

His breathing was heavily laboured now, and though he tried, his voice could no longer negotiate the deep crimson curdling in his throat. It wouldn't be long.

I kept a tight hold of his hand, and we waited.

31

Light drizzle swayed in the wind, one way and the next, settling gently on the blackened congregation below. It was the first time we'd had rain in weeks, if not months.

Colin never caught up with those men, and they left nothing to tell us who they were. The house had been sold privately a few days prior, cash, but the new owners were still in Dubai and yet to set foot in the place. McIntyre, along with Katya and Tony, had completely disappeared. Travis was the only known mole still visible, if you believed Fergus was on the home team, but there was no value in exposing him even if there was someone to tell. In the five days since the chief's death I was still the only suspect in Bingo's murder, and now, in the total absence of any evidence to the contrary, Fergus had pinned me as his No.1 for Straughan. In all likelihood he was briefing officers that *I* was the one working for McIntyre. I was all over the news, but there was nothing to be gained by my surrender and incarceration. I had no choice but to drop off the radar completely and hide.

Considering the incredible risk to their own freedom, Colin, Jen and Vicky had been amazing. Colin procured me a basic pay-as-you-go Nokia. Unlike contract phones, they're next to impossible to trace, so conversations were possible in relative safety. Initially I was staying further down the coast in a caravan that belonged to my grandfather. I hadn't been there for years - I forgot I had the key. It was meant to have been sold after he died but we never got around to it. All his furniture was still in place. His favourite armchair sat waiting patiently for his return, still holding the giant remote control for the ancient television. On the windowsill, under a thick blanket of dust, was the only other picture in existence of us as a family, all slightly older than in the photo I carried.

Unfortunately, my stay was cut short. On only the second night I returned from the local shop to find the entire area illuminated in blue flashing light. I was forced to retreat to the beach to spend the night in a small cave, losing the sniffer dogs as the tide rose to lap my scent from the sand.

The next morning, after just under three minutes sleep, Vicky put me into contact with one of her old friends, though when I say old, I mean eighteen, and when I say friend, I mean prostitute, with four children, on the Black Rose Barton estate. To maintain what little harmony there was in the brief intervals between Kelis shouting at her kids, her boyfriend, the dog and her other boyfriend, I pretended to be a teacher, recently made redundant. All things considered, it wasn't a bad couple of days. I was happy to teach some basic reading and writing – even the kids got involved. But when a little late-night reconnaissance confirmed Building Twelve had been emptied ahead of schedule, I knew I couldn't delay any longer. It was time for one last roll of the dice.

I watched from a distance as the chief's sons led his coffin through the mourners to a space next to their mother. Together again. I wish I believed that.

When I was a kid, an elderly couple we used to live next door to would take me to church on occasion, particularly for the ceremony where you're given a candle stuck in an orange, the significance of which has long since escaped me. I remember everyone was very warm and welcoming, but when it came to my questions they were always laughed away as the naiveties of a child. Then one day you realise just how much everyone lies, not always maliciously, but consistently and to themselves. There are no answers, and even if there were, the questions are stupid.

As the last flower was thrown onto the coffin, the crowd began to disperse. I waited until the cortège had pulled away before I made my way over to the grave, remaining in the shadows among trees as far as possible.

I stood to watch the last glint of polished brass disappear beneath the earth. In the decade or so we'd worked together I knew nothing of the chief until the end, only that he was ten times the man I could ever hope to be. It's funny how someone dies and all of a sudden there are a thousand questions you wanted to ask. My mind kept replaying that scene on the kitchen floor. What else he was trying to tell me in those final moments?

The rain grew more intense. I looked up to let it cool the deep bags under my eyes. For a minute or so I let it drip down my neck and soak my chest.

One of the gravediggers was looking at me.

'Do I know you?' he asked.

I shook my head. 'No.'

He looked about eighty and wasn't about to give me any trouble. He held out his umbrella.

'Take it,' he said. 'It's pouring.'

'No, I'm fine. Thanks. It's nice sometimes, don't you think?'

Clearly not.

'Berk,' he murmured, returning to his shovelling.

After two or three more minutes, saturated and beginning to feel the cold, I said goodbye. I turned to walk for the gate, looking over my shoulder one final time.

I was going to meet with Jen in a local park. She'd secured some cash for me to keep me going for a few days in London while I watched Jones' place on the docks. I'd hide out there all week if I had to. I owed it to Straughan. I owed it to myself.

I was almost out of the churchyard when I felt a presence closing in. Before I could see who it was my head jolted forwards. A warm, tingling sensation rushed downwards through my body from the back of my head and I dropped to the floor.

My eyes stayed open long enough to watch a big man produce his phone and hold it to his ear.

'Found 'im,' he said.

32

My head bobbled about in the back seat. It felt like the worst hangover ever. I was one speed bump away from a shower of puke.

We were near the seafront, passing lavish, detached houses, interspersed with hideous new bespoke atrocities; Wendy houses for businessmen that spent most of the year abroad. We stopped on the driveway belonging to one such place. It was Mediterranean white with tacky blue glass at the balconies. Nothing as vast as McIntyre's former mansion, but the location guaranteed it was just as expensive, if not more so.

My door opened and I was pulled out by an old friend. I don't think he recognised me without the penguin suit, though.

Inside we gathered in a bright white kitchen-diner, which only served to make my headache worse. It was spotless. Nothing arranged on the shelves. No boxes to suggest this was a permanent move, just like Katya's place.

'I believe you know my other guests,' said McIntyre.

To my surprise, Fitch was sat at a table with his girlfriend, Marilyn. They were half way through a bucket of chicken, covered in oil. The hefty woman still looked uncertain which dimension she was in.

'Well, well, well, look what the cat shat out,' said Fitch. 'What are you doin' here, Rose?'

'I just came to borrow some sugar,' I said. 'Have you got any?'

'Fuck you.'

The pathetic weasel snarled behind a piece of chicken, anxious not to have us pursue that particular line of conversation and pique Sammy's interest. He chomped into

215

the dense meat, almost immediately doubling his weight as he gulped it down.

McIntyre opened the door to a massive fridge.

'Drink?' he asked me.

'Yeah, why not,' I said, checking my head for blood.

He cracked the tops off two bottles of beer and we both threw it back, neither of us pausing for breath. Without saying a word he returned to the fridge and handed me another.

'Sorry to hear about your boss,' he said. 'If it's any consolation, I don't believe you killed him. Maybe if you guys would just knock once in a while these things wouldn't happen?'

I ignored him, looking around for clues as to what was going on. Several of his heavies were present in various rooms. There was a large group in the back garden, chatting and smoking. This was an army ready to march.

'Downsizing?' I asked.

'No, this is just a rental.'

'Beautiful view.'

'Nothing compared to the one I'll have soon.'

'Oh? Going somewhere nice?'

He smiled. He was arrogant but he wasn't stupid.

So, to what did I owe the pleasure of his company and more excellent beer? McIntyre finished another big gulp. The bottle made a sucking noise as he pulled it from his lips.

'I need you to do me a favour,' he said. 'I need something your colleagues took off my friend at the warehouse.'

'What?'

'That doesn't matter. You just need to pick it up for me.'

'Any property will probably be in the secure lock-up.'

'I happen to know that's exactly where it is.'

216

'Well then you should know that even if I wasn't suspended, they won't just let me walk in. Only a couple of people have access to that room.'

'We aren't going to ask for it.'

McIntyre momentarily disappeared into the lounge and returned with a lengthy metal case, similar to that I'd seen on the night of the party. Still holding his beer, he flicked the catches at either end and flipped open the lid. Inside was a huge pump-action shotgun. It was brand new, jet black, sat next to a full box of red and gold cartridges. He had another swig of beer and used the bottom of the bottle to point at the gun.

'You ever used one of these before?'

'*Me*? Forget it. I'm not touching that thing,' I said.

'Don't worry, it's going to be fun. I know you like dressing up, so we got you this…'

He gestured at one of his guys who brought over a large plastic bag. From inside emerged the head for a fluffy blue penguin suit, almost identical to the one I was wearing at the party. McIntyre held it up next to his face and smiled like an idiot.

'Now, here's the really fun part,' he said. 'A couple of the lads have rigged this up with mikes. You've even got a little fibre-optic camera in the beak. It's brilliant. We tried it out earlier. We'll be able to see everything you do.'

I tried to laugh it off but McIntyre leant against the counter, fixing me with that famous glare.

'If anyone tries to stop you,' he said, 'in fact, even if they don't, you're gonna shoot 'em. Dead. No exceptions.'

What the hell was so valuable? I thought back to everything that had been confiscated from the Sri-Lankan following the warrant. His laptop had been handed back; we couldn't keep it once it was clear there were no charges were being brought. He had some company ID and a wallet, but I'm sure that was returned as well. I didn't think there was anything else.

217

Whatever it was, I'd have to massacre almost everyone I knew to get to the lock-up, along with anyone who might be visiting on the day.

'It's not going to happen,' I said. 'Forget it. You're insane.'

'Am I?' he replied, apparently pausing to mull the notion over. 'I might have had my moments a few years ago. Helped with the brand. Have you ever Googled insanity?'

'I haven't really needed to.'

'What *is* sane? Is it smashing your head off a brick wall every day for people who couldn't give a toss whether you live or die? Is it living in the same shithole your whole life, bent over a desk by Dave Martin for another 10p every year? If I killed you now, who'd notice? Who'd care? Maybe the landlord at your local when he realised his profits were down by half each week.'

'Three-quarters. I eat there, too.'

'I know you, Rose. We both want the same, the difference is that I went out and got it. I'm the sanest person you'll ever meet.'

'I'm really happy for you. But you can shove that gun up your arse, I'm not going anywhere.'

McIntyre didn't bat an eyelid, continuing with his train of thought.

'Psychology is an interesting topic. 'Course, I don't discuss it with these lads. Loyal as they are they're not really what you'd call academic. Look, I knew you'd be a bit nervous, so Fitch here is going to help me out with a little demonstration in focus.'

Fitch looked terrified.

'Sammy?'

McIntyre walked behind him, taking a position as if he was about to massage his shoulders.

'I understand you two know each other quite well,' said McIntyre. 'In fact, I understand you're so close, you even like to share a few secrets.'

Fitch furiously shook his head. 'No, Sammy, it 'aint like that.'

McIntyre waved another of his men over.

'Really?' he said, taking delivery of something behind his back.

'I didn't say anyfin! He tried to force me, he threatened me, but I dint tell him anyfin, I swear!'

McIntyre's face darkened.

'No, please, Sammy, I promise! Tell 'im, Rose. I didn't say anyfin!'

There was nothing I could say even if I wanted to defend him. He was a grass and McIntyre knew it. Fitch started to panic, then laugh, then panic again, watching for some hint in Sammy's face as to what he was going to do. Marilyn was completely oblivious, gnawing on a chicken bone.

Fitch was nearly crying now. I could almost hear his heartbeat pounding off the brittle twigs in his chest.

McIntyre took a few moments to study Fitch's expression. He began to nod gently as if in understanding, perhaps even forgiveness. He moved from Fitch's shoulder.

Then he jumped back into the little man's face on his other side.

'Hey!' he shouted, wide-eyed.

The spindly skank nearly fell off his chair. McIntyre laughed, joined by a couple of his suited dogs from another room.

'You had me, then,' said Fitch, trying to slow his breathing.

'You're so highly strung,' said McIntyre. 'You need something to calm you down.'

One of the men stepped in and two huge hands held Fitch's pathetic arms tight about his body. McIntyre gripped a handful of Fitch's hair and yanked his head back. His other hand was in the air clenched around a loaded syringe. He swung it down and buried the entire needle into Fitch's right eye. There was a pop as the pressure gave way and a burst of blood and fluid shot in my direction. The scream nearly destroyed the windows. Everyone outside turned to look in. McIntyre pushed down on the plunger with his thumb, emptying enough brown to kill a horse. Fitch was pinned over the table as McIntyre was handed another syringe. This time the needle went straight into the jugular vein and the entire contents disappeared within two seconds.

Barely audible over the terrible noise, McIntyre said: 'There you go, mate. That's on me.'

The big man let go. Fitch struggled for air. His neck visibly tightened and he started to convulse. He pushed away from the kitchen counter, overwhelmed by panic. I heard several crunches as his torso seemed to implode. He fell to the floor, shaking violently, uncontrollably.

McIntyre watched on with his arms folded, like a scientist observing a reaction in an animal. Everyone else had gathered round, inching nearer with each second.

For a full ten seconds Fitch shook like crazy, smacking his arms and legs of the stools and the counter, before the last of the oxygen left his lungs with a spurt of blood.

It was over.

What was left of his right eye dribbled onto the floor. A shattered nervous system provoked a twitch every few seconds, expanding the remaining lifeless eye into shock and back again.

Marilyn stopped chewing to look down at her dead boyfriend. Then she reached into the bucket for her chips.

McIntyre tutted. 'The gear's definitely gone downhill since I left the game.'

He turned to me.

'Killing me won't get you anywhere,' I said.

He laughed. 'I don't wanna kill you, Rose. If I wanted to do that, I'd have done it a long time ago. And anyway, when you've slaughtered half your own station, I won't need to. But, just for insurance...'

Two men wrestled a woman each into the kitchen - Jen and Vicky. They were gagged with thick strips of gaffer tape and their hands were cable-tied far too tightly behind their backs. They tried to scream at the sight of the body on the floor, pushing back into their heavy chaperones.

'We didn't know who was who, so we brought both of them,' said McIntyre.

I wanted to run to them but he stopped me in my tracks.

'Uh, uh, uh,' he said. 'Not now. We can all have a cuddle once this is over.'

'Alright, look, I'll do this,' I said. 'I'll get your stuff. No one has to get hurt.'

'No, they don't,' said McIntyre. 'It's just one of life's little bonuses. Consider it my way of saying thank you to the police for all your support over the years.'

He reached back for the penguin head, letting it dangle off his finger.

'Time to suit-up.'

33

With every second of that journey to the station I was trying to think how I could get out of it. How could I get people to run without saying anything? My instructions were to shoot on sight, no warnings. I could cut a man in half with that gun. McIntyre had travelled with me and two of his men. He had a monitor rigged with a microphone. The picture was perfect. There was no hiding.

The rain had given way to thick humidity. I was sweltering in the back of the van. They'd pulled the flippers off the costume, but otherwise I was pretty much dressed as I was at the party.

Jen and Vicky were tied tightly together on the floor next to me, almost unconscious with the heat. McIntyre warned me that if I missed any target he'd start with a knife, and let me listen to the girls scream in my ear.

We were on the driveway leading to the main station car park. I had ten seconds left and no answers. There was nothing I could do. If I killed myself he'd only slaughter the girls and get one of his boys to go in anyway. The whole thing was just a game.

We came to an aggressive stop. Sammy swiped open the side door and pushed me out onto the concrete in one fluid motion.

'Remember, I'm watching,' he said. He picked up the shotgun and threw it at my feet. He hit the panel behind the driver and the tyres shrieked a laugh as the van sped off.

I got to my feet and picked up the gun. It weighed a ton. I had eight rounds loaded and another twenty four strapped to a belt. I could kill everyone on duty in the building at that time of day, and still have enough left to deal with the witnesses. The ARVs would be called in once it was confirmed shots were fired, but standard containment and hostage concerns meant they'd spend the first hour fannying around, trying to cordon off the nearby roads. It would all be over by then.

'*Christopher*,' said McIntyre in my earpiece, '*are you receiving me?*'

'I can hear you,' I said.

'*I told you this would be fun. We're parking up nearby. You've got fifteen minutes.*'

The duty guard at the desk had heard the commotion and was standing at the counter. I didn't know him. He was just one of the civvies we employed for their ability to phone people up scared when things went wrong. He was easily in his sixties, hunched, and looked about as frail as a recently divorced lemming. If I stomped my foot on the floor he'd probably have run away, but the main entrance is controlled by a switch on the desk after six O'clock and I didn't have my card. We were going to have to become friends very quickly.

I tapped on the glass door, trying to hide the long metal lump behind my back. The guard frowned at me. He must have thought the drunks had started early. I tapped again and he looked annoyed if anything, hoping I'd go away.

'He's not going to let me in,' I said to one side.

'*You've got a very good key there if he doesn't. Ask him nicely. Go.*'

I pressed the button on the intercom. The old man eyed me suspiciously as he spoke.

'Can I help you?'

'Hi, I'm a PC with Special Ops. Sorry about the outfit, I'm on my way to a party. I just forgot something downstairs when I left.'

'Where's your ID?'

'I don't have it with me. You can check me out on the personnel database. I'll give you my details.'

'*We haven't got time for that. Shoot the door open.*'

'I won't be five minutes, I know what I need.'

The guard fell back into his chair, fumbling around for his glasses. After a lengthy squint at the screen he began to enter a password with single-finger typing.

'*I've got the knife, Rose. Five seconds. Shoot the door open.*'

'He's doing it,' I said.

A scream in my ear. It was Jen.

Without another thought I swung the shotgun up to my waist and took aim. I scrunched my face up, turned my head to one side and pulled the trigger. The gun nearly flew out of my hands. Contrary to everything you see in films, a shotgun shell releases a very tightly packed group of ball-bearings, and the force, like the noise, is incredible. Glass smashed all the way up the lobby. There was an almost perfect circular hole where the lock was. After a few moments, the door wobbled and fainted onto the hard, laminate tiles. The guard jumped from his seat and ran.

'*Shoot him,*' said Sammy.

'I'm in. I'm on my way.'

'*Shoot him.*'

'He's gone.'

Another terrible scream.

'*Last chance!*'

I ran around the reception desk to see the terrified old man trying desperately to force the fire exit. He slapped the bar release down, just as I pumped the angry mechanism and fired. The door smashed clean off its hinges and out into the car park, coming to rest on the guard's back.

'*That's my boy!*' said McIntyre. '*Did you see that old duffer fly? It's what he would have wanted.*'

Only an arm was visible, protruding from under the wood. He was completely motionless. I couldn't see any blood, but there was no time to check. If he'd managed to trigger the silent alarm the entire station would be on me in seconds. I ran back to the desk to check the computer. Next to the monitor was a picture of that poor man's family; a wife, children. His mug read: 'The World's Greatest Granddad.'

'*You can bury him later,*' said Sammy. '*Get on with it. And when I say shoot, you shoot.*'

There was no indication the alarm had been triggered, but someone had to have heard the shot. I pumped the next round ready and the empty flew across the foyer, landing to smoke gently in a puddle of glass.

The lock-up was in the basement at the end of a long corridor. I had to pass several offices – potentially twenty to thirty people. I had to warn them, and well in advance. I looked down at the line of ammo on my belt. It was time to use it.

Going for the central staircase I turned my eyes but not my head to look at the guard. To my relief he was moving. He was alive. I pretended not to notice as he looked around and I ran down the stairs.

Halfway down I could hear footsteps slapping towards me, then a shadow encroached on the landing below. Before I could see who it was I fired into the wall. Plaster puffed in all directions and the person jumped backward and scampered away again. I descended another few steps and fired again, then another few steps and fired again.

There was a stampede as I arrived at basement level. I could hear people trampling each other, trying to force the emergency exits and throwing chairs through windows to escape. It was like extreme cattle herding. I deliberately held my head still, focused on an empty office, trying to avoid anyone crossing my line of sight. More terrified screams echoed off the walls as I blew the lighting away from the ceiling. Cheap tiles fell in a fantastic shower of sparks. I smashed the water cooler to pieces, watching the remains of the giant plastic bottle jump all around the corridor.

The screams were becoming more distant. Through a window I saw people working in pairs to help the slow and less able to the main road. I just had to hope that no one had stayed behind to be a hero.

'*You're enjoying this, aren't you?*' said McIntyre.

He's was right. In a way I was. There was a delicious, perverse satisfaction in destroying anything I wanted. Nothing could withstand the awesome power in my hands. I paused to reload, looking around at the doors in the corridor. All those pointless jobs and departments; millions squandered on new systems unfit for purpose; Personnel drawing up ever more sinister shift patterns that they never had to suffer themselves; managers inventing another senior role for the thick bitch who looks the best bending over her desk.

Surely now it didn't matter if there were nine holes in the wall or ten?

I turned into the Duties office. *Chuk-chuk.* I took aim at a computer on the desk.

'Leave approved!' I shouted, and blasted the whole thing out of the window. 'In fact, make it two weeks. You've been working hard.' I fired again at a second computer on the neighbouring desk and it joined its dead friend on the lawn under a blanket of glass.

The next door was for Payroll. The fat, expenses-claiming face of the woman who ran the office looked smugly back at me from her official photo.

'What's that? No overtime despite a seventy-two hour week? Wrong answer!'

Only a small portion of the picture frame still clung to the wall as I showered myself in splinters and tiny crystals of glass. That was better than drawing on a moustache.

I backed out into the corridor and within a few steps I was in the canteen. There I was witness to the most disturbing sight of all - salad. Or to be precise; browning, dying, putrid salad, ladled from a compost heap somewhere by our fucking useless catering contractors, the cheapest in the known universe. I was about to blow all that crap back to hell when I noticed a figure cowering behind the counter. It was Mariusz, the alleged manager of that particular eatery. He was easily twenty stone, wearing a once-white t-shirt with most of the month's inedible menu stained down the front. His fire escape was padlocked shut. It was all about my charity.

'Please! Don't shoot!' he said, shaking with his hands in the air.

'That depends,' I said. 'What's on the menu this week?'

He looked confused. 'Vegetable lasagne.'

I loaded the next round into the chamber.

'I'm going to ask you that question again, and I want you to think very carefully about the answer. What's on the menu this week?'

'Steak!'

'That's better. What kind?'

'Sirloin!'

'What kind?'

'Fillet!'

'*What* kind?'

'Rump?'

'Good. Cut it the right thickness, it's beautiful, bags of flavour. You don't need to waste money on anything more expensive. And what are you going to serve me with my rump?'

'…Salad?'

'*NO!*'

I blasted the fleshy, decaying meld of dark greens and browns loose from its heated glass capsule on the counter.

'Get out! You're a disgrace,' I said, shooting another round into the wall as Mariusz waddled into the corridor like a bus in loafers.

I could hear McIntyre chuckle in my ear.

'We'll definitely get two-hundred-and-fifty quid for that one,' he said. 'I'll even let you off the fact you didn't shoot him. But if you don't mind, maybe you could just write the rest of your grievances down in a letter and we can return to the plan? You're making yourself very popular.'

I stopped to listen. There were sirens in the distance. Lots of sirens.

I ran out into the corridor again. The lock-up had been left open as everyone inside had run for their lives. Inside were boxes, crates, metal baskets, drawers, cabinets and exhibits with their court tags attached. I knew well the entire corner for articles relating to McIntyre and it didn't take long to find something I didn't recognise in a clear evidence bag – a small, unassuming memory stick.

'Let me see.'

I held the bag out in front of me for the camera.

'That's it. Don't lose it.'

'Let the girls go.'

'Not until I've got it in my hands.'

What the hell was it? Instructions? Codes for a bomb? Was it a memory stick at all? What if it was actually a component for a device?

I knew what I was about to do had a very low probability of success but I had to try. I filled the gun full of red and gold and placed the memory stick on the desk where it would be easy to see.

'What is this thing, Sammy?'

'It doesn't matter.'

'I want to know. Or I might just shred it here and now on the table.'

I drew the big black barrel into view, hovering over the frail nugget.

'Don't try and get clever with me. You're not in any position to make demands.'

'You think I won't destroy this thing? The mood I'm in.'

'*I'll throw these bitches at you in pieces.*'

'What are you doing? Tell me, *now*.'

I pumped the gun hard. My finger wrapped around the trigger, one millimetre away from critical pressure.

McIntyre spoke plainly: '*I expected better from you.*'

There was an incredible scream in my ear before the line crackled to a death.

I kept listening. 'Sammy..? Sammy..? Wait!'

What had I done?

I snatched the memory stick from the desk and ran, crunching plaster and glass almost every step of the way back to the main entrance.

If he'd hurt them. If he'd *touched* them.

Now it was about damage maximisation. As soon as he opened the door to that van I'd open fire. I'd kill him, and the two men with him, I didn't care.

But as I ran through the foyer and out into the car park my plan was already in pieces. I froze solid as every single armed officer in the force was looking down their guns at me, leaning on bonnets for cover.

Bloody public inquiries. They shouldn't have been anywhere near me.

'Put down the gun, now!' shouted one of the officers.

'On the floor, face down, hands behind your head!' screamed another.

If I twitched I was dead. But I couldn't let go of the gun. If I did McIntyre had won and the girls had died for nothing.

There was a crackle in my ear.

'*You know the drill*', said McIntyre, '*They can't shoot unless you're a direct threat. Turn around slowly. We're just off the rear car park.*'

The officers kept screaming for me to hit the floor. I was the live target on a firing range. I had to make sure that barrel didn't lift, not even slightly. I turned in tiny, incremental steps, keeping my arms straight at my sides. I daren't breathe. The shouts became louder and more insistent.

'On the floor, now!'

'We *will* shoot!'

I began to walk for the back of the station. Ten paces felt like ten miles. I could hear the officers encroach from all sides. Two of them were almost either side of me, using cars as cover, looking down their sights.

'Drop to the floor, now!'

I ran.

As I rounded the corner a shot aimed for my leg clipped the brickwork and ricocheted off the floor in front of me.

Behind the station the van screeched alongside me and the side door swung open. Sammy was already pointing a handgun at me.

'Throw it behind you,' he said.

I nearly swung the gun up for a shot, but I saw his grip tighten on the pistol. I'd be dead before I could get the barrel at forty-five degrees. I had no choice. I crouched to lay the gun behind me.

The officers were closing in over my shoulder.

'Memory stick,' demanded McIntyre.

I took it from my pocket and threw it over.

'Thank you,' he said.

I looked over my shoulder again. When I turned back there was a bright flash. Then the sky. I tried to lift my head, but...

34

It was bright. Bright walls. Blurry. I was tired. The sun was more white than yellow. It was morning.

I went to rub the bridge of my nose, trying to coax some eyesight back but something stopped my right hand from rising. I pulled and there was a clank of metal. My left hand was free and I reached over the feel the cold bracelet. A handcuff. They'd nailed me down.

I was in my own private room. Hospital gown; IV line; heavy bandaging across my abdomen with a small, dark red patch at the left-hand side. The window told me I was on the fifth floor at least. Miserable grey concrete towers stared at me from the estate over the road.

And then I remembered.

What had happened to Vicky and Jen? Where were they? Did he let them go? I had to know. I had to find out. I had to get out of there.

I looked at the door and the shadow behind the frosted glass. I listened for a moment. No conversation. It was just the one person. It'd be a guard; an officer or one of McIntyre's men. Probably one and the same thing.

It took all the energy I had to lean forward, fighting against the tight material wrapped around my body. I swept the blanket away and dropped my right leg onto the cold floor. My left leg followed and I had to take a moment to steady myself. I felt dizzy and really quite sick. I slid my fingers across the bandage. No exit wound at my back. I eased the IV line out from the vein in my hand.

I dragged the handcuff along the bed rail, one way and the next, looking for some way I could pull it free, but the solid steel laughed off that idea. I looked at the cabinet next to the bed. With my left hand I hit the head on a soap dispenser. I rubbed the goo around my right wrist and under the bracelet. I tried to make my hand as narrow as possible, pulling and straining, but the metal only bit angry red rings into my hand. I applied some more soap and tried several different angles, until fatigue told me to give up. It was too tight.

I slumped forward, leaking sweat from my forehead onto the sheets. I crouched at the bedside, now extremely light-headed. I was at risk of doing some serious damage, whether I could feel it or not.

I pulled myself back onto the bed, allowing my head to sink into the heavy feather pillow. My left hand slapped into my face.

McIntyre was always going to win. I should have destroyed that memory stick when I had the chance. He'd be in London. There was nothing I could do but watch the news like everybody else and wait for him to play his hand. I should have shot him. I should have tried.

I watched dark blood creep silently through the fibres of my bandage. The emergency button was within easy reach of the bed, but I wouldn't even try for it. I didn't deserve any help. I pulled the sheets back up to my chest. What will be, will be.

Then I could hear voices outside the door. One of them was female, with an insistent pitch.

Jen?

The door opened and I shook my head to try and recalibrate my sight. It was the woman who had come in. She shut the door behind her, stopping to look me over.

Her face came into focus. It was Penny. She edged towards me like someone uncertain of a wild animal.

'I wanted to know if it was you,' she said. 'You're a policeman. Why didn't you tell me?'

'I'm sorry, Penny. I didn't want to put you in danger.'

Penny looked back at the door.

'You were right,' she said, 'They made the death certificate up. A kick, like you said.'

I nodded.

'I was right, too. Cardiac embolism. What was he going to do?'

'What d'you mean?'

'The swabs. It was a compound I wasn't familiar with...'

'What compound?'

Penny was hesitant. She looked frightened.

'I had a senior colleague check the results for me. They had to evacuate the lab for six hours before they knew it was safe...'

Now she was almost tearful. I leant up on my elbows.

'Penny, what is it?'

'Some type of explosive. It wasn't a massive sample but everyone was terrified. They kept asking me where I got it. I told them I was doing work for you, Professor Smith, and they said they'd never heard of you. Dr Wells denied all knowledge and now senior management are involved. I've been moved off my section. I might lose my job.'

Penny held her hand to her face, trying to hold back the tears.

'Hey, you're not going to lose your job,' I said. 'You've been amazing. You might have saved hundreds of lives.'

'Really?'

'What have you done with the results?'

'Analysis is saved on the machine. I printed copies off. One's in my desk. I took the other one home. Different places, like you said.'

There was no time to explain anything. No one would believe me anyway. There was only one other person in the world I could trust.

I asked about the man on the door. Penny said it was a policeman with a gun. The description sounded like a guy

233

called Mike, but we didn't really know each other and he wasn't about to do me any favours. He thought Penny was coming in to check the IV lines and solutions. He was bound to radio Fergus once it was clear I was conscious and lucid again. They'd be anxious to secure me properly this time. I needed the key to those 'cuffs, and then I needed a distraction.

'You're leaking,' said Penny.

I looked down. The dark patch was expanding. I could feel the cool liquid running over my stomach and down one side.

'I think I might need another plaster.'

Penny leant in to help and then stopped herself. She took a step back.

'They say you've killed people,' she said. 'You shot someone at your own station.'

'To be fair it was mainly computers and salad... but yeah. I had no choice.'

'How do I know you aren't going to kill me?'

'You don't have to do anything you don't want to, Penny. But there is a man out there with a lot more of that explosive and I don't know what he's going to do with it. It may already be too late, but I have to try and stop him.'

'Why don't your colleagues do anything?'

'They aren't my colleagues.'

I was starting to feel faint again. The blood was forming droplets on the surface of the bandage.

'You must have pulled your stitches out,' said Penny. 'You can't go anywhere like that. We need to patch you up. Stay here.'

'Wait! D'you know if two girls were admitted with me? A brunette called Jennifer, and a girl of fifteen, Vicky?'

'I can ask.'

Penny ripped open the door and I saw the officer stand at his chair, watching her run down the corridor. He turned to look at me as I eased myself down again, trying to relax my erratic heart that quickened and slowed, panicking for more blood.

The officer nudged the door open and pulled his gun on its strap to rest at his back. He stood there with his hands on his hips. He was enjoying my predicament, smiling at my blood-stained sheets.

'Just do us all a favour and die, you bastard,' he said. 'Prison's too good for you. I should have taken you out at the station.'

It was always the most caring people that ended up in the firearms unit. Ex-military types that may have witnessed friends killed in conflict, frustrated by the rules of engagement and desperate to unload an entire magazine into someone at the first excuse. He'd have done that then if he could, and I understood entirely. I'd be the same. He only knew what he was told.

Another minute or so and Penny burst back through the door with an arm full of medical paraphernalia, dumping it all on the bed next to me. She picked up a sterile syringe and tore open the packaging. Picking the plastic safety guard from the metal pin, she flicked the solution and tested a squirt in the air. I pulled the sleeve back on my hospital gown, when, to my surprise, she turned and plunged the needle into the back of the officer's neck as he went to leave.

He spun around. '*What the..?*'

He tried to activate his radio, but his body was quickly falling limp. His eyes rolled back into his head and he fell lifelessly to the floor.

'What was that?' I asked.

Penny checked the corridor and locked us in.

'Just a little anaesthetic,' she said, starting to pat down his pockets. Then she stopped. 'Though I really should have asked him if he was allergic first of all.' She shrugged. 'Where do they keep the handcuff keys?'

'Try the little pocket on his belt.'

'There's been no one admitted by the name of Jennifer in the last twenty-four hours. There's a Victoria, but she's in her sixties.'

'Okay. Thank you.'

'Who are they?'

'Friends.'

'Are they alright?'

'I don't know.'

Penny popped open the officer's leather belt pouch and smiled, shaking the shiny little key in her hand. She almost tripped as she hurried to unlock the cuffs. She held a palm to my chest before I could move.

'We need to sort this or you won't get very far,' she said.

I lay flat as she slowly peeled away the sodden bandaging to reveal a surprisingly small and almost perfectly round hole.

'You need sewing up again,' said Penny.

'We'll have to worry about that later,' I said. 'Do what you can for me.'

'I can't let you leave like this.'

'Don't worry'

'You're just going to keep bleeding.'

'Then I'll keep bleeding. There's no time. Please.'

She unpackaged sterile pads and bandages.

'You better not have AIDS,' she said. 'I couldn't find any gloves.'

I could see why she worked in the lab and not on the wards. She wasn't exactly Florence Nightingale in her bedside manner, but the solid, tight dressing she wrapped around me was certainly secure and reassuring. She opened another syringe and stroked the edge of my shoulder with the side of her finger, injecting me with a booster of some kind. Stepping over the officer again, she retrieved my clothes from a wardrobe on the other side of the room. I was helped to my feet and I held her hands for a few moments to

236

steady myself. She tried not to look as I slipped into my trousers, but as I shrugged into my shirt I triggered the first pangs of pain and she assisted with the buttons.

'It's just a flesh wound,' she said. 'I've got my car downstairs. Let's go.'

'No, you can't.'

'I'm near the entrance.'

'No, Penny, they'll come after you.'

'Well, where are you going to go? How are you going to get there?'

I thought for a moment. 'Can I borrow your car?'

'You can't drive.'

'I can.'

'You won't be insured.'

'Believe me, if I get stopped, 'no insurance' is a long way down the list at the moment.'

I found a piece of paper and pulled a pen from Penny's coat pocket.

'Look, here's where I'm going. It's a friend's place. Your car will be parked outside. I'll leave the keys. Collect it when you're ready.'

Penny was genuinely disappointed to miss out, reluctantly extending her arm to give me the key for her car.

'D'you have any leave left this year?' I asked.

She nodded.

'Take it. In the meantime keep those results locked up. When they ask about this guy, tell them I threatened you, but one way or the other, if you have to go off sick, get out of here until I can make contact with you again. Or if you hear that something has happened to me, go to the police and explain what you know.'

'What do I know?'

I paused, trying to get my arm into my jacket. 'I don't know. Give them everything you have and hopefully someone'll figure it out.'

Penny straightened my jacket and adjusted the collar on my shirt.

'Be careful,' she said, biting her bottom lip.

I smiled and held a hand to her face.

Then she flung out her arm and hit the fire alarm.

'Oops.'

35

The street was quiet. At that time of day everyone should be at work, therefore anyone sat in their car could well be an officer lying in wait. Anyone out for a walk could suddenly turn and run for me.

I crawled past Colin's house. I thought I could just make out his nan in the living room watching TV.

Up ahead I noticed his garage door was halfway open. I sped up and parked opposite to observe a single pair of jeans. Colin was putting something into cardboard boxes, taping them shut.

Deciding it was safe, I got out of the car. Within six feet of the garage door, the excitable jangle of a collar transformed into enthusiastic, black-and-brown muscle. I tried to keep Bollocks on the ground and off my bandaging, pressing down on his wide, flat head and slapping his side.

'Chris?'

'How are you doing?'

'Shit, the whole world must be looking for you. Come inside, quickly.'

I left the garage door at enough of an angle to make out any approaching vehicles.

'How's he been?' I asked, nodding to the dog.

'He's fine. Very quiet. But I can't keep him with nan for much longer.'

'He doesn't like her either, then?'

'Oh no, he loves her – follows her around the house. But she hates him. She locked herself in the toilet for three hours yesterday while he just sat outside the door. He thinks she's playing.'

'I would have thought he's doing you a favour.'

'The worst thing is taking him for walks and having to shout, "Bollocks! Bollocks!" across a park full of families and children.'

'We need to give him a new name.'

'I've tried. He won't answer to anything else. I'll take him to the dogs' home when I get the chance.'

'No, don't do that. As soon as we're sorted I'll take him.'

Colin cocked his head. 'Will this be sorted? What the hell happened at the station?'

I stopped giving the dog attention and straightened up.

'He's got Jen and Vicky.'

'Oh no. Are they okay?'

'I don't know. He wanted a memory stick we seized from the Sri-Lankan.'

'Why?'

'I was hoping you'd tell me. What was on it?'

'Nothing. According to our high-tech unit it was riddled with a virus.'

'They couldn't recover any of the files?'

'No, it nearly destroyed the system. They had to take the computers offline and reboot them. No one touched it after that.'

'Was it some type of encryption?'

'I don't see how. Encryptions just show up as nonsense unless you have the means to decode them. They shouldn't attack the host computer.'

A car approached and Colin pulled me further into the garage. It was just a neighbour parking up.

'Has Fergus spoken to you?' I asked.

'They phone me practically every hour.'

'What have you said?'

'What can I say? He doesn't believe my statement. He's convinced you killed Sewell and the chief. They've forced me to take leave until the investigation's over.'

240

'And Katya?'

'No one's seen her. Or Tony.'

'What about Travis?'

'Usual shifts as far as I know. Are you sure about him?'

Another car was closing in and we crouched to look under the garage door. Just someone passing.

I stood upright too quickly, provoking a few painful twitches. Lifting my shirt the first pin-prick of red was already visible. It was going to get much worse the more I moved about. I was feeling dizzy again and leant against the wall.

'Are you okay?' Colin asked.

I nodded, though my pained expression disagreed.

'We need to get you back to the hospital.'

'No, we need to get to London.'

'And do what?'

'He'll be at Jones' place by now.'

'No. No way.'

'Colin...'

'*No*. I'm putting my foot down this time. We're going to get killed. You nearly were killed.'

'I need to find Jen and Vicky.'

'I'll call it in.'

'He's got explosives. Penny found traces of it on Bingo's swabs.'

'Penny? Who's Penny?'

'Grab your keys and secure that old wench in her armchair. We're leaving.'

'Alright, suppose he has got a bomb. Tell me what one-and-a-half unarmed policemen are going to do about it.'

'If they're on site we'll flood the place with officers.'

'They won't touch him.'

'But they want me. They'll have to come if they know I'm there.'

Colin was not going to be moved so easily this time. He wanted to say something but struggled to let go, angrily ripping gaffer tape from the roll to seal up another cardboard box full of junk. He leant on it with his back to me.

'He was right you know,' he said. 'It won't bring her back.'

'What are you talking about?'

'Your sister. You have to move on.'

'This has got nothing to do with my sister.'

'Hasn't it? How did Sewell get in the river, Chris?'

'I don't know.'

Colin looked at me.

'You were with me that night,' I said. 'You know I had nothing to do with it.'

'I read your statement, that's all. I don't know what happened in the garden.'

'So you think I killed Bingo?'

'… No.'

'Well, say it like you mean it, won't you? Where's all this suddenly come from?'

'I'm just scared. This is crazy. I don't know who to trust anymore.'

'Me. That's who you trust. And no one else.'

'McIntyre isn't worth getting killed over.'

'Well I'm afraid that's a choice the girls don't have. Look, you can stay here another night, boiling cabbage for that knackered old bint, or we can do something with our lives for once.'

Colin turned again, leaning on the boxes.

I continued: 'The last thing the chief said to me was that he was proud. I really don't know what of. I can't think of a single thing I've done that's worth a toss. Maybe I can change that. You're the only person I can trust. I need your help… the dog's farted again, hasn't he?'

Colin smirked. Bollocks stopped panting to give me his best innocent expression. I pushed the door up and stepped out for some air, but as I looked down the street I saw Edith and ducked away again.

'What is it?' asked Colin.

'Your nan. I think she saw me.'

Colin looked out. I peeked around the wall. She'd gone back inside.

'You better stay here,' said Colin. 'She's seen you on the news, she might get funny.'

Colin swiped his hands down at his sides, looking up to the gods of how-did-I-get-into-this-shit? He was right. We really could get killed. I certainly wasn't going to get a second chance. But I was ready.

I had never previously understood the notion that something was worth dying for. Surely suitable effort and a modest amount of running away to achieve around seventy-five percent of any given objective was perfectly acceptable? How would you know if all your hard work had paid off if you were dead? But that day, and possibly owing to the sheer volume of powerful drugs my body was saturated with, I understood perfectly. I would do whatever it took to free the girls and destroy McIntyre's plans. I would die happy, knowing that he would live in misery. There was no greater achievement.

'Give me a few minutes,' said Colin, taking Bo – as I would refer to him from then on – by the collar.

I gave Colin Penny's keys with a brief explanation and he jogged with the dog to his house.

It was nearly midday. According to the estate agent the keys for Sammy's rented place only went back over the desk that morning. There was still time. We could be at Jones' yard within two hours. Even if the main players had gone, someone had to be on site we could batter for information; there had to be at least a trace of evidence we could use to warn everyone what was going to happen. Jen

243

and Vicky might even be there. Then I'd call it in. Here I am. Come and get me.

I saw Colin hurry back out of the house towards me. I ducked back into the garage as his nan appeared in the doorway again.

'We better get going,' said Colin.

'Does she know I'm here?'

I heard another car pull up. Then another. Then another. This time it *was* the police. All marked cars bar the one with a windscreen filled with DIs Martin and Fergus. A uniformed PC went to Colin's door and I saw Edith point in my direction.

'Time to go,' I said. 'Where's your car?'

I watched Edith gesturing in our direction as Colin secured the padlock on the garage door. The officers ran for us as we disappeared behind the block. Colin fumbled for his key as I waited on the passenger side of his car.

'Today, Colin.'

They were nearly on us when the locks flicked up on the doors. We dived in and slapped them back down again, just as we were being surrounded at all sides.

Fergus stood over the bonnet. 'Step out of the car please, gentlemen.'

I looked at Colin. He started the engine.

Fergus flashed a warning with his eyes. '*PC Whyte…*'

Colin put the car into gear and took the handbrake off.

'We *will* put the windows through,' said Fergus.

Colin slammed his foot down and the front wheels spun. Fergus leapt to one side and Martin, who had only just managed to catch up, almost fell over backwards. The rest of the officers flung themselves against the garage doors as we sped straight through them. I looked back to see everyone running for their cars.

I exchanged a snarl with Edith as we passed. Miserable cow.

We turned out of the road into heavy traffic, just as flashing blue hit the rear view mirror. Until London there was no such thing as a red light.

'Nice getaway,' I said.

'I never liked this job anyway,' said Colin, swerving through a line of stationary cars at a junction. 'And I'm not losing my no-claims bonus for that bastard.'

36

There's nowhere like London. You can almost hear the thump of imperial kettle drums as terrified rural types cower in the Victorian shadows. Millions of people rushing around in every direction; red platelets coursing through the mighty fanged animal that is nine-to-five, only slowing to circumnavigate the occasional clot of tourists.

Part of the reason I joined the police was to avoid people, at least some of the time. Shift-work may often feel like some kind of communist torture, but days off during the week are a god-send for anyone who doesn't want to go shopping with a machete. The standard week that everyone seems to crave is undoubtedly one of the largest contributors to our mood in this country. Everyone goes to work at the same time, comes home at the same time, they go to the pub to stand in endless queues for a drink at the same time. There's no escape.

We passed through Purfleet, moving east into Grays. Colin had planned the most convoluted route possible, staying off the major roads to avoid the ANPR and any premature local attention.

Fergus and Martin lost us early. We spun into a field off the A-road not far from Colin's house and waited for everyone to pass. But we didn't want them too far behind. With any luck they'd quickly radio-in for Jones' address and catch up just as we were pointing at the evidence, wagging our tails. That said, if Sammy had already gone; if the place was empty and the plan was already in motion, then I had to concede we'd have no choice but to hand ourselves in. They were going to need every single officer free and available. As long as I knew where the girls were I didn't care.

'This is it,' said Colin, gesturing out his window, 'Tilbury Port.'

We were driving parallel with an endless security fence. I watched a mosaic of coloured containers climb high above a ship's deck, fed by giant derricks. In one corner, rows of brand new vans looked like a wave breaking onto the concrete, while in another their forebears lay in mangled, rusting towers. Crates were wedged into every last available inch, heavy sacks of materials littered warehouse doorways, and in no particular hurry, blackened hands smeared overalls in readiness for cigarettes. It was an immense operation, with just about every single multinational that new what a boat was camped out somewhere on site.

I assumed the security would comprise of the usual high-vis and indifference, so I was surprised to see an entire police station just off one of the main entrances.

'Oldest force in the country,' said Colin. 'Pre-dates the Met.'

'They're proper police?' I asked.

'Similar principal to the transport guys. They have jurisdiction over the immediate area. If anything serious crops up, Essex take over.'

'D'you think they know anything?'

'They might, but I bet they won't tell. Company that runs this place literally owns them. Probably explains how Jones has run a scrap business here for the last six years, selling stolen lead to China.'

'How d'you know all this?'

'While you were playing hide-and-seek with Fergus I did some research. Jones also owns Building Twelve. McIntyre pays him over the odds for it every month to secure his gear, or at least he used to. Looks like it's being handed back as part of the deal.'

'So I hear. But what's Sammy getting out of this?'

'Who knows?'

'Well has your research determined how we get into this place?'

Colin smiled. 'We're police officers, aren't we?'

With every passing hour that seemed a title I was increasingly unlikely to hold ever again.

We stopped at the last security barrier. Colin got out to speak with an officer emerging from the checkpoint. It was quieter at this end of the compound. I couldn't see a single person moving. Very few vehicles. No obvious spotters.

Suspicious eyes climbed Colin's shoulder. I leant into the palm of my hand, trying to obscure my face without letting on that I was trying to obscure my face.

I caught the officer's eyes as we drove through the barrier, and again as I looked back a few moments later. He thought I looked familiar. A few moments longer and he may have realised why. Hopefully he was in the middle of a suitably involving crossword puzzle and wouldn't keep thinking.

We drove a careful course between abandoned loading trolleys on the acned concrete. A tipper lorry passed us in the other direction, but otherwise all remained still. Colin slowed down and gestured to the far end of a wide concrete jetty. Beyond a couple of newer buildings sat an ancient, corrugated heap, scarred with the signwriting of several companies that had owned it and left over the years. It was surrounded by mountains of scrap. No one could see in.

Colin pulled the handbrake up fifty metres or so away.

'That has to be the place,' he said

For a few moments we looked about us, trying to gauge the threat, waiting to see who might emerge from the twisted metal.

'Look, there's no sense us both going in,' said Colin, 'especially in your state.'

248

'I'm fine,' I said.

'You're not. Stay here.'

'Don't be daft.'

'Let me confirm it's the place. I'll come back for you.'

'We need to watch each other's back.'

'What, like we did at Sammy's? Like we did at the warehouse? You risked your life and I just sat there. It's my turn.'

'You could get jumped from anywhere around here.'

'I'll be five minutes. Wish me luck.'

Colin sprung his door open. I went to reach for him but the seatbelt dug into my side and sent pain in every direction. I unfolded again to look over the dashboard. Colin scurried to the corner of the first building. With one last look around he disappeared out of sight.

He may have been right, it probably was his turn, but ultimately there was a reason I was usually the one on infiltration. Colin was the technical man. He had a superb eye for detail and a comprehensive knowledge of all things law. But he was a horrible liar if he got caught in a tight spot and he certainly wasn't a fighter. He was scared of spiders. And thunder. And people.

It was a bad idea, and two minutes later I started to panic. I'd have been there and back in that time if I was fully fit. I leant out of the window and closed my eyes, trying to focus on any sound, but the background clanks, drills and hydraulics coughed over everything.

Three minutes. Four. Four-and-a-half.

He was in trouble, whether he knew it or not. He probably thought he'd found a decent vantage point, crouching behind a knackered old car. He'd eventually turn to see McIntyre's nuts.

I opened my door and gripped the frame to pull myself upwards. I could only jog a few paces at a time, parallel to a wall with my hand outstretched as a stabiliser. I kept my phone in my hand with 999 punched into the keypad.

On the other side of a deep tunnel of scrap I tip-toed up to the old workshop. Everyone was on the other side of the building, next to the water. I could hear voices. Several trucks had backed up to the loading bay, engines running.

No sign of Colin. There had been no commotion, I was sure of that. No cries from a beating or gunshots. But then they probably just walked up to him, asked for the time and hit him over the head as he looked at his watch. You don't need to shoot Colin. That's like using a bazooka to swat a fly.

Satisfied everyone was suitably occupied I eased an industrial wheelie bin under a window and struggled on top. Luckily the constant diesel chug of the trucks was ample cover for any strained whines I may have let out.

I wiped a century's worth of dirt from a small pane of glass and peered into the building.

'Hello everyone...'

37

At first it looked like I was spying on a makeshift mosque. The Middle-Eastern men were all in traditional flowing dress and turbans, barefoot and knelt in prayer, including the two from the house the night the chief was murdered. One took the role of a decidedly animated cleric, chanting and furiously gesturing. They rose and fell, time and again, as the sermon became louder and more intense. Next to them several of the metal cases lay open, but it was too dark and I couldn't angle my head to see what was in them.

Completely oblivious across the room, Jones' boys were loading the trucks with the boxes from Building Twelve. It took two men to carry each one but they weren't using the forklift. Whatever the contents were, they were light. But contained with sufficient pressure, in a sealed trailer, you wouldn't need much explosive, and I counted at least five boxes in each lorry.

Lee Carr watched on from a gantry connected to an old dredger. Two shipping containers were loaded at the mid-section. It wasn't fast, but there'd be more than enough fuel on board a boat like that to leave Europe well behind. On deck, several of Sammy's security team laughed, smoked cigarettes and threw empty beer cans into the water as if they were about to start out on a booze cruise.

I instinctively ducked as McIntyre appeared with Jones from an office at the far end of the workshop. He stood over the foreigners, impatiently waiting for them to complete their prayers, repeatedly looking at his watch. As the rant ended the men took turns to embrace one another.

McIntyre stepped in, clapping his hands together. 'Okay. We're almost set. Your gear's arrived. You guys okay? Ready?'

A few nodded, just about understanding what was being asked of them. They looked anxious, sweating heavily despite a strong sea breeze. They paced around in their group exchanging little in the way of conversation, like athletes on the one-hundred metre starting line. Even stone-cold Sammy was visibly unnerved, fidgeting from foot to foot. I followed him to the other side of the workshop and there was the Sri-Lankan, straightening his tie at what was left of a mirror. He was dressed in the suit he had hanging at the warehouse with an ID lanyard around his neck. He and McIntyre exchanged a nod.

As the last box was loaded onto a truck, every tailgate slammed shut.

'That it?' Jones asked McIntyre.

'That's it. Ship your boys out.'

'Payment?'

'Two hours. It'll come up as a stock transaction. Close the account when you've emptied it.'

Jones stopped McIntyre in his tracks. 'I want cash.'

'I told you; I don't deal in cash.'

'You're six months behind and I've got no guarantees.'

'So what d'you want me to do, Jonesy? Go to the cash point and withdraw a few hundred thousand?'

'Two of my boys will go with you until the deal's done.'

'Will they fuck.'

'I'm not asking.'

'I've been on this for two years. I'm not going to cock it up now, babysitting your idiots.'

'Then I want a deposit. I don't care how you get it, but you get half the cash to me now before you disappear in a puff of fucking smoke. Either that or you take a couple of lads. Decide which, here and now.'

'Arthur, how many times do I have to explain this to you?'

'You think I'm a mug? I give you my warehouse, my yard, I move all your crap half way across the country. Stop playing fucking games and start handing over some money.'

Jones' men closed in, all armed as before. It'd be over before any of Sammy's guys on the boat had a chance to look up.

With a shake of the head, McIntyre's shoulders dropped. 'Okay, Arthur, okay. You win. Can you start the drill up please, Lee?'

On the other side of the workshop, Carr started an old generator and heaved a pneumatic drill to his waist.

'*Drill?*' said Jones. 'What are you drilling for?'

'Nothing, it's just to cover the noise.'

'What noise?'

Jones followed McIntyre's line of sight to find the foreigners standing in a line behind him, every one of them holding an AK-47 ready at their hips. Without another word, McIntyre leapt to one side. The drill screamed the place down just as the men opened fire, ripping white hot lead through bodies. I dropped away from the window as blood and pulp flew up the walls. Ricochets jumped everywhere, crunching plaster and smashing glass. Two rounds pierced the wall next to me and I fell onto my back. Through the holes I watched a man being smashed up against the office. Another lost both arms. I had to turn away as another hit the floor, screaming with his wounds until a shot to the head splashed his brain across the floor.

The guns stopped.

Carr dropped the drill and cut the generator.

I climbed back to my feet, fearful of provoking the slightest creak on the bin. Jones had fallen to one side, his life spurting free from his neck with every last heartbeat. Unblinking eyes watched McIntyre approach and kneel next to him.

'*That* noise. Too bad, Arthur. Thanks for your help.'

McIntyre stood up, wiping blood from his face with his sleeve. Everyone from the boat had gathered in stunned silence. One or two tried and failed to look amused. Over the years those thugs would have punched anyone in range as a conversation-starter. They'd have beaten people over debts and stabbed their relatives. Maybe even one or two got to hold a gun once. None of them would have seen anything like this. Congratulations boys, you've just graduated to terrorism. There's no going back now.

Then I could hear footsteps behind me.

Someone shouted: 'Armed police!'

I almost fell off the bin, slamming my back against the wall. In the face of several guns I uselessly held my finger to my lips and frantically pointed behind me. The officers encroached, emerging from the scrap at all sides.

'Armed police! Get down on the floor, now!'

'Oh – *don't you know another sentence?*' I said.

It was too late. From either side of me, McIntyre's men fanned out from the workshop, every single one of them armed with at least a handgun, leaning on barrels and bonnets for cover. The clicks of guns being cocked on both sides rang out across the entire yard.

There would be no survivors. In the hail of bullets I was inevitable collateral.

'Put 'em down, McIntyre!' shouted a familiar voice.

It was DI Martin, hiding behind the scrap. I could just make out Fergus crouching next to him.

'Let's all be sensible,' said McIntyre. 'There are no winners here.'

'Lay the guns on the floor, *now*,' said Martin.

'You know I can't do that.'

'I've got more people at the gates. We *will* kill you.'

'We can all back away from this.

'*Five seconds*,' said Martin.

No one moved. Every gun on both sides flicked left and right, trying to judge the most immediate threat.

254

Three.

Two.

One.

'Okay!' said McIntyre.

To my surprise, he lowered to his knees, placing the gun on the floor in front of him. Everyone, including the maniacs in their robes, speckled with blood, followed suit.

Martin emerged from the twisted wrecks with Fergus. Side-by-side they walked to stand triumphantly over McIntyre as a wall of armoured officers built behind them, still twitchy, looking for any sign of movement.

Martin picked Sammy's gun off the floor while his fellow inspector produced a pair of handcuffs.

'You're under arrest,' said Fergus with a broad smile.

McIntyre looked up. 'Oh. I don't think so.'

There was a single bang out of nowhere and I braced against the wall.

Martin had shot Fergus. Immediately he turned on the spot and fired several more times, killing another two of his own officers.

No one else flinched. Within moments everyone had emerged from their cover, safety catches on and guns holstered. Those on their knees climbed back to their feet. Everyone met around the bodies, shaking hands and slapping shoulders.

'Christ, Dave,' said McIntyre, 'what d'you do? Stop for a coffee and a Danish?'

'I think you'll find I'm making good time under the circumstances,' replied Martin.

'Were you followed?'

'No. But we don't have long. You need to get those things moving and drop your man off.'

'Get your guys inside.'

'One last thing…'

'Dave' turned his attention to me, double checking the gun he had was still loaded.

I checked my footing. If I jumped the whole bin would move from underneath me. If I was lucky I might land where I could push one of the officers into Martin, maybe buying just enough time to snatch his gun and kill him in the confusion. But only him. Or did I ignore him and run for the workshop? I could grab one of the AKs and back myself into the corner, picking them off as they gave chase. But I had nowhere to go at the end of that jetty. They only had to wait for the empty click and I'd be surrounded in moments.

Martin stepped closer, looking down his sights at me. I was ready to jump when McIntyre gripped the gun barrel and brought it down.

'No, no, inspector,' he said. 'Things are hot enough. Come on, inside.'

Martin didn't want to walk away. He wanted to do it. He wanted to pull that trigger. Only after a good few seconds, mulling over our every previous confrontation did he think better of it, slapping the gun into McIntyre's chest. He gestured for his bent officers to follow him inside, but he couldn't resist one last dig at me.

'You never were good enough, Rose,' he said. 'Thank you for making it so easy.'

That was my cue. Martin passed within eight feet of me and I launched off the bin, crashing him into the ground. It felt like punching a space hopper full of water. I tried to make each of the three swings I had time for connect with more and more force until I was pulled off him and we were dragged apart, spitting venom at one another across the yard.

Twisting and kicking out, I was hauled into the workshop and held against the wall by two men. McIntyre followed, drawing the slide back on the gun. I threw speculative head-butts either side of me, for which I was awarded a massive fist to the gut. That was the end of my fight. My arms were pulled straight from either side as I coughed and spluttered. McIntyre took position in front of me.

'Drill please, Lee,' he said.

Martin watched on, wiping blood from the corner of his fat mouth.

'Have you really got more people at the gates, Dave?' asked McIntyre, looking down the gun at my face.

'No,' replied Martin.

'Good.'

The generator shook into life and Carr hammered the drill into the concrete.

I flinched as a single shot pierced the din.

I couldn't feel anything.

After a few moments I released one eye from its tight squint and looked down my body. No wound. No more blood.

Then I looked up to see Martin fall backwards onto the crimson sludge. His officers turned to find the foreigners had reformed behind them.

A storm of bullets thumped against their body armour, penetrating and pureeing organs. I turned my head, closing my eyes tight, as blood pounced at me, dribbling down my face and neck until the last man fell onto the ragged pile.

The six, smoking gun barrels closed in, scanning for any remaining sign of life. No one had survived.

Carr dropped the drill and cut the generator once more, stepping back to look over the wider docks and check for interested parties.

He nodded the all-clear.

'Right,' said McIntyre, 'That's enough excitement for one day.' He beckoned Carr over. 'Get this lot on board and get going. Make sure they're secure in the crate and don't dump them until you're at least five miles out. Sorted your travel?'

'Yeah. They don't really do First Class, but it's got wings, I'll get there.'

Sammy winked. 'I'll see you in a few days. Cocktails are on you.' Then he turned to the Sri-Lankan, cowering behind the wall at the far end of the workshop. 'Ash, if you want to wait in the car. I'll be two minutes.'

Carr signalled and one by one the trucks found first gear to leave the compound - without the foreigners. I was dropped to the floor as everyone was needed to load corpses onto the boat. Martin slid past me, painting a thick smear of blood on the floor with the back of his head.

From my knees I fell back against the wall. McIntyre was smirking at me like a parent amused at a child's misdemeanour.

'PC Rose,' he said. 'Truly you never give up, do you?'

He checked the time again before he lowered himself next to me. We watched the butchered bodies as they were dragged past us. I recognised at least two of the officers. You'd need a dentist to tell you who two or three of the others were. The liquid floor shimmered a perfect red.

Sammy nodded to my wound. 'You gonna be okay?'

It was almost genuine concern. Now I was still again my whole body was aching.

'Is it my turn now?' I asked.

'No,' said McIntyre. 'I'm a man of my word. You're too good for 'em, mate. I snap my fingers and all the other coppers kill each other for the right to crawl into my arse. But not you.'

'What have you done with the girls?'

'You'll see.'

'If you've touched them...'

'Yeah, I know, blah, blah. I'm not a monster.'

'Where's Colin?'

'Colin? I nearly forgot.'

McIntyre looked up and I saw Colin standing in the office doorway.

'Run, Colin!' I shouted. 'Get to the station!'

He didn't move. He just stood there, seemingly unable to look at me.

'*Run Colin, run,*' mocked McIntyre. 'You know, for an intelligent guy, you can be pretty stupid sometimes.'

I felt an unusual sensation flow through me, like I was being emptied.

'Colin?' I said. 'All this time, you..?'

He looked like a child being scalded, head bowed, nothing to say.

'You never knew?' asked McIntyre. 'He was really worried, bless 'im. Trouble you cause, having to rearrange everything at the last minute.'

I looked at Colin. 'The whole time..? *You pathetic fucking -*'

In my anger I tried to get to my feet and run for him, but McIntyre yanked me back down by my arm and I crashed against the wall.

'Now, now,' said Sammy. He turned to Colin. 'Would you mind escorting our foreign friends to your car and hand them their gear? Leave the guns in the boot.'

He had the bombs all along. We'd brought them with us.

'Don't be too hard on him,' said McIntyre. 'We didn't give him a lot of choice.'

I fell onto my back, looking for the sky through the dirty corrugated iron. On the dredger I watched a pair of feet disappear into one of the shipping containers. I could feel a fine mist of water as Carr hosed the floor down. Blood ran thick into drains at all sides of the workshop.

'What are you going to do?' I asked.

'Me? I'm not going to do anything,' said McIntyre.

'What are *they* going to do?'

'To be honest, I don't know. And I don't give a shit. They can blow this poxy island off the face of the earth for all I care. Fifty years and it's all theirs anyway.'

'Hundreds of innocent people... for what?'

'Are they innocent? Bankers, lawyers... *police.* At least these guys believe in something.' McIntyre pointed at the boat. 'Your boss would've strung up his whole family for another fiver. Whatever I paid him, few months and he'd have sold me out to the highest bidder. You don't have to thank me.'

McIntyre kept looking at me for some kind of reaction. I clawed my face, trying to tear the stupidity from my mind.

'I want you to know something,' he said. 'I'm glad Bingo's dead, and his brother. Neither of 'em were good enough for Emily.'

'Don't you talk about her.'

'I'm serious. She never deserved that... Chris, get out of here. Fuck the rules. Go somewhere you're still allowed to have fun – somewhere with some *fucking sun.* We don't have long. You know that better than anyone.'

Again he waited for a response that never came.

A short way off the foreigners were getting into a car.

'Allah be with you!' shouted Sammy. 'Or whoever it is this week. Blow something up for me.'

McIntyre had one more look at his watch. He slapped my shoulder and got back to his feet. Turning me over he secured my hands with a cable tie. I couldn't have resisted if I had wanted to. I was escorted quicker than my legs wanted to move into the office and thrown onto the floor.

Jen and Vicky were tied together, back-to-back, gagged with tape. They were dirtied, eyes red and stinging, but otherwise unharmed. Vicky kicked out as McIntyre came close.

'Reminds me of your sister, this one,' said McIntyre, staying just out of range. 'Look, I've got to go, but more of your useless colleagues will be here soon. In the meantime, think about what I said. Please. It was fun knowing you, Rose.'

The door locked and the key flew into the dark seawater. Carr finished with the hose and jumped on the boat as it began to gurgle away from the jetty. On the other side of the workshop I heard a car door close. The engine revved and McIntyre was gone.

38

It was so obvious. At the fancy-dress party that night – how did McIntyre know I was looking at that computer? I didn't say anything. The guys who dragged me in didn't say anything. I was never going to get near anything important. I was just allowed to play until I strayed too close. Colin reported back with every detail, every change of plan. He was already at the house the night the chief died. For all I knew he was the killer. And all the while Fergus was being briefed against me; a perfectly innocent, honest copper just trying to do his job.

I couldn't lift my legs up and through my arms. I turned to face the wall and pushed myself along the floor towards the girls. Jen kept trying to tell me something. I leant in and bit at the end of the tape wrapped round her face. I tugged sharply but only succeeded in head-butting her, provoking muffled complaints. Changing the angle I tried again a few times until the tape hung loose to one side of her mouth.

She gasped for air. 'Where the *hell* have you been? What the *hell* is going on? I thought you said the police was all paperwork?'

'Are you okay?' I asked, shuffling along on my bum to Vicky.

'You lied to me.'

'What?'

'That Russian slag turned up again the other night.'

'Polish. When?'

'The other night. "I really need to see him. Tell him to call anytime".'

'Jen, she's one of them.'

'One of who? What do they want? I thought we were dead.'

I looked up and around the office. There were several ricochets embedded in the walls. It was only pure luck that none of them struck any lower.

I ripped the tape from Vicky's mouth and spat it away. She stretched her neck, taking in a deep breath.

'Are you okay, Vicky?'

'Yeah. Thanks for letting me stay with you, I feel so much safer.'

'I'm sorry.'

'I think I understand why you drink now.'

'How do we get out of here?' asked Jen.

I pushed my feet into the floor, trying for purchase on the smooth concrete to force my back up the wall. Standing, I kicked the door, but it held firm. I tried again and again with more force, but the reliable old lock braced against me. After several more attempts I started to feel dizzy and I slid back down the wall. It wasn't going to move.

'Have you wee-d yourself again?' asked Jen.

'What?'

'I can feel something wet down here.'

'That's not wee, it's blood.'

'Blood? From what?'

'I just need a new bandage. I've been shot –'

'*Shot*? Oh my God, you're bleeding to death!'

'I'm fine.'

'Heeelllp! Heeeeeelllp!'

'No one will hear you.'

'Heeelllp!'

'Jen, there's –'

The door crashed through, slamming against the wall. I looked up to see a man in a suit, rigidly clasping a handgun.

He shouted over his shoulder, 'Clear! Three hostages here.'

In amazement, Jen and I said: '*Travis?*'

'Hi guys,' he said, holding up a friendly hand and lowering his gun. He spoke with a lisp I'd never noticed before.

There were several pairs of feet moving to surround the building. Soon the entire workshop was full of suits and earpieces.

'What are you doing here, you bastard?' asked Jen. 'And where's my loofah?'

'I'm with the National Crime Agency,' said Travis. 'We've been watching you for a while.'

'Watching *me*?' I asked.

'Where's McIntyre?'

'You missed him.'

I could hear more cars arriving, braking sharply. Doors flew open and within moments we were surrounded again; ten, fifteen, twenty people approaching from all sides. Trev's men wedged themselves into any cover they could find in the workshop and trained their guns at the doors.

'Armed officers! Put down your weapons!' shouted someone from the far end of the room.

'We're civilians!' Jen shrieked. 'Don't shoot!'

Travis was knelt behind the doorframe.

'We're officers with the NCA. Lower your weapons!'

'We're MI5, lower yours!'

'Let's see some ID!'

'You first!'

Travis held up his hand. 'I'm going to reach down and slide my badge over...'

'Okay, I'll do the same.'

'Easy.'

'*Easy.*'

I shook my head in disbelief.

Warrant cards slid across the wet floor. After a few moments the guns were lowered on all sides. Slightly confused, everyone began to congregate in the middle of the workshop, nodding and exchanging simple pleasantries.

A pair of women's shoes approached the office. The owner had another familiar voice: 'What the hell are you doing here? Where iz everyone?'

'Gone,' said Travis. 'I need a medic here.'

Trev stood aside in the doorway and Katya appeared. Her face lit up when she saw me.

'Chrisz!' she said, holstering her own gun as she came to kneel at my side.

'*Oh, Chris, Chris,*' mocked Jen.

'When I heard about Straughan I feared the worst.'

'There's still time,' Jen muttered.

'You're MI5?' I asked.

She nodded. 'Where's McIntyre?'

'I don't know. But Martin and about twenty others are on their way to the bottom of the Atlantic.'

'Dead?'

'In pieces.'

Katya looked at her watch. 'He's always on time. He must have suzpected me.'

Another agent called from the workshop: 'Ma'am, we've found someone in a bin with a gunshot wound. Area's clear, but there's a lot of blood out here.'

'He's zstarting early,' said Katya. 'Contact the Met. We need every officer on the streets visible, now. Zirculate the registrations on the target vehicles – white, unmarked box vans. Sightings only. Evacuate the banks.'

'Wait, wait,' I said. 'What are you doing?'

'I'm sorry Chrisz. I wanted to bring you in, but your raid on McIntyre's place threatened my cover. When did the trucks leave?'

'About twenty minutes ago. Why are you evacuating banks?'

'He's going to blow them up.'

'What?'

265

'He's going to bet all his money against the markets as they fall.'

No he wasn't. Killing traders and destroying a few computers was no plan. He might make a few quid on the initial blip, but it was nothing worth this kind of risk. Even if you took out the entire Stock Exchange, trading defaults to one of two back-up systems elsewhere. I knew that from at least two well-publicised reports about the dodgy computers they had installed. The LSE, like every other company in Britain, tried to do things on the cheap and outsource their IT… to Sri-Lanka.

'Ashane!' I said.

'What?' said Katya.

'The man in the warehouse.'

'You've loszt me.'

'You don't know? He works for a Sri-Lankan company. He's part of the cell. He has a memory stick on him with a virus.'

'What good is that?' asked Travis.

'He's going to corrupt the system. They can take all the money they want. No one will even realise.'

'So where are the trucks headed?' asked Katya.

'Forget the trucks, they're decoys. He probably used those boxes to test shipping lanes when he brought the men over.'

'Chrisz, I've been undercover for eighteen months. I know he has explosives, I've seen them.'

'I know, but they're not in any lorries. They're strapped to six religious nuts.'

'Suizide bombers? You're sure?'

'Colin had their rig in his car.'

'Colin?'

When this was over *I* was going to stop paying my council tax. Eighteen months and the country's leading intelligence services still didn't know what was going on, having spent half their time watching me eat beans on toast night after night. McIntyre had expertly fed them just enough bullshit to keep them onside and working for his cause, and when they had served their purpose, they were discarded like a teenage fling without so much as a 'sorry, you're frigid' text.

Katya had a call over her radio. The first truck had parked up near Buckingham Palace.

She looked at me. 'What's he doing?'

'Diverting attention.'

'I can't take that riszk'

'I'm sure he's counting on it. But you need to find those men and their real targets.'

'What are the real targets?' asked Travis.

'You tell me, Trev, you're the intelligence.'

The bank evacuations were cancelled. Katya advised the Met control room to set up perimeters around the trucks as they were discovered, but not to commit any more units than were absolutely necessary. Every single police officer in the county and the neighbouring forces were put on the highest alert. Leave was cancelled, shifts extended and lethal force was authorised. A press release would detail the cancellation of all non-essential travel throughout the city, including the tube, trains, buses and flights until further notice.

The terrorists would not surrender. If they realised they were being obstructed from their targets they would simply detonate in the most populous area. It was hard to see how the day could end without significant casualties.

When Katya let go of her radio she was shaking slightly.

'Eighteen months down the drain. This is real, iszn't it?'

I nodded.

'Where's he going to go?'

Nobody knew. He never told anyone.

Except I did know. I'd known all along. I just didn't know.

'Costa Rica,' I said.

Katya and Travis looked confused.

'*Costa Rica*,' I repeated.

Still only blank expressions.

'Doesn't anyone watch documentaries except me? What idyllic, cash-strapped state doesn't have an extradition treaty with the UK? We need to get to the airport.'

Jen and Vicky were cut free while Katya helped me off the floor, holding me at the waist. It was then she noticed the blood on my shirt.

'Chrisz, what happened?'

'Ah, small bullet problem,' I said.

'Go with one of my guys, we have first aid in the cars. We'll fast-track you to the hospital.'

'No, I'm staying.'

'You can't.'

'We need everyone up and running. Patch me up and give me a car and a phone.'

'I'll take him,' said Travis. 'Our car's the quickest way across town.'

'*No one's taking him anywhere*,' said someone behind us.

We turned to find DI Fergus standing in the doorway, covered in dust and oil, bleeding heavily from a similar wound to mine. He was trying to hold a gun straight at me.

'Rose, you're under arrest.'

'DI Fergus, I'm an officer with M15. Put down the gun,' said Katya.

'I don't care who you are, this man is wanted for murder. I'm bringing him in.'

Fergus had a wild look about him, almost delirious with blood loss. I knew exactly how he felt. But as he struggled with the weight of that gun, I was increasingly worried that he was about to give me the fastest vasectomy in history.

'The real zsuspect is getting away as we speak, Inspector,' said Katya, trying to be delicate. 'Please, put down the gun.'

'Put these on him,' said Fergus, throwing his cuffs onto the floor in front of me.

'Inspector –'

'Do it! Now!'

'*Inspector…*'

Fergus was going to shoot me. He rattled the gun in his hand like a geriatric trying to force the TV remote to work. Before he could pull the trigger Travis stepped in between us and knocked him clean out. A medic rushed to his assistance on the floor.

Travis turned to me and took me by the shoulders.

'Are you okay?' he asked.

I forced a brief smile. 'Yeah. Thanks.'

'Look at you, you're all leaky,' he said, still holding me.

Katya looked at him, then at me as I lifted my shirt.

'Chrisz, he's right. That wound isn't going to heal –'

'That's right, it won't...'

She knew what I meant. Our eyes locked for a moment and I was back on the sofa at her house. If that was her house.

'Is Tony one of your guys, too?' I asked.

'You're joking aren't you? He's in cusztody.'

I nodded. Finally something made sense.

Another marked police car pulled up in the compound, lights flashing. The doors opened either side and John and Ross got out to find themselves staring down several gun barrels as Trev and Katya's men formed up.

'Woah, woah, woah!' said Ross, raising his hands.

Katya walked out in front of her people. 'Zstand down,' she said.

'Lower you weapons,' said Travis. 'It's okay.'

John kept his hands in the air. 'What the hell is going on?'

'What are you doing here?' I asked.

'We're supposed to be looking for you. Radio's gone crazy.'

'Perfect timing,' said Katya. 'We need every available pair of hands.'

John and Ross were briefed on the story so far. In turn they told us that there were several other units out looking for me across five forces. Ross radio-d our Control Room and did his best to explain, but the duty inspector repeatedly demanded my arrest and return to the area. To his credit, and my relief, John leant into the car and turned the radio off.

'NCA will take the airport,' said Travis. 'Katya, take your guys to sweep for the terrorists.'

'Excuse me, but this operation is under MI5 juriszdiction. I'll make the calls on who goes where.'

'I think you'll find we got here first,' said Travis.

'And how's that working out for you?'

'We've brought down the biggest dealers this country has ever known. What has MI5 ever done?'

'We deal with terroriszts. If I want a spliff I'll call you.'

'And about those terrorists,' I said. 'Travis is right. You've got more men to cover the town. We'll chase McIntyre down at the airport. Have one of your guys take the girls for me.'

'Take the –? You can piss off,' said Jen. 'I'm not waiting around to get tied up and shot at again. Where you go, I go.'

'Then take one of our radios,' said Katya. 'Stay in touch.'

'We will,' I said. 'But Travis...'

'Yes?'

270

'Take your hand off my bum, please.'
'Sorry.'

39

I tried to keep still in the back seat while Travis ploughed left and right through the traffic, sirens blaring. Another car full of NCA officers followed close behind, with John and Ross just behind them. I was slouched between Vicky and Jen, trying to avoid using any muscles. The new bandaging was tight again but it felt like the wound may have widened.

'They're not moving fast enough,' said Jen, leaning out of her window. 'Beep the horn, Travis. Come on! Faster! Police!'

I caught a look from Trev in the rear-view mirror and we synchronised a roll of the eyes.

I was on hold to a travel company Vicky had found on the internet. We needed to confirm which airport sent planes to Costa Rica. I was fairly certain it'd be Heathrow, but if it wasn't we didn't have long to guide any other units.

'*Hello?*' said a chirpy, customer-service voice on the line.

'Hello?'

'*Mr Rose, we've checked our flights, and the best we could do for you is next Wednesday.*'

'No, you – I've explained this. I just want to check when the flights are leaving.'

'*Next Wednesday.*'

'There are no earlier flights from Heathrow.'

'*Yes.*'

'Yes what?'

'*There are earlier flights.*'

'Today?'

'*Yes, but the only seats left are First Class and that's very expensive.*'

272

'I don't want to get *on* the flight, I just want to know when it leaves.'

'*Are you aware that it's the rainy season in Costa Rica? Have you considered the Canary Islands?*'

'I don't give a *shit* about the weather; just tell me when the fucking plane takes off.'

'*Mr Rose, there's no need for that type of language. I'm only trying to help you.*'

'There is *every* need for that type of language. I don't want to go anywhere, I just want to know what time the plane leaves today for Costa Rica.'

'*Why did you phone a travel company if you don't want to go anywhere?*'

'Oh, *I hope they blow the shit out of your office!*'

I squashed my thumb hard on the button to hang-up and dialled the next number. After a couple of rings an automated voice said, '*Hello, and welcome to Lo-Cost Travel. Please listen carefully to the following seventeen options…*'

I hung-up again.

Vicky offered to try and took the phone, searching various sites.

We were nearly at the airport. The car radio was on and we had all exchanged various handsets so every unit could talk and listen out for updates. Three of the five trucks had been located. Two of them were found outside the Houses of Parliament and the London Eye. It was all headline-grabbing stuff, perfect for diverting attention away from the real targets.

'Here,' said Vicky, showing me the phone. 'London Heathrow to Costa Rica, leaves 14:15. No flights from Gatwick or Stansted. The other airports don't go to Central America. Has to be this one. What do these symbols mean?'

'It's a private plane,' I said. 'He's chartered a flight.'

Naturally. He doesn't want to be turned around on a commercial plane while he's still in international airspace.

'Which terminal?' asked Travis.

Vicky scrolled through the details. 'Four,' she said.

Travis turned off the sirens but left the lights flashing as we pulled into the Departures strip, parking half on the pavement. Our doors flew open and we ran inside, followed by John, Ross and the men from the second NCA car. Immediately we had to dodge trolleys, children and baggage at all sides. It was absolutely heaving, peak-summer travel. If you lost someone they stayed lost. The situation was compounded by mass confusion as one after another, every flight was delayed or cancelled. There was nothing I could see listed for chartered flights and the information desks were swamped with queues a mile long.

'Travis, go and find the duty plod and brief them on what's going on,' I said. 'He's probably at his gate already. I'll find out which one and call you. But be careful, he might be armed. Sight and contain for now.'

Travis nodded and ran to the escalators with his colleagues.

How were we going to get through all those people?

'Police! Excuse me, sorry, excuse me, police, excuse me...'

Everyone was understandably reluctant to move and lose their place in one of several queues I was trying to wade through. We'd only managed to get through the first few layers of people when someone caught my eye leaving one of the check-in desks.

'That's his wife,' I said.

'Where?' asked Jen.

'Bottle blonde, tits, over there.'

'I'll distract her,' said Vicky.

'How?'

'I'll get her talking, slow her down. Keep going, I'll find you.'

Vicky unapologetically fought her way back out of the tight crowd, shouting, kicking and punching at anyone stupid enough to stand in her way. Free of the tangle, she ran towards Pamela McIntyre, who was now dragging a garish pink suitcase towards the duty-free shops.

There were hundreds of eyes fixed on us. We were walled in at all sides by anger, every route sealed off. I looked at my watch. 14:06. I tried to push through with more pleasantries, but several families had deliberately huddled together and left luggage obstructing the area along the queue barriers. Jen looked at me and shrugged, pushing back against a huge, sweaty man.

I jumped as John boomed at my shoulder: 'Ladies and gentlemen! I do not wish to cause alarm, but we are police officers and I need you to clear the desk.'

Nobody cared. They'd been standing in that queue for half their lives already. There was no way anyone wanted to lose their place.

John tried again: 'Please clear the desk for me!'

Several parents snorted with derision, muttering among themselves before turning with their children to face forward again.

'Right,' said John. 'You want to see some police brutality? You got it!'

Waving his baton like a six-year-old Jedi, John steamed into the crowd. He looked like an oil tanker crashing into its dock, kicking bags and suitcases onto the main concourse and dragging the entire queue barrier with him. Those who weren't quick enough to move were knocked to one side by a giant thigh, or a push with a bear-like palm. One man, desperate to defend his position, quickly found himself gripped in a tight headlock, screaming as he took half a canister of CS spray to the eyeballs, before being thrown onto a pile of abandoned luggage.

Finally at the desk, John turned to address the now-terrified masses again: 'Thank you for your co-operation. The Independent Police Complaints Commission number will be made available to you in due course. In the meantime, stay out of our way or I'll fucking tazer you!'

Ross jogged to the desk and instantly hit suave. 'Hi, what's you name?' he asked the checkin-in girl.

'Laura.'

'Laura. Can you check a chartered flight for me, please? Should be taking off in the next few minutes.'

Laura tapped at her keyboard.

'Gate twenty-four. It's leaving now.'

Ross smiled. 'You're beautiful. Thank you.'

I grabbed Jen and we ran. I pulled my phone from my pocket and dialled. 'Gate Twenty-Four,' I shouted to Travis.

'We're on our way.'

'*We're already there,*' he replied. '*He's seen us. He's on board the plane.*'

Barging through yet more queues, jumping luggage and leapfrogging kids, we eventually met Travis with the airport officers and bypassed security. We were almost at the gate when my phone rang – Katya.

'*We have the Sri-Lankan, but he's already uploaded the virusz. McIntyre will have what he needs. Where are you?*'

'At the airport. He's on the plane.'

'*If he leaves now, we'll never get him back.*'

'What about the bombers?'

'*Four down. Two failed to go off. The Met killed two getting onto the tube. There's a fifth contained in Waterloo zstation, the media are all over it.*'

I looked up to a TV screen to see the 'breaking news'. Pictures showed one of the men running into the bowels of the station. Hundreds of people were fleeing in panic. Armed officers were closing in but there was no way they'd risk firing their weapons in crowds like that.

'*You have to stop him, Chrisz.*'

'I'll try.'

40

We watched the plane backing away from the gangway, readying for take-off.

'Call the tower,' I said. 'Get them to stop it.'

'We already have,' said one of the airport officers. 'They're ignoring us.'

'Look,' said Jen, pointing, 'he's got a gun.'

Sammy was crouched between the pilots, casually drooping a handgun at the captain's shoulder. That plane was going to take off, one way or the other.

'How did he get a gun on board?' asked one of the officers.

'How does he do anything?' I said, 'This is Samuel McIntyre.'

Vicky appeared at my side, closely followed by McIntyre's wife.

'He's going without me?' said Pamela. 'No, Sammy, wait! I'm not on the plane!' She jumped up and down on her ridiculous high-heels, waving her arms. 'Wait a minute; I see what's going on here. You're police, aren't you?' She turned to Vicky. 'I thought you were small for a Jehova's Witness.'

McIntyre was disappearing out of sight.

'Can't we block the runway?' I asked.

'No chance,' said the officer. 'Planes are landing every few seconds, it'd be carnage.'

My phone rang again: *Chrisz, we've had sightings of the last man on the Piccadilly Line. We think he's hijacked the train. He's headed to you at the airport. Look out.*

The airport officers overheard that and started running back through the terminal. I told Travis to go with them and help evacuate the area. There was a dense, panicked atmosphere building amongst the travellers, compounded by the scenes on TV.

Then something shot past the window. I turned to see a set of mobile stairs race towards the plane. I pressed my face against the glass.

It was Colin.

I dialled his number.

'*Hello?*' he shouted over the noise of wind and engines.

'Colin, what the hell are you doing?'

'*I don't know.*'

'How did you get out there?'

'*Don't ask me stupid questions. Grab some stairs and help me chase this bastard!*'

I spun round. 'How do I get on that runway?' I shouted to the officers.

'You can't go – '

'How?'

'Back through the building, down the stairs -'

There was no time for that. I was going to run down the gangway when Jen grabbed at my arm.

'Wait!' she said.

'What?'

'You're an idiot.'

'… Thanks.'

'Be careful.'

It was a fifteen foot drop to the floor. Lowering onto my stomach peeled most of my bandage off. I hung from the gangway by my fingertips, waiting for my momentum to steady so I could drop straight, but my weight became too much and I fell onto the concrete, falling forwards and rolling. A hot, sharp pain burned through my feet and shins. As I stood I realised I'd twisted my ankle.

I limped over to another set of mobile stairs. There were a surprising number of pedals and buttons, but I figured out forwards, left and right and began following Colin to the runway. He was just behind the plane as it taxied to the far side of the airport. I cut across the grass and pulled alongside him.

I shouted: 'What's the plan?'

'I'm open to suggestions.'

'Do you have any idea what you've done?'

'I didn't know! I'll explain later, I promise.'

The plane began to turn and we had to take evasive action to avoid colliding with each other under the tail fins.

'He has to use that runway,' said Colin, pointing to a strip of tarmac in the near distance. 'Let's try and block him off.'

I moved to the left and Colin to the right. If we could brake into the wings we might have been able to divert him off course. Maybe we could cause some damage and prevent takeoff altogether.

We were beginning to gather some serious speed. The nearest engine roared in my ear. We were almost around the wings when I heard gun shots and the pang of metal being struck. McIntyre was leaning out of an open door, shooting at Colin, who ducked and swerved. I veered right to slam into the fuselage, hoping to put him off, but the plane was too heavy and I nearly capsized.

Colin had fallen back, just off the tail.

'Stay back!' I shouted.

Colin accelerated again, going for the wing flaps. McIntyre reloaded and fired another three rounds. I saw the windscreen shatter on the cab as Colin hid in the foot well.

'Colin, *stay back!*' I shouted.

McIntyre fired two more rounds and a tyre burst. Colin wrestled for control, helplessly trying to counter the steering as he swerved left and right. The stairs jumped from the wheels on one side to the next. McIntyre fired again and Colin turned too sharply. The stairs skipped and flipped over onto their side, sliding on a wave of sparks. Small pieces of debris bounced in every direction.

Checking my position next to the plane, I looked back. Nothing moved.

I looked back again. The cab was on fire.

A third time. Colin hadn't got out.

I was nearly alongside the cockpit. I started to break gently into the wing, when a door burst open on my side and a flash of gunfire sent me diving for cover. The bullets hammered off the chassis around me. Scrunched into a ball, I reached out an arm to push the brake pedal. The stairs wobbled above me as the plane struggled with the obstruction. Two more shots pinged just above my head before Sammy was out of ammo and threw his gun at my windscreen.

I hauled myself back onto the seat and slammed the brakes hard, stretching my leg rigid. The tyres were squealing. Smoke poured out from all sides underneath me as I bounced along the tarmac. The plane was pulling to the left. The pilot tried to move away from me, driving out to the far edge of the runway, but I went with him, holding my position in the middle of the wing.

The engines began to die down.

We came to a complete stop. I watched and waited, keeping a tight hold of the steering wheel and my foot firmly on the brake. I leant out of the cab to look back for Colin when a sharp pain pulled me back into my seat. The lower half of my t-shirt was saturated in blood. The bandage had completely come away.

I tried to look out again and I saw the plane door was open. The stairs had been lowered.

A grip tightened on my collar and I was thrown out onto the concrete. I fell flat on my back, smacking my head. Another plane that had come into land screamed just metres above us.

McIntyre's foot crunched into my stomach. As I lurched forward his other foot connected flush with my face and knocked me flat again. He picked me up at the lapels and shook me ferociously.

'*Why, Rose? Why d'you do it?*'

Upright, not quite standing on my toes, I could feel blood stream down my thigh and leak from the back of my head. It dripped from my nose and my mouth.

The few remaining muscles working in my face tried to shape a smile.

'I'm a police officer,' I said.

There was the faint sound of sirens and Sammy turned with me still in his grasp. Half of London's emergency services were hurtling towards us from the horizon.

He dropped me on the tarmac and got into the stairs cab, moving them clear of the wing. Jumping out again he signalled to the pilot to re-start the engines.

I dragged myself along the floor, trying to intercept him as he walked back to the plane.

'Sammy!' I shouted through the blood, just as his foot hit the first stair. '*Sammy!*'

He stopped, looking over his shoulder at me. I pulled myself to within a few feet of him until the last of my strength had gone.

McIntyre looked at the advancing vehicles. They were still a way off. In minutes he'd be free forever; outrageously rich, completely untouchable; living the ultimate lifestyle. He'd beaten the police. He'd beaten the security services. He'd won. Just as he knew he would.

He had time. I'd earned it.

He released the banister on the stairs to saunter over to me. He came in close, kneeling at my side.

'Wanna come with me?' he asked.

I wanted him nearer still. I beckoned him down with my finger.

He leant me his ear and I said: 'You're under arrest.'

A pronounced click.

McIntyre looked down to see I'd cuffed him to my wrist with the irons Fergus had dropped.

'NO!' he shouted, almost yanking my arm out of its socket. 'NO!'

I was laughing when I wasn't coughing up blood.

He stamped on my arm, trying to snap it. He thrashed left and right. He kicked me one way then the next, my head reeling from side to side. He tried to drag me up the first few steps onto the plane, and when he couldn't lift me he shouted and swore, kicking me again and again and again.

Still I laughed. I didn't care. I couldn't feel it anymore.

Everything slowed down as a wide net of flashing blue drew in. Sounds distorted. There were voices but no words. Blurred silhouettes created a dark canopy and I felt my arm fall limp to the ground.

Still he thrashed as they pinned him to the tarmac. I saw him look at me as they pressed his face into the floor. His eyes tried to finish me off. After all the reprieves, the stories, the advice, finally he wished me dead.

I smiled back.

They took him away and I saw Jen. She was crying, screaming, terrified. Well-meaning arms reached out to hold her back as my body rose level with a stretcher.

I felt completely at ease as I was wheeled away. A beautiful sense of calm tingled through me and I forgot everything. I looked up to smile at the lady walking at my side and she returned the gesture. She reached down to rub a single red tear from my cheek. She stroked my forehead with the back of her fingers.

'Always covered in cuts and bruises, Chris,' she said. 'What would mum say?'

Then I recognised her.

I knew her.

Emily.

She watched as I was loaded into the back of the ambulance. It took all the strength I had left to lean my head forward. I wanted to call for her but I couldn't make a sound. I tried to speak but I couldn't draw the words from my throat. I could only look at her smiling back at me as the last fifteen years ran clear from my eyes.

'Thank you,' she said.

And the doors closed.

41

It was a few days later when the Chief Constable took his place at the press conference, almost blind with the lightning of photography. The room was packed with journalists from all over the world.

He pulled his glasses from his pocket and began to read the statement: *'Good afternoon. As was reported last week, in a joint operation with the Metropolitan Police Force, MI5, and the National Crime Agency, several of my officers were engaged across London in the biggest anti-terror operation this country has ever known. Having identified a number of suspects, the officers moved quickly to nullify their threat in the city's streets, train stations and at Heathrow Airport. In the course of their duty, trained marksmen were forced to fire upon, and kill, four of the suspects. A further seven were arrested and taken into custody, among them, Samuel Richard McIntyre. His business associate, Lee Carr, was detained by a South African naval vessel yesterday, along with a number of other persons on board, en route to the Middle-East. The suspects are all to be charged with offences under the Terrorism Act, and in connection with several murders, including those of Detective Inspector David Martin and Detective Chief Superintendent Barry Straughan.*

It is a testament to the incredible professionalism of those involved that there was not a single serious injury to a member of the public during this operation. We owe an enormous debt of thanks to all our officers, and in particular, PC Christopher Rose. If it were not for his selfless actions and determination, we would be gathered here today mourning the loss of hundreds of innocent lives. His bravery will never be forgotten. Thank you.'

The clamour for questions began as the Chief Constable and his team tried to leave the room.

'Chief Constable! Chief Constable! Is it true some of your own officers were among those arrested?'

'I can't comment on that now.'

'Can you confirm that the terrorists were targeting government ministers?'

'Not at this stage.'

'Chief Constable, isn't it true that PC Rose had been suspended for drunken antics dressed as a duck?'

'You can turn the TV off now, thank you,' I said to the nurse.

'Someone's in for a promotion,' she smiled

'I hope not.'

As the nurse walked out of my room, Jen walked in, immediately less than impressed that Katya was sat at the foot of my bed. She dropped her bags on the floor and practically jumped on me, squeezing me hard about the shoulders. She turned to Katya, exaggerating clearing her throat: 'Uh-*huh*.'

Katya looked at her.

'Look, I don't know what 'uh-huh' means in Poland, but in this country it means bugger off.'

'*Jen.*'

'It's okay, I have to go,' said Katya. 'I'm glad you're feeling better. I'll see you back at work.'

'Will you?'

'Zsure. We haven't even started. There's a long road ahead if we want to keep that man and his friends behind bars. I'll brief you properly soon. You rest for now, hero.'

Katya left and closed the door.

'I'll brief *her* properly soon,' said Jen.

'Oi, you're a bit feisty today.'

'Every time I leave you for five minutes you've got another woman with you.'

'Well that's because I'm phenomenally attractive, especially now I'm famous. You're lucky I had time to see you at all today.'

Jen smiled, laying her head on my chest and I reached up to stroke her hair.

285

For all the grief we were to each other; the drinking, the arguments, the jealousy; maybe it could still work. For some reason we never wanted to admit it, but we had fun together. I wouldn't try to second guess anything this time.

I'd lost nearly five pints of blood by the time they wheeled me in to A&E. I'm told I was pretty much dead on arrival. I didn't come round for two days, and when I did, all my ribs were broken, as was my arm and my nose. I had a fractured skull, and cuts and bruises on every single inch of my body. But I felt surprisingly good. Everything was wrapped up tight and I was morphine-d to the hilt. I could have used a drink, though.

If the plan had succeeded, Ashane Gunasekara would have sent millions upon millions to a network of al-Qaeda cells and Taliban sympathisers all over the world, under the cover of a viral meltdown. Before the blood had time to dry on our streets, he would have returned to the Middle-East to help orchestrate the next wave of attacks. McIntyre had met him quite innocently at a FTSE dinner some two years prior, and appears to have become taken with the *hypothetical* boast that Gunasekara could acquire almost infinite cash, if he had the initial capital for the tech to bypass one of the world's most stubborn firewalls. Tired of what he saw as an increasingly oppressive state, and in the interests of securing one last incredible payday, Sammy handed over almost everything he had. In addition he managed the protection, logistics and travel for six extremists to meet a home-grown terror cell in the Midlands who were already making the bombs. In return, McIntyre could retire to paradise, never to want for anything again; a king among paupers that would defend him, holding him aloft on their perfect beaches at the promise of a handful of coins. The outside world couldn't touch him. We could only raise our pointless comedy threat level from 'General Naughtiness' to 'Beware the Koran!' and wait in silent fear for the next disaster. It was an audacious goodbye that tied the security services in knots, and but for a few more minutes, it would have worked.

Someone appeared in my doorway. He was heavily strapped himself and only just able to push his wheelchair. It was DI Fergus.

'I'm sorry,' he said, 'I didn't realise you had company.'

'No, no, it's fine,' I said. 'Come in.'

Jen stood, straightening her top.

'I'm going to grab a coffee,' she said, and left the room.

Fergus looked over my unexpected haul of get-well cards, flowers and presents, piled high on every surface.

'How are you doing?' I asked.

'Fine. Thanks,' he said. 'I've got to have another operation soon, but I'll be okay. How about you?'

'Business as usual,' I smiled.

His head dropped. 'I just wanted to say sorry. I shouldn't have said the things I did in that interview.'

'Forget it.'

'McIntyre played us all. I should have realised. Sewell… Straughan…'

'Sir, it doesn't matter now. We've won. We had to pay the highest price, but there was never going to be another way. I think the chief knew that.'

'Well, I just wanted to say well done.'

Fergus extended his hand and I took it. Without another word he wheeled himself into the corridor and disappeared.

Perhaps we were friends after all. Certainly I knew now which side he was on. But would he still trust me in the months ahead, when the dust had settled and the emotions had died?

The revised official final word on Bingo was to be death by misadventure; effectively suicide, following a cocktail of drugs, but I knew there was still some doubt surrounding that verdict. There would be those who were still convinced it was murder, and maybe it was. Maybe someone had Sewell alone in McIntyre's garden that night after all. Maybe someone injected air into his blood stream with his own insulin syringe and held him down in the river until he was dead. Maybe it was justified revenge for all the hurt he caused to countless families in the past, including mine.

Maybe we'll never know.

The night drew in as Jen left and I was alone in my thoughts, looking at my reflection in the black window.

For once I couldn't hear anyone moving about on the ward. I tied my gown loosely at my waist and shuffled into the corridor. There was a little room just down the hall from mine. The guard had temporarily left his post, probably in search of more caffeine. The reading light was on.

I pushed the door open and Colin looked up from his book. He was handcuffed to the bed as I had been.

'D'you like grapes?' I asked.

'No.'

'Neither do I. I've got thousands of them. What's wrong with Malteasers? Bloody hospitals.'

'How are you feeling?' he asked.

'Yeah, fine. Nice to have a kicking in my own clothes for once.'

Colin's lip began to wobble and he filled with tears.

'Chris, I'm so sorry. I had no idea what he was planning. It was only supposed to be money. He never said anything about terrorists and suicide bombers. I couldn't get out. Martin threatened me. Said they'd kill us both if I said anything. I swear I never knew those men had a knife when the chief died.'

I had no reason to doubt Colin's honesty. He was hardly the first to succumb to the lure of easy money, and he wouldn't be the last. DI Martin, Katya, Riley, Jones – everyone who thought they knew what was going on only held a single piece of the puzzle, and they were all as expendable as each other. Even McIntyre's own wife didn't make the plane in the end. You may not come to realise it for a while, but you always paid for your association with that man.

'I just wanted a life,' said Colin. 'If I had the cash I could put nan in a home where she'd be looked after. I could have a place of my own.'

'I trusted you,' I said. 'You're just lucky none of those bombs went off.'

Colin smiled. 'It's not luck. They gave me the vests that night you turned up at the house. When I got home, I replaced the explosives with sand.'

'What?'

'Same feel, same weight. There was no way I was going to let them blow anyone up.'

'Seriously?'

We laughed.

'Well what the hell did you do with the explosives?'

'It's in my garage, in Tupperware.'

I laughed again, stopping immediately when a thought suddenly hit me.

'Hang on; you put explosives in sealed containers?'

'Yeah. Clipped tight.'

'In the garage where your nan chain-smokes?'

Colin's smile dropped.

42

The explosion could be heard from five miles away. The immediate area surrounding Colin's garage block was reduced to smouldering rubble and there wasn't a window left on the street. Fortunately there were no serious injuries. Edith, who inadvertently triggered the blast with the casual toss of a cigarette butt, was up the road and almost in her front door when the shockwave knocked her to the ground. She was taken into hospital with cuts and bruises, but appeared to be in fine, cantankerous order. I offered her several hundred grapes when I was discharged, but she politely declined, telling me to fuck off.

Sadly, a couple of days later, complications with her heart arose, that may or may not have been exacerbated by events. Either way, and despite the surgeon's best efforts, Edith died on the operating table.

Colin was ecstatic.

Under the circumstances the courts were expected to be fairly lenient with him. Regardless of his involvement and whether he was negligent in trying to send his closest relative into orbit, removing the explosives was the real reason no one else was killed that day. Perhaps a short prison sentence would toughen him up. It might give him that edge he was missing to attract the ladies. Either that or a dodgy home-made tattoo and a gaping arsehole.

'Here's to you, Chris,' said Keith, holding up his pint at the bar. 'The world's best copper.'

'To you, Kiss!' said Mae Su, and everybody around me joined in with the toast, including a bus-load of people attending another gay wedding.

Jen and Travis hugged me from either side and I nearly choked on the accumulative toxicity of hair care products.

'Well done. You were amazing,' said Travis.

'Thank you,' I said. 'But still don't touch my bum.'

'Sorry.'

It was a strange sensation – actually being liked - and for once I dropped my guard and just went with it. It wouldn't last long. Roughly up until McIntyre's first day in court I suspected. There was no way he planned to fester in a jail for five minutes longer than he had to, and he was sure to still have friends we were yet to become acquainted with.

Hopefully I wouldn't have to dress up in future, but my undercover work was going to be a lot harder for a while, what with my face splashed all over the news. Still, it's a fickle world. In time people would forget. The following week the media would have moved on and the police will have done something wrong again. I'd be another face in the crowd. Just the way I liked it.

I watched the bubbles in my beer rise to the surface and pop. Whether it was the morphine or delirium brought on by my injuries, I was glad to see my sister one final time. It was real enough.

I looked up to her, nodding at my pint. 'It's just the one, I promise.'

Vicky and I were going to complete our counselling, and then we were going to find her a stable place to live. Her step-father wasn't just going to disappear, but we were more than ready for that.

'I'm sorry I dragged you into all my crap,' I said.

Vicky looked at me incredulously. 'Are you joking? That was amazing! I'm definitely joining the police.'

And management think I'm trouble.

We all laughed and joked for another hour when the pub door flew open. A young woman practically fell into the room, scanning the crowds until her eyes met mine. It was

291

Penny. Before I could say anything she ran over, jumping into my arms and sticking an enormous kiss on my lips. The crowd fell silent as Jen slapped her wine onto the bar.

'Now who the hell is *this*?'

Oh shit.

Chris Rose will return in *Fall of the Penguin*... And so will Bollocks the dog. And Colin. And Samuel McIntyre.

Basically, a lot of the people you've just read about will be in the next book.

Contact Adam Brett and find out more about his work at www.adam-brett.co.uk

13732523R00175

Printed in Poland
by Amazon Fulfillment
Poland Sp. z o.o., Wrocław